PEACE AND PRISONERS OF WAR

PEACE AND PRISONERS OF WAR

A South Vietnamese Memoir of the Vietnam War

Phan Nhat Nam

TRANSLATED FROM THE VIETNAMESE ORIGINAL
"Tù Binh và Hòa Bình," Saigon 1974

Introduction by Senator James Webb

NAVAL INSTITUTE PRESS
Annapolis, Maryland

Published by the Naval Institute Press, 2020

Library of Congress Cataloging–in–Publication Data
Names: Phan, Nhật Nam, author. | Webb, James, (date)– writer of introduction.
Title: Peace and prisoners of war : a South Vietnamese memoir of the Vietnam War / Phan Nhat Nam.
Other titles: Tú binh vá hóa bình. English
Description: Annapolis, Maryland : Naval Institute Press, 2020. | "A hardcover edition of this book was originally published by Khang Chien, Publisher. First edition published 1989."
Identifiers: LCCN 2020021800 | ISBN 9781682476314 (paperback)
Subjects: LCSH: Agreement on Ending the War and Restoring Peace in Viet–Nam (1973 January 27) | Vietnam War, 1961–1975—Prisoners and prisons.
Classification: LCC DS559.7 .P4813 2020 | DDC 959.704/37—dc23
LC record available at https://lccn.loc.gov/2020021800

A hardcover edition of this book was originally published by Khang Chien, Publisher.

First edition published 1989.

10 9 8 7 6 5 4 3 2 1

To all Americans and Vietnamese
who struggled at great cost
to secure freedom for the Vietnamese people.
And in remembrance of my beloved country,
the Republic of South Vietnam.

Contents

About the Authors

PHAN NHAT NAM is a soldier, a renowned writer, and a political commentator. A graduate of Da Lat, South Vietnam's equivalent of West Point, he served for eight years as a soldier in the Red Berets, South Vietnam's elite airborne division, during the Vietnam War and after that he became the country's best-known war reporter. Following the Communist takeover in 1975, he was imprisoned in Hanoi's infamous "re-education camps" for fourteen years, eight of which were spent in solitary confinement. He was allowed to emigrate to the United States in 1993 under the Orderly Departure Program, and he has continued to write and speak about the war and its continuing aftermath, remaining one of the most influential voices in the worldwide overseas Vietnamese community.

For his combat service as a Marine Corps rifle platoon and company commander in Vietnam, JAMES WEBB was awarded the Navy Cross, Silver Star Medal, two Bronze Star Medals, and two Purple Hearts. He is the author of ten books, including the classic Vietnam novel *Fields of Fire*, and he has widely traveled as a journalist, receiving a National Emmy for his 1983 television coverage of the Marines in Beirut, Lebanon, and as an embedded journalist in Afghanistan in 2004. In government he served as a full committee counsel in the House of Representatives, as Assistant Secretary of Defense and Secretary of the Navy in the Reagan administration, and as a U.S. Senator from Virginia.

Introduction

Senator James Webb

FEW AMERICANS KNOW of Phan Nhat Nam. But in many ways he is a historic icon.

His service as a dedicated yet independent soldier in the cause of South Vietnam's quest for a free and democratic system, his brilliance as that country's most respected war reporter, and the personal suffering he endured once the war was over, have earned Nam the perhaps unwanted title of the very symbol of all that was possible, all that was lost, and all that was painfully exacted over many years by the cost of that loss. Because of the way the Vietnam War ended, anonymity became his fate both inside postwar Vietnam and even among American academics and media commentators, contrasted with the enormous respect that he receives in the Overseas Vietnamese community.

This dichotomy itself is emblematic of the gaping hole that exists in the way the history of the Vietnam War has been debated and which, after fifty years, has supposedly been resolved.

In 1970, after eight years of infantry combat in one of South Vietnam's most respected airborne divisions, Nam began writing while remaining in the army as a soldier. His writing style, which he himself termed *but ky*, was a melding of strong emotional feelings that carried with them the heart of a novelist, along with the detailed, factual reporting of an on-the-scenes journalist who knew his subject matter from direct experience on the battlefield. In addition to spending many years as a soldier and filing numerous magazine and newspaper reports from some of South Vietnam's most bitter battlefields, by the time South Vietnam fell to the communists in 1975 he had written five well-received books. *Peace and Prisoners of War* is the only one that has thus far been translated into English.

Phan Nhat Nam, whose birth name was Phan Ngoc Khue, was born in 1943 in the old Imperial capital of Hue. In 1950 when he was seven years old his father abandoned him and his mother in order to join the communist Viet Minh. His mother died just as he finished his high school studies in Quang Nam's capital city of Danang. Trained in Da Lat at South Vietnam's equivalent of West Point, from 1961 until 1970 he served with distinction in combat as a soldier in South Vietnam's elite "Red Beret" Airborne Division. As the war progressed, he displayed unusual writing talent and acute insights that gained wide recognition in South Vietnam as his stories spilled out onto the public pages with words and observations that could only come from one who had lived through much of what he now was observing.

Through his gutsy and insightful commentaries from many of the most brutal battlefields of the war, Phan Nhat Nam became South Vietnam's most respected war reporter. Renowned South Vietnamese writer and literary critic Vo Phien commented on the emotions that propelled Nam's "violent, stormy" writing style: "Phan Nhat Nam was an army officer known for his honesty and . . . insubordination to higher ups whom he despised . . . He wrote because after eight years in the army and in the war 'what I have seen and heard has had such an effect on my mind and soul that I cannot help writing it all down . . . To write as a kind of prayer in the darkest loneliness, to write so that the tears may pour out from behind my clenched teeth and my dried out lips, I write *but ky* as I have sighed in despair night after night.'"

From 1970 to 1975 there remained plenty of carnage and despair on the battlefields of Vietnam, even as the United States steadily disengaged from its commitment to the people it had left behind. Very little of this continuing combat received major attention in an America that had grown weary of what they viewed as an unwinnable and overly costly war where American lives were no longer at the same risk as a few years before. By 1972 for many Americans the Vietnam War seemed to be over except for a small contingency force inside the country and a bevy of diplomats reaching toward a final political solution at the Paris Peace talks. But in that year alone, 39,587 South Vietnamese soldiers were lost, mainly while repelling a full-scale offensive where the North Vietnamese threw almost its entire army into the south, including 14 divisions, 26 independent regiments, and several hundred Soviet tanks.

When one measures these losses against South Vietnam's 1970 population of only 19 million people, this was the equivalent of the United States losing 400,000 soldiers in one year—as many as were lost in all of World War Two. The ARVN's willingness to fight, hold and counterattack in such landmark battles as the successful eighty-day fight for the city of Quang Tri, and the historic breaking of the North Vietnamese siege at An Loc, were a shock to the invaders, whose official records admit to having lost 100,000 soldiers in their miscalculated attacks during that same year.

During these months Phan Nhat Nam was present on many battlefields, providing real-time coverage of the difficult and costly combat. His book *The Fiery Red Summer*, published the same year, was vastly popular in South Vietnam. In many chapters it lauded and recorded the heroism and humanity of his comrades, defending them from anecdotal American accounts that demeaned the courage and competence of South Vietnamese military commanders. Quang Tri and especially An Loc had enormous significance in a South Vietnam that was increasingly being left on its own. Historian and Vietnamese linguist John C. Shafer wrote in 1999 that "by all accounts, American and otherwise, the Battle of An Loc was the most important single engagement (at least symbolically) of an offensive that was itself arguably one of the most, if not the most, important campaigns of the war... General Paul Vanuxem, former Commander of the French Mobile Units during the First Indochina War and a trusted adviser to President Thieu, ... claims that 'An Loc should have fallen at the first impact. Two months later, An Loc still stands. Everything being equal, with the exception of Stalingrad only, there is simply no equivalent feat in the military history of the contemporary world.'"

The new cohort of South Vietnamese military leaders in these battles were separated by a full generation from French colonialism. Trained largely with the assistance of American advisors, and above all hardened by nearly ten years on a brutal battlefield, they had proven themselves. But this was a war that on both sides was sponsored by major powers. Over the next two years the American support steadily receded while the support for the North Vietnamese from China and especially the Soviet Union steadily increased. Soviet assistance to the communist regime in Hanoi was not merely philosophical. By 1987, when this writer was Secretary of the Navy, the Soviet Union was subsidizing the Hanoi government to the tune of billions of dollars a year, and on any given day twenty-five Soviet Navy combatants were operating out of Cam Ranh Bay, Vietnam, realizing the historic Russian dream of holding warm water ports in the Pacific.

Unfortunately, few people in the outside world were listening, and especially in war-weary America. The international community, indoctrinated over many years by the highly disciplined and persuasive messengers from Hanoi, saw things differently than those South Vietnamese who were now entering their tenth year of an exhausting combat that would eventually take the lives of 1.4 million communist soldiers, 58,000 Americans, and more than 220,000 South Vietnamese. Success-oriented and always future-looking America was largely moving forward, past what was viewed by many as the irritatingly unending war in Vietnam. As the battles continued in Vietnam, America in 1972 found itself embroiled in the ever-widening Watergate scandal, President Richard Nixon's new initiative toward China, and, when it came to Vietnam, the hope that the Paris Peace talks might extricate this country from the unending arguments and protests over a war that now had few prominent supporters.

In the middle of all of this repositioning and search for the future were the South Vietnamese, trapped by the reality of America's growing abandonment of its commitment to their pursuit of democracy and unable to grasp what the future might hold. And among the South Vietnamese who were struggling to determine what these adjustments might mean for their personal lives as well as their country's future was the iconoclastic yet emotional voice of Phan Nhat Nam. When the Paris Peace Agreement was signed In January 1973 Nam was appointed Secretary to the Joint Military Committee, whose principal task was to negotiate the exchange of Prisoners of War among four different contingents: the North Vietnamese, the Viet Cong, the South Vietnamese, and the Americans.

At the age of thirty, Nam became the youngest negotiator on either side during the intense and frustratingly kabuki-like deliberations. Beyond doubt, one of the key reasons that Nam was treated so harshly after the communist takeover was the blunt and insightful manner in which he described the robotic behavior of his North Vietnamese military counterparts during the negotiations in which he participated in 1973 and 1974, which were recorded in this book.

Unlike so many other books about war, *Peace and Prisoners of War* is not a novel or a carefully couched, retrospective memoir. It is a series of essays that were written in "real time" during the fateful gap between the withdrawal of American military support in January, 1973 and the overwhelming, fifty-five-day North Vietnamese offensive that brought the final fall of South Vietnam in April, 1975. As with his other books, Phan Nhat Nam wrote the essays from the perspective of a soldier-scholar who was loyal to the goals of South Vietnam's incipient democracy. But in this book we are seeing and feeling the author's sense that things are not going to end well either for him or for the country on whose behalf he had already spent more than twenty years of his life supporting on a very costly battlefield.

For his honesty in this book and for his caustic, honest portrayal of his North Vietnamese adversaries who sat across the table from him, once the communists took power Phan Nhat Nam richly paid.

In Phan Nhat Nam's essays we can sense his palpable love for his country, tempered by an unspoken but very real sense of impending doom. By 1973 when these essays begin, the American military had left Vietnam, and military assistance of any sort was strictly reduced by the mandates of a war-weary Congress. By 1974 the presidency of Richard Nixon, who remained the main American guarantor of the terms agreed upon in the 1973 Paris Peace Accords, was under irreversible political attack, and by that summer his presidency had ended altogether. In November 1974 the so-called Watergate Congress was elected, its new members having run on a promise to end all aid to South Vietnam. Their first formal vote once the new congress convened in January 1975 was to cut off a vital emergency appropriation to the South Vietnamese military. This vote served as a moral blow and a strategic nightmare for the struggling South Vietnamese government, which began repositioning its military, catching them on the move just as the North Vietnamese offense began.

In the essays of this book we follow the observations of a brilliant writer-soldier as he participated in and reported on the false, tedious formalities of the prisoner of war exchanges that were mandated by the 1973 Paris Peace Accords. These formalities quickly revealed themselves as little more than a mockery as the South Vietnamese became politically irrelevant while the Americans withdrew and the North Vietnamese prepared for a final offensive.

In retrospect a reader can only imagine how difficult it must have been for a battle-hardened, thirty-year old soldier and writer to suppress a mounting sense of frustration and uncertainty about his country's future without conveying a sense of hopelessness to his loyal readership. Indeed, many of them were still fighting at the far edges of a brutal war that they still had hopes of winning or at least drawing down to the kind of territorial and political stalemate that twenty-two years earlier had marked the end of hostilities between North and South Korea.

By walking through this reportorial balance as Phan Nhat Nam lived it, readers in this day and age might come to understand the sense of doom that was growing every day inside an abandoned South Vietnam, measured against the determination of South Vietnam's new generation of military leaders who believed that if the Americans would only continue to assist them logistically and with air support, as had been the case during the brutal campaigns of 1972, they could prevent such an outcome.

As one example of how desperate the situation had grown for our South Vietnamese allies, during the 1975 "final offensive" one of this writer's friends who had already spent twelve years on the battlefield and was then serving as a thirty year-old regimental commander in the central highlands was reduced to fighting the attacking North Vietnamese with an average of only two artillery rounds per gun per day at his command. Needless to say, his unit was eventually overrun by the refurbished North Vietnamese. He was wounded and carried by his soldiers for three days as they retreated, and eventually ended up in communist reeducation camps for more than 13 years, five of them in solitary confinement.

On April 29, 1975, the day before the final fall of South Vietnam, Phan Nhat Nam wrote his last posting as a reporter on the war. As later related in the New York Times, Nam watched as the North Vietnamese shot down a South Vietnamese C-119 gunship that was protecting South Vietnamese who were fleeing from the communist advance on Saigon. According to John C. Shafer, "Phan Nhat Nam went to the wreckage, took some photographs, and began to cry. 'At that moment,' he says, 'I realized that I was dead. In my mind I had died in the war. And in my mind, I have been dead from that moment until today.'"

After the communist takeover of South Vietnam in 1975, like hundreds of thousands among the leadership of South Vietnam, Phan Nhat Nam was sent to the infamous prisons that were euphemistically termed "re-education camps," which in reality were Southeast Asian gulags put together in order to separate the former leadership of the South from their supporters in order to allow the communists to take control over the populace and ostensibly to retrain these former "puppets" in the principles of communism. Nam was incarcerated for fourteen years, eight years of which were spent in solitary confinement. And finally, in 1993, he was permitted to leave Vietnam under the Orderly Departure Program (ODP) which allowed those who had been imprisoned in communist reeducation camps for more than four years to emigrate to the United States.

Following his 1993 arrival in the United States Phan Nhat Nam has continued to write regularly, including the Vietnamese language publication of two new books. In the prologue to his 2002 book *The Stories Must Be Told*, Nam comments, "I continue to write about soldiers. To write about war and suffering. About people who have suffered. I cannot write about anything else. There is nothing else. If I don't write about these things, I will prove myself ungrateful and people will have the right to curse me."

This book, and his other writings, will keep Phan Nhat Nam alive for a very long time. Its honesty rises above the reconsidered and carefully polished thoughts that appear in so many memoirs. Like a treasured jewel discovered after being lost in the attic for many years it is an unvarnished observation frozen in time, devoid of spin or false retrospective wisdom, written while the war was still being raged, in support of the cause of a country that no longer exists. And it is filled with a frank and clear-eyed cynicism directed at the often robotic communist representatives who were sitting across the table, conducting the communist version of a filibuster as their armies refurbished and the world grew tired of how long it seemed to be taking for the South Vietnamese to finally surrender.

Not coincidentally, these were the very people that Phan Nhat Nam must have known would seek revenge, not if but when the course of the war played out to their advantage.

It has been extremely difficult for the post-war debate about the Vietnam War to include such raw commentary about the political motives and day to day struggles of our South Vietnamese allies during the final months as the country and political system they were trying to consolidate was crumbling before their eyes. Inside Vietnam, those voices were brutally silenced from the moment the communists took control of the country on April 30, 1975. In addition to the suppression of internal dissent a Bamboo Curtain fell over the country, separating Vietnam from most of the outside world for fifteen years. More than a million South Vietnamese were sent into re-education camps, some for a few months and others incarcerated for as long as eighteen years. And inside Vietnam, any vocal support for the motivations of the previous regime is still met with quick political reprisals. In America itself, the informational gateways that should have allowed a balanced accounting of why and how the war was fought (as well as its brutal aftermath) have long tilted toward a "default" setting that the war was unwise, unwinnable, and fought on the anti-communist side by the philosophical remnants of the former French colonial regime or by an unrealistic premise that reunification of the country under a communist regime was unpreventable.

All of this, given the years that have passed, is actually something of an unnecessary shame. The great irony of the Vietnam War among the Vietnamese who fought it was that both sides could find moral justification in the causes for which they were willing to fight. Ho Chi Minh often proclaimed that his over-arching goals were for "*doc lap va tu do*," Vietnamese for "independence and freedom." Setting aside Ho's long affiliation with the international communist movement, including many years residing in Moscow while studying revolutionary practices at the Soviet Comintern, it is understandable that after more than a century of colonial rule many Vietnamese were drawn to the notion of national independence and reunification.

On the other hand, having watched the stark political division of Germany following World War II into the repressive communist East and the democratic West, plus the continuing brutality of a murderous regime in North Korea, it is also logical that many Vietnamese were willing to fight for the same notions of freedom that then were embraced by citizens of South Korea and West Germany.

Over the years, many Americans who fought in this war have come to terms with its results, and continue to view Vietnam as one of the three or four most strategically important countries in Asia. We have worked hard to build strong relations with Vietnam's present government, and to cement personal relations with its leadership. Years ago, we shook the hands and made peace with our former enemies. But we will know that this peace is real only when our former enemies and our long-time allies can respect one another, and especially when the history of how and why this war was fought is fairly and honestly portrayed.

Phan Nhat Nam has carried this awesome burden in his heart and in his brain for many years. In the pages that follow, those who read this book might come to understand why.

One

Peace

January 28, 1973

I HAVE USED this date as a point of reference—The Day of Peace. An unusual peace it is, as bitter as the medicine that we, as a patient on the point of dying, had to take. The militiamen go about knocking on doors and urgently calling on the heads of households to display the national flag in front of their houses. The President reads his televised message to the people—a historical message announcing the portentous coming of peace, a message that contains heated words and simple phrases full of suggestive images, a message that is delivered breathlessly, which is quite unusual from any head of state. . . . The Vietnamese motherland welcomes peace with fear and misgivings.

I walked in the streets of Saigon on Jan. 28, feeling strange and troubled. The long months and years of fighting had made the war a permanent fact of life, and to be rid of it was like being removed from a familiar environment. And yet how miserable that environment had been! In Tay Ninh, the Communists encircled the Cao Daiist Holy Temple on all sides. Route 15 was blocked north and south of Long Thanh. The road to Central Vietnam and to Da Lat was again unsafe. The Communists tried to hold on to a stretch of Highway 1 near Trang Bom. Peace had come with a series of violations that took place simultaneously in all four Corps areas. Was there peace?

. . . Still a great consolation, though: No large-scale battle beyond the battalion level had taken place: as heartening as when you see the seeming revival of a dead body letting out its last gasps while life has gone out of its limbs.

—

But it seemed that the broken pieces of "peace" were being reassembled. The Indonesian and Canadian delegations on the International Committee for Control of the Cease-Fire were coming to Saigon. Men clad in Mao suits made of khaki were present at Tan Son Nhat. For the first time, the Communist cadres from Hanoi, from Paris, and from the secret zones converged on nationalist territory. The historic meeting took place. A new phase had begun for the nation. And the new road that stretched before us seemed lost in the fog of the battles in all four Corps areas. Peace had come to the men who lay dying, an uncomprehending look on their faces. Meetings were held around a table covered with green felt, in a room with all doors closed. In a mellifluous voice and with polite manners, the men who had fought with each other as recently as the previous day, or the day before, now exchanged views on a tragic issue—the prisoners, direct and most painful victims of the war, piteous offerings for peace, now chips in the bargain.

Today, the first day of a silent drama, the prisoners started to be released so that they would be left in peace in some void space, or would be issued again a new combat uniform to put on their body and a weapon to hold in their hands and pushed back on stage to resume their parts in a never-ending tragedy.

As a witness and participant in this silent and pathetic "battlefield," the writer of this memoir, who could still claim to have retained enough righteousness and loyalty in his heart, has attempted to present an account of his experiences, in the rush of the moment and with unavoidable subjectivity, at least as a Vietnamese.

. . . I opened the door and I was met with an enjoyable rush of cool air. There was a brown polished wood paneling on the walls, carpeting on the floor, and a table covered with green felt. The place had a quiet comfort and solemnity that was typically American, 100 percent American, with the air being deodorized, sanitized, and purified. In this small, neat, and well-designed room, where everything shone, the thorniest question of the Cease-Fire Agreement was the problem of the prisoners of war consisting of 30,000 prisoners of the two Vietnamese sides and 561 American P.O.W.s. The fates of these prisoners would be decided as the prisoners would be the subject of the discussions and, in the bargaining process, would be "measured out" by the hundreds, or by the dozens, or even individually, depending on the pace and mood of the negotiations. Man had become a mere number. Prisoner, what are you thinking at this time?

". . . Gentlemen, let me introduce Captain Nam. . ."

I stood up and bowed. . . . They were looking at me with watchful eyes. . . I was now confronting real Communist cadres, middle-aged men, solemn and rigid in their olive drab uniforms made of the khaki from Nam Dinh. They were core cadres of the middle level, fresh from the Paris negotiations, the expert negotiators, men who could sit for a long time, discoursing at length on vague, vain, and contradictory issues . . . the born actors, the professionals, men who knew how to remain cool under any circumstances. That was my first impression of them as I saw their unsmiling faces.

The session began. Colonel Dat, who headed the South Vietnamese delegation, was the colonel of the colonels, with his fifteen years of rank seniority, and the officer who had first begun to deal with the problem of prisoners and prison camps twenty years ago and whom no one could best in his present position as an expert on prisoners. The meeting started with a review of the activities during the day, followed by observations on the releases of prisoners, and exchanges of lists of prisoners between the two sides. . . .

The speakers took turns clockwise, beginning with the Republic of Vietnam, the U.S., the National Liberation Front,[1] and North Vietnam. Views were exchanged in a measured tone, quietly, soberly, and unyieldingly. The arguments followed different lines of thought, and were not necessarily the answers to the questions asked but were presented according to the strategy of each side. The Republic of Vietnam announced the number of prisoners scheduled to be released during the day, but up until the time of the meeting the release was still delayed because NLF representatives at the Thach Han River refused to cross the river to receive the prisoners and because the prisoners in Bien Hoa refused to board the plane for Loc Ninh. . . . Colonel Russell of the U.S. raised the issue that the NLF had not released the American prisoners in Loc Ninh as scheduled. The problems were presented clearly and neatly like the little cakes brought in to serve as snacks for the delegates. . . . I waited for the answers from the two Communist sides. As the delegates proceeded with their meetings, you began to see more and more of the evasive tactics, and attempts at avoidance so clumsy that they made you laugh. Colonel Le Truc, head of NLF delegation, turned to the issue of the civilian prisoners and Lieutenant-Colonel Tan, head of the North Vietnamese delegation, announced that the Hanoi government had unexpectedly released an American Lieutenant-Colonel in Gia Lam earlier in the day because of a human consideration—his mother was seriously ill!

1. National Liberation Front of South Vietnam, National Liberation Front for short, formed in the end of 1960 to wage an open war in South Vietnam, was an extension and under total command of the Hanoi government. Its descendant "Revolutionary Provisional Government of South Vietnam" was dissolved in 1976 after the Hanoi government's 1975 complete takeover of South Vietnam.

Like stones bouncing freely on a bumpy incline, the proposals, questions, and issues brought up by the Republic of Vietnam were turned into other questions, or shelved as part of some general problem that could only be solved some time in the future. You could expect no direct answers to the questions raised during the meeting.

I listened attentively, taking notes and feeling curiously relaxed with cold indifference. . . . So, that was the original strategy of the Communists: never give a direct answer to a question, keep turning around aimlessly, for as long as possible and as far away as possible from the real issue at hand, and be as vague as possible. The Communists would always create difficulties and blur the issues even though they only had to do with the technical or procedural matters. As solemn as an old clerk, as clever as a professional gambler, the Communist delegate always tried to prolong the meeting in order to intentionally and systemically wear down the adversary. The Paris Talks could have gone on for four more years or forty more years with these expert negotiators. In a serious tone, they always tried to evade or to shift the problem rudely and in complete disregard of the undeniable facts. Colonel Dat presented the incident that took place in Bien Hoa on the morning of Feb. 12, 1973: Communist prisoners refused to board the trucks that were to take them to the airport and demanded to meet a representative of North Vietnam to give them assurance and guarantee their release. The representatives of the prisoners declared that they did not trust the representative of the NLF (Col. Le Truc). That was the fact: the North Vietnamese P.O.W.s did not trust the representative of the National Liberation Front. . .

Confronted with the facts, Tran Tan slowly opened his notebook and, after clearing his throat, said, "Gentlemen, according to Articles 1 and 2 of the Annex on the question of the prisoners-of-war, there are only three categories of P.O.W.s: prisoners of the U.S. and other foreign countries, prisoners of the Republic of Vietnam, and prisoners of the Provisional Government of Republic of South Vietnam.[2] Therefore, according to the content of these Articles, and the agreements at the Paris Peace Talks, we affirm that there are no North Vietnamese prisoners in South Vietnam!" That was absolutely in the book and in conformance with the

2. The Revolutionary Provisional Government of the Republic of South Vietnam was a self-proclaimed body derived from the National Liberation Front in an attempt to confuse the non-Vietnamese public and to strive for a governmental status when the war was on course to be settled by political solutions.

strategy! I had to try to restrain my laugh at his straight-facedness, his eyes sparkling with self-satisfaction, and his "sharp reaction" in accordance with the "spirit of the annex." The agreement, a tricky design forged by eminent crooks, would often be used as a basis for arguments and frequently repeated with the solemnity of a sacred teaching. Most of the meetings would proceed in that way, aimlessly, uselessly, and characterized by the polite shamelessness of the Vietcong side, and four hours would pass without a hitch.

So they were Communists, the authentic Communists, the Class A Communists, the core cadres who could hope to become Central Committee members in the future. Le Truc, secretary of General Tra, the Defense Minister of the Provisional "Government," was an expert in three issues: supplementary lists of military prisoners, the release of 140 civilian prisoners to the South Vietnamese government, and demand for more releases of prisoners held by the Saigon side in addition to the ones that had been scheduled for release. Truc tirelessly went back and forth with the three issues during four full hours, ignoring the question from Colonel Dat of the Saigon side: Why did you not receive the prisoners that we have brought up to the Thach Han River for release? He also ignored the question from Colonel Russell: Why did you not release our American P.O.W.s exactly at 8:30 at Loc Ninh as you had promised? In complete disregard of the clear and sharp questions hurled at him Truc took time dwelling on the three problems in his field, like a duck frolicking by itself in a separate pond. The fact was that the north bank of the Thach Han River was under the control of the North Vietnamese Army and Truc could not send out instructions directly to them, nor could he receive instructions from them without intermediaries. That helped to explain the pitiful show of arrogance that Truc put up while discoursing on unrelated issues to evade the facts. How long did he manage to stay in Paris, I wondered?

I faced the Communists, I listened to their empty answers, their vacuous arguments, their play-acting of anger and tasteless pleasantries. . . . I saw clearly the whole strategy and tactics of the enemy senior cadres—an enemy about whom so many myths had ben weaved. Knowing the enemy in order to know ourselves. Neither a superiority complex nor an inferiority complex is advisable, I concluded. They are just ordinary experts, I told myself, ordinary in their appearançe, in their speech, in the tone of their voice, in the intensity of their looks. After all, they are just desk men, knowing their lessons, doing their homework, obedient to their superiors, faithfully carrying out their instructions, and performing their duties by rote and by routine practices rather than by skillful and flexible initiative. . . . This is a football team consisting of average players specializing in teamwork but there are no outstanding athletes among them allowed to develop a personal style. In a general way, and without risk of error, that was basically the main characteristic of a Communist cadre.

The war, and the peace, had been carried out and managed by these senior cadres. They were the rigid and single-minded executors. The men who looked upon the tragic history of the people as coldly as if they were just juggling with numbers and categories . . . I had faced them on the battlefields. I had known their brutalities and cruelties. I now ran across them again, an obdurate adversary sitting across a large table covered with green felt. The rude brutalities on the battlefield and the rigid radicalism in the conference room belonged to the same nature, the nature of systemic reflexes built in after long periods of trials and control. I was not being confronted with a different breed of people. These men were only good cadres who knew how to follow instructions, and how to keep their personal emotions, if they had any, from influencing the proceeding of their duties. My impressions were taking shape, like the spirals of cigarette smoke that cannot disperse in the still air of a closed room. There was a lurking pain that obsessed me, though. This war certainly had its own logic. The Communists apparently could only live in a world of conflict and strife. Isn't it true that the philosophy of dialectic materialism is built upon the concept of an explosive clash between two opposite elements? In the conference room humming with air-conditioners, there is suddenly something like the portentous moment of silence after a shell has been hurled out from the innards of a cannon. . . .

[FEBRUARY 1973]

Two

The "Kaolo" Pen

SUDDENLY I SAW a whole series of my youthful days unfold before my eyes when I flipped through an old album looking at old pictures. Across from me, a little to the right, Lieutenant-Colonel Tuan Anh, of the North Vietnamese delegation, laid his pen on the negotiating table. It was a snorkel pen, brown with yellowish stripes. It has been such a long time! Twenty years ago, as I recalled, as a reward for having successfully completed my elementary education, I was given a "Kaolo" pen, the most expensive gift I had ever received until then. It was heavy and unwieldy in my small hand. As I carefully applied a rotating motion to one end of the pen, the writing tip, a glass cone with helical threads was slowly twisted out of the tube, amid murmurs of appreciation of the kids who were looking on and were greatly impressed by the performance. The pen cost seventy-five piasters, it could write on any side, and the nib remained fine even after long use. As I gleefully reversed the rotating motion, the nib gradually retreated into its nest. Twenty years. The kid who, until that day, had never tasted crushed ice, had grown into a man, and had witnessed the climactic upheavals that defied his sense of fairness and credibility, the strange, sudden, and explosive changes that came about day after day, year after year. Changes that took place in the material world outside as well as in the minds of people, in the way they look at the world, in the way they think, changes that affected each nuance of thought, even in the way people react to changes.

In 1950, Mr. Nixon protested Secretary of State Dean Acheson's conciliatory policy toward Communist China. In 1972, that same strongly anti-Communist politician was seen delicately fixing the jacket for Chau En Lai, a most affectionate gesture beyond the requirement of diplomatic courtesy. In 1950, Senator McCarthy achieved notoriety for his Communist witch-hunting tactics. Less than twenty years later, the pendulum had swung to the opposite direction in the person of Mr. McGovern. In the early 1950s, bicycles with tubeless tires were considered a mark of social status in Saigon. In 1972, Solex and Sachs motorcycles were becoming antiques, and even the Mustangs had lost their original glamour. Ex-emperor Bao Dai, despite the recent exploratory articles by the French *Figaro* paper—and the support by some Saigon papers—remained an old has-been, a thing of the past. There can be no Peronist phenomenon in Vietnam where twenty years of war have brought about a complete upheaval in the life of the people and in the values of society. If anything, the Vietnamese people have proved to be the most resilient people in the world.

But the Communists in North Vietnam apparently have remained immune to change. There is something of a "deja-vu" in the way they dress, in the way they go about doing things, in the way they express their ideas and present their arguments, in the way they smoke, and exhale the smoke, and put their hands on the table, and straighten their glasses. . . . In 1950, at a war zone upstream of the Perfume River, in the A Shau valley, I asked a prisoner of war, "Uncle Nhan," "Why is your rifle so big?" and the immediate reply was "I need a big rifle to shoot the French." I got the same retort when I asked a Communist cadre at Loc Ninh airbase recently, "Why do you all have baggy pants?" and the retort was: "The baggy pants give us ease of movement in our fight against the Americans." After more than twenty years, we are now facing the same people, with the same way of thinking, the same propaganda line, the same jargon (resistance, country-selling clique, peasant-and-worker struggle) that is so confusing and ear-jangling uttered by people with hair parted in the middle and shaved close to the scalp on the sides. . .

Lieutenant Colonel Tuan Anh, the one with the most placid and intellectual appearance in the North Vietnamese delegation, had a bright smile. His smile, however, seemed to be well calculated, well prepared. Do you think that Indochina could be balkanized, with some possibility for progress and freedom? The smile, which had been measured out, vanished on his lips, with astonishing suddenness. But watching him solemnly positioning his pen on the table, and gravely twisting out the tip of his pen, I understood immediately. The twenty years that had passed had not brought about any changes in the immutable and strictly organized Northern part of the country. The 138 pages of Vo Nguyen Giap's *People's War and People's Army* (Su That Publishing House, 1959) contained nothing but vague and crude arguments. On page 112, Giap defined the People's Army as an army that is truly of the people, "of the working people, basically the peasants and workers, an army led by the proletariat!" Then Giap went on to talk about the People's Army under party leadership. And what is Giap's Party? It is the Indochinese Communist Party founded in 1930. And the Party, Giap wrote, concluding his argument, represents the whole people. Giap had the wisdom of not trying to tie the knot of this argument.

I marched on the road to An Loc in June 1972, I went into Quang Tri with the paratroopers in the last days of July of the same year. Plodding up Route 13 and Highway 1, the roads strewn with dead, I was constantly tormented with several questions: How can the Communists be so cruel? How can they murder innocent civilians with such cold-bloodedness? But now I believed I understood the Communists had acted in strict accordance with the directives of their doctrine, which had thoroughly impregnated their thinking, even their breath. "The People's Army takes charge of the armed struggle to realize socialism. The People's Army fights for the interests of the revolutionary working class, with the support of the people of the U.S.S.R., and the progressive and peace-loving peoples in the world." Therefore, the people of South Vietnam, who are not revolutionary, who are not class-conscious, who do not support that struggle, will be considered as enemies and traitors that have to be destroyed.

We in South Vietnam will probably never accept this kind of strange, stupid, and wicked argument. We cannot even conceive that such crude and destructive thinking could have been used as guidelines for so many murderous acts. But such are the realities, as terrifying and shocking as they appeared. They have been seen during the Tet Offensive in Hue, in the battle of Quang Tri in April of 1972, on Route 13 to An Loc and Chon Thanh in March of 1972. Even though as a combat soldier I have many times brushed with death during my long years in the army, I still could not understand the mind of the adversary, and these questions continued to bother me, until today.

As I sat in this closed conference room, and watched the old pen being laid on the green covering of the negotiating table, the realization came to me as a flash. I understood the truth of their murderous system. It was a terrifying discovery: the Communists kill as a result of definitions, born from their Autumn Revolution and refined after more than nineteen years of socialism. These definitions were raised as old banners leading the way to ruthless massacres. I understood that Mr. Ngo Dinh Diem,[1] the last mandarin of a bygone era, as symbolized by his heavy desk in the style of Louis XIV, had to pay the price with his own life for his incapacity to bend with the wind.

How can the Communist officer sitting across from me, handling his old pen with so much care, catch up with the world? How can he understand the mind of the South Vietnamese people when his brain is so thickened with outdated arguments of comrade general, a history professor from the 1930s, who concocted directives for the conduct of the war by such vacuous arguments as this one: "The success of the armed struggle of the Vietnamese people is due to the victory of the Red Army over the Japanese and the German fascists." Enough, comrade general! It is just because of that miserable victory (!) that the French were able to return to Vietnam and share with you, over nine long years, the bloody feast where the Vietnamese people were the victims.

But these arguments have been written down on paper, and dirty mimeographed copies of the book have been widely distributed to each "Combatant," to each cadre down to the village and hamlet level, to people whose minds are as closed and heavy as bricks, to be made even more impervious by the fire of the Communist furnace, so much so that, in this year 1973, in Loc Ninh, or in Thach Han, or wherever you go, you would run against the same theme: Marxism-Leninism has taught us this, Marxism-Leninism has taught us that. . . . That war, the state, the army are all historical phenomena of class struggles which would come to an end when there are no more classes in society, that is when Communism has achieved victory all over the world! Marxism and Leninism and the October Revolution belong to history, but "Colonel" Nam Tich, commander of the Loc Ninh airbase, that peasant who turned his back on his rice fields to join the Communists, is never tired of repeating the lessons that he has learned. Is it true that socialist ideology has finally penetrated his thick head, as acknowledged by the rank of lieutenant colonel given him?

[MARCH 1973]

1. Ngo Dinh Diem was the President of the First Republic of South Vietnam from 1955–63, executed together with his brother in the 1963 U.S.-backed coup by a military junta headed by General Duong Van Minh.

Three

White Hair on the Green Felt

SITTING ACROSS from me are two white-haired men, a Colonel and a Lieutenant Colonel of the National Liberation Front. Both of them are over fifty, their hair is overwhelmingly white, they have pallid complexions and strange looks in their eyes. The man with the rank of Colonel is named Nguyen Hoan, a native o Ben Tre. He has a bright smile, which he rarely uses, but he often affects a self-confident attitude by sitting back in his chair and directing his strange look straight into the eyes of the interlocutor facing him. It is a strangely wicked look, emanating from a pair of eyes that are adorned with blue half circles and that shine as if through a thin veil of liquid, a look that is obviously the reflection of a sick man and violent temperament as of a sadist enjoying the sight of a victim writhing under tortures. In fact, that look denotes a supremely violent nature, a kind of absolute inhumanity and coldness of the likes of Goering and Rudolf Hess, of those who are supremely confident in their own doctrines and the righteousness of their own acts. His is the look of a man who is no longer a human being, since he has agreed to become a non-entity in his complete immersion in the flow of historical movement. Nguyen Hoan's are a pair of electronic eyes ever watchful of other people's reactions. The second man is named Bui Thiep, a native of Quy Nhon province. Thiep has a heavy, diffident face circled with wrinkles that run from his forehead around to the corners of his mouth, like the stripes on the head of a tiger. Thiep is a melancholy and wearied tiger, which is to say that signs of violence can still be detected lurking behind the tired mask. Thiep is like a beast waking up from a doze after a bloody meal.

I am not exaggerating in my description of the adversary. I am just trying to express truthfully my impressions of the Communist cadres who confronted me, whom I have talked with for a protracted period of time. I believe the images and metaphors I have used to describe Nguyen Hoan and Bui Thiep do reflect their personalities. On the other hand, I am not even sure these are their true names. Perhaps they are only their noms de guerre, but they no doubt belong to the generation of cadres issued from the Autumn Revolution of 1946 and are probably card-carrying members of the Communist Party from before 1946. Both of them were given military ranks after the military congress in Hanoi in 1956. They are cadres from the South regrouped to the North in 1954 to prepare to return to the South according to the terms of the 1954 Geneva Agreement. Although they did not return to the South in 1956 as had been planned, they nevertheless were the first cadres of the National Liberation Front at its founding a few years later. Before coming to Saigon, Thiep and Hoan spent several long months and years working in the Paris negotiations. In short, both of them are core cadres of the National Liberation Front, possibly with many achievements during their long years of struggle under the leadership of the Party.

Their experiences are reflected in their self-control and the strictness of their behavior, as well as in the way they present their arguments seemingly in accordance with the theories of dialectic materialism. Their speeches are well rehearsed, their presentations and counter-arguments at the negotiating table follow a simple, easily identified pattern. This is an example. The Government of South Vietnam denounced the fact that both military and civilian prisoners of war were still being detained by the Communists in several places scattered all over Indochina. As supporting evidence, the GVN delegation quoted prisoners' messages broadcast over Hanoi and NLF radios, letters and pictures transmitted through released GVN P.O.W.s. Apparently, it would seem that this evidence would be hard to reject. However, Hoan and Thiep (or any other member of their delegation, including Hoang Anh Tuan, or Si, or Giang, who are at the level of heads of delegation) managed to successfully evade the issue in accordance with their instructions. First of all, they rejected the denunciation by claiming that the charges were "blatantly made up" by the South Vietnamese side. Then, quoting from the opposition press in Saigon, such as the Catholic *Doi Dien* paper, from the "White Papers" by Ho Ngoc Nhuan, from the various protest notes by international organizations calling for improvement of the prison system in South Vietnam (always stressing the accuracy and reliability of the documents since they were issued from Saigon or from the Free World), they launched into the countercharge that hundreds of thousands of people were still being detained and subjected to harsh and brutal treatment by the Saigon government, which therefore, has seriously violated the Paris Agreement, and the Annex Agreement on the Release of Military and Civilian Prisoners!

The arguments seemed to be logical, the presentation was made smoothly, and the tone of voice was determined enough without going beyond the prescribed spirit of reconciliation. . . . Communist cadres used the same phraseology, the same way of presenting a problem and concluding a speech, according to the guidelines and instructions given them during their study sessions. At first, I felt some admiration for the methods of work of the Communists because obviously they always did a lot of homework before coming to the negotiating table, where their performance was quite homogenous. But after six or seven months I became utterly bored with the Communist jargon, their mania for using obscure words to express such simple ideas as "presentation of a problem," "development of the issue," "outlining the issue," "recapitulating the proposed solutions," etc., and their tireless repetitions of such phrases as "spirit of national reconciliation and concord," "serious observance of the spirit and letter of the Cease-Fire Agreement," "struggle for peace and freedom."

I became suspicious: Are these all the strong points of the Communists? I have come to see that their way to analyze a problem is based on certain simple, elementary rules and their vocabulary consists of a certain number of obscure phrases and words apparently good for use in any circumstance. From the soldier standing guard on the north bank of the Thach Han River to the general sitting at the negotiating table they all have the same way of talking, the same phrases, the same crude arguments good for all occasions. Doubt became conviction, the initial feeling of admiration was altered into complete boredom. "The struggle of the patriotic and revolutionary Vietnamese people has received the enthusiastic support of the peace-loving peoples in the whole world."

How many times have I heard such overused phrases, which probably were coined as early as the 1940s? Although they have lost virtually all their meaning and effectiveness after their almost three decades of overuse and abuse, these phrases, like rocks polished by the years, continued to be solemnly inserted in any talk, any article from the theoretical texts in the Party's *Hoc Tap Journal*, to remarks by Vo Nguyen Giap on People's War, to the scribbling of a Communist reporter filing his stories from somewhere in the mountains of Quang Tri for publication in the *Giai Phong* paper—"Giai Phong" meaning liberation, another overused word!

It is strange that the Communists built their doctrine on theories of conflicts, the process of destruction through theses and anti-theses, the materialistic explanation of history. But in many aspects, they seem to be most conservative and most determined to stick to a spiritualistic point of view. In the first years, after the Labour Party had been renamed, a Party Congress was held at the foot of a banyan tree, near a cave, somewhere in the year 1940 or 1941. Many of the phrases used by Communist cadres today were invented in that Congress more than thirty years ago. I wonder how those same words can reflect the new realities of today? It is true that the Communists have not achieved any real progress in the way of language and, in a more general sense, they have not been able to contribute anything new to culture. We cannot judge the enemy through a few obscure and crude phrases which are probably mainly intended for propaganda. But we have to recognize the truth, and the truth is that each period, each phase of history has its own language, its own vocabulary that keeps pace with changes in society, and while the Vietnamese language, as we compare the state of the language now with the state of the language thirty years ago, has proved its wonderful capacity for evolution, the Communists have ridiculously continued to use words and phrases that have been emptied of all meaning. That is why, in the year 1973, they continue to repeat such phrases as "the cordial and friendly relations between Vietnam, China, and the U.S.S.R.," "the great brotherly country of the Soviet Union," "the peace-loving brotherly countries in the world."

Is there any more "brotherly country" in this era of treachery and deceitfulness? Is there still a "great and brotherly Soviet Union" in light of the brutal suppression of Poland and Czechoslovakia by the Red Army, under the pretext of safeguarding the Warsaw pact? It is not even possible to argue that these words and phrases, however devoid of meaning they have become, are only used for mass consumption, for propaganda purposes aimed at the foot soldier, the artillery man. Because the same words are used in the will of Ho Chi Minh, in the remarks of General Giap, in the pronouncements by General Secretary Le Duan, the same language is being spoken by General Tra and Colonel Si, the same phraseology, the same jargon, is still being maintained as the linguistic framework of the Vietnamese Labor (Communist) Party in their proletarian struggle.

Language is the reflection of the spirit, and a spirit, if it can call itself "progressive," cannot be contented with a language that has been kept unchanged for thirty years, just as it is not possible to use one of the first Ford automobiles in a twenty-five-hour auto race. The style of the critic Truong Tuu may have seemed original in the years 1930–31, but this criticism is totally out of place when it comes to understanding the novels of the 1960s and 1970s. The worker and the peasant class cannot launch their struggle in a society where the new and principal victims are the intellectuals constantly threatened both physically and mentally.

The Communist regime in the Soviet Union was shaken in 1973 not because of the outstanding success of the American Skylab, or because of the deployment of Chinese troops along the Issouri River, or the unrest of workers in Siberia, but because of a few hundred words by Solzhenitsyn and a few statements by the scientist Andrei Sakharov. That is why, in the new realities, the old Communist societal construct has become so unrealistically constrained. But at the end of his will, Ho Chi Minh, the most brilliant mind of the Vietnamese Communists, still wrote: "After I pass away, I will be able to rejoin comrade Karl Marx and comrade Lenin." (!) Karl Marx and Lenin are towering figures who have greatly influenced contemporary history in the Soviet Union—but their roles, their thinking are being reassessed in their own countries. But in Vietnam, half a world away from the capital of the proletarian revolution, and half a century away from the start of the Communist revolution, President Ho Chi Minh still firmly believed in the ultimate victory of a doctrine that had run its course. It is indeed a most serious mistake. . . . The Vietnamese Communists will not open their eyes to the blinding light of history.

"My dear nieces and nephews! In our struggle, we have to shed our blood, we have to turn our rice fields and out gardens into battlefields, we have to make swords out of plough shares, to turn peasants into combatants. . . ." Thus spoke Ho Chi Minh to a group of cadres on the way to war. I would not believe that these words are the reflection of a violent nature because I cannot think that an old man of over sixty could still harbor the wish to see the shedding of blood. But this pronouncement reflects the unshakeable belief in ultimate victory, in the course of history, not only for his people but for the whole of mankind as well. Because of this belief, from Ho Chi Minh down to the members of the party's Central Committee, to the members of the National Liberation Front, such things as the cold-blooded massacres in Hue during the Tet Offensive have happened. It is because of that belief that as early as the years 1964–65, a man named Nguyen Van Hang, a native of Nam Dinh province in North Vietnam, was given the Cambodian name of Thach Met and appointed village chief of a Cambodian village in the Parrot's Beak area. That belief in ultimate victory also moved the Communists to accept the slogan "Born in the North to Die in the South."

The Vietnamese Communists have forgotten that the war in Vietnam is no longer a war against the imperialists or the feudalists, that there can be no liberation when the world powers have decided to pick Vietnam as a place for reconciliation. (!) The atomic bomb in 1945 signaled the end of the people's liberation war against the powerful imperialists and colonialists. (?!) That bomb was the first clash of two conflicting ideologies which were looking for ways toward peaceful coexistence over the blood and bones of the Vietnamese people. The Vietnamese Communists cannot understand, cannot bring themselves to accept reality. It took the world twenty-eight years after the end of the Second World War to get out of the Cold War, with its balance of terrors, thanks to the final explosion in Vietnam.

The world is safely held in equilibrium over the body of our country. The Vietnamese Communists cannot understand these simple facts. Likewise, they did not know that their general offensive against An Loc, Quang Tri, and Kon Tum only served to open wide the gates of the B-52 ammunition depots where the bombs had been stacked to the brim after a period of waiting. They did not know that one B-52 shot down in Hanoi did not mean anything in the 24-hour continuous attack on Dec. 5, 1972, by the terrible armada of 200 B-52s and 500 jet fighters and bombers. That was a demonstration that an all-out, massive air attack could be mounted against any objective on the Asian continent from the invulnerable island bases of Guam, Midway, and Wake. Then the Americans quietly withdrew from Vietnam and Thailand after completing the military exercise for which the target was North Vietnam. The Americans made an outstandingly successful show of force to the Russians and the Chinese, while at the same time demonstrating their restraint. The two Communist powers, reassured, pushed North Vietnam to sign the Agreement.

That was it, the war in Indochina was, for all purposes, over. The North Vietnamese and the Khmer Rouges are threatening Phnom Penh? Laying siege to Battambang? Units of the North Vietnamese 320th division are attacking the Le Minh base camp? The Rangers at the Tong Le Chan camp are encircled by the Vietcong's 9th Division for 16 months to this day? But these are only small clashes in a local conflict lost in the three immensities which are the Soviet Union, China, and the United States. The Vietnamese Communists would not believe this and are determined to make the last steps in their path to victory: liberation of the

South, reunification of the country, and domination of Laos and Cambodia under the dark shadow of the Indochinese Communist Party. The Vietnamese Communist is like an ant which has managed to climb up to the rim of a cup and thinks it has succeeded in staying away from the abyss. Ho Chi Minh, if his soul could come back, would certainly feel bitter to see Kissinger riding on a Volga from Gia Lam airport to Hanoi, past the ruins of the Central Station destroyed by the bombing of 1972. It was as if it were only yesterday, but Ho died on Sept. 3, 1969.

—

Across the table from me, the two white-haired Communist cadres are again repeating a number of familiar phrases (which I know by heart after three months in this place): "In serious observance of the Agreement, we take note of your proposal concerning the issue of the Government of Vietnam's P.O.W.s captured in Lower Laos. We also demand that you release unconditionally 200,000 political prisoners. We would cite as evidence the 'White Papers' of Mr. Ho Ngoc Nhuan,[1] the statement of Gen. Duong Van Minh,[2] the appeals from Representatives Truong Gia Ky Sanh and Ho Huu Tuong,[3] and from the Committee for the Improvement of the Prison System in South Vietnam. . . ."[4] I looked at the minutes of the meeting on April 20, 1973: all that had been brought up during that previous meeting.

What changes can we expect from these Communist cadres? They are continuing: "Article one of the Paris Agreement guarantees the right for self-determination. Vietnam is an independent, unified country, as stipulated in the Geneva Agreement of 1954. Therefore, there can be no such thing as an invasion by North Vietnam against South Vietnam. How can you use the word 'invasion'

1. Ho Ngoc Nhuan was an anti-government activist and left-leaning representative of South Vietnam's National Assembly. After 1975 he was selected to be a member of the Vietnamese Communist National Assembly.
2. Duong Van Minh was a general who led the November 1963 coup that terminated the First Republic of South Vietnam and in which president Ngo Dinh Diem was executed upon his surrender. Considered neutralist and soft-headed, he was chosen on April 28, 1975, as an acceptable figure for surrendering to the Communist troops two days later.
3. Truong Ky Sanh and Ho Huu Tuong were Fourth International-influenced socialists.
4. Committee for the Improvement of the Prison System in South Vietnam was a Vietcong front set up to disinform the foreign media and to denigrate the South Vietnam government.

for people in the same country?" Words and words that I have heard so many times, I have known so many absurdities, but what can you expect from these men when they remained mute to the questions: How can a man be "liberated" out of a community of his own choice? How do those so-called "liberated cases" square with more than 300,000 "liberated" people who broke their ranks to defect? Why did the inhabitants of the "liberated" villages in Loc Ninh, Dakto, Gio Linh, and Dong Ha brave death to flee to the government-held areas?

These are very concrete questions, but I do not have any hope for any satisfactory answers—and I don't expect any changes from them. Their reflexes have been conditioned by training, indoctrination has taken the place of private thinking, and directives and instructions have overpowered their minds. What can we expect from these men who have more than twenty years of party membership to their credit? Their hair has turned white after thirty years in the proletarian revolution, they have climbed to the rank of colonel in the army and senior political commissar in the Front's Central Committee. It is "their promised land" now . . . what can they do outside it? What will they become other than reverting to what they truly were: a teacher of elementary school, a complete failure thrown out of the mainstream of great change and progress? Let's imagine the return of Bui Thiep to his native village in Binh Dinh, with his khaki bag on his shoulder and his rubber sandals made out of old tires on his feet. Without the badge rank and without the authority that goes with it, what is he going to do in his village, where many local inhabitants have moved away, where no wife and no children wait for him? He is going to be alone with his own shadow lengthening on the yellow and dry ground in the dying light of the day. . . . Without the "proletarian revolution," without his rank of Colonel, Bui Thiep will fall into a terrifying nothingness. There will be nothing left for him, nothing, except some white hair in the palm of his hand.

[APRIL 1973]

Four

Up to the North, Back to the South

FOR MORE THAN A MONTH now I have been feeling turgescent, like a balloon fully inflated, like a person brimming with energy without knowing how to expend it. After long years as a career combat soldier, I was suddenly picked out to participate in the quiet battle around a felt-covered conference table in a room filled with the humming of air conditioners. On certain days, things are happening around me at a hectic pace. On others, it is just plan boring, such as sessions which, after four long hours of inconclusive talks, could be summarized in just one sentence: The session is adjourned for the delegations to receive new instructions. The battle takes place behind closed doors, but it can also reach out as far as the Phu Quoc Quan, and as far up as the north bank of the Thach Han River.

I have to write—I am thrilled with the possibility that I will be able to sit down quietly with my pen to begin my memoirs, "P.O.W.s and Peace." Details are falling in place while I am aboard the U-21 on an outgoing trip early in the day or on a return trip from Loc Ninh airbase at sundown. My mind is being filled with outlines, subdivisions, images, materials, and they all wait for me to have a propitious time with my pen to come out on paper. But no, I still have to hold it back, because the story is still developing, because of the requirements of my duties, and because the situation is still too confusing for me to feel independent enough and clear-minded enough to begin. I am telling myself that I will have to wait until the sixtieth day, or the ninetieth day, or perhaps some day not so far away.

But today is the day I will have to use my pen. The upcoming trip to Hanoi is like a glaring light flashing into the forgotten corners of my mind where layer upon layer of primal impressions have quietly settled down all these years. Old images suddenly come back to mind of an ancient native country, where history goes back to the very birth of a whole people. Hanoi, that sacred land of the impressionable mind, the source of vibrant emotions for so many outstanding writers and poets of the romantic era . . . Hanoi, a geographical name that calls to mind, for many people living below the Seventeenth parallel, some vague reminiscence of a place that can only exist in a dream.

But I have come to that place. I belong to the South, and I have grown up in the South, but I have come to the capital of the North. I have come, and I have returned laden with strange emotions and melancholy. It is an undefinable feeling, a gnawing emotion, a pensive mood, a dizzying weariness. I have to note these emotions. I have to write. I have to dedicate my book to that mysterious and sacred land that has fallen in ruins, and to the South as well, that glorious land that has nurtured us, that has never yet received our praise, that has been so generous to us without demanding anything in return. On the plane this evening, I was suddenly seized with a vague feeling of guilt, as I looked down: the plane was turning in from the sea; in the west, the sun, a dazzling red, was sinking into the horizon; the darkened stretch of land in Long Khanh was dotted with some small forest fires here and there—the South.

I must say that I am just jotting down the first impressions of a young man from the South after a trip to the North, and as such I am writing what I think and in complete freedom, and this certainly is not a report from a member of the South Vietnamese delegation to the Joint Military Commission, and this has no propaganda purpose. This kind of clarification may seem comical to the readers in South Vietnam, but this is most necessary for the North Vietnamese readers—those who have read and dissected the articles by Duong Phuc and Pham Huan and pronounced their judgment with sharp and misleading criticism. In short, the people who have their own views of "good performance" of duties and activities of all kinds.

Glancing toward land, I saw the dark outline of the Hai Van Pass above the graying horizon. At this cruising speed, we would be flying into the airspace of North Vietnam within the next fifteen minutes. In 1967, leading a unit moving up to the Demilitarized Zone, I stayed up all night to wait for the first light of day so that I could look to the North. I still remember the strong emotions I felt that day when I saw the beach front from Cua Tung curving up in the golden light of the sun toward Vinh Linh and Dong Hoi and reaching further up out of sight. That emotion has lain dormant within me ever since. "That is the sense of the indivisible motherland," I had very sincerely written down in my first notebook. But today, flying over the North and looking out of the porthole, I saw the white sand beach all the way from Quang Tri to Quang Binh and strangely, I felt nothing within me. . . . Have I changed so much? I was feeling as if I were a stranger to myself. Here I am, flying over the Northern part of my motherland, passing Cua Tung, and then over Dong Hoi, and I am feeling so calm, so indifferent. How can I explain to myself this lack of emotion? It is really strange because all night yesterday, I was still feeling so restless in anticipation of the trip. Now, at this very minute, the North is right here, below me, but all the emotions stacked up within me have evaporated. Why? Ever since I was a kid, and perhaps to the end of my days, I have always had the biggest wish, and that is to set foot in every corner of the country. Foreign lands, foreign scenery never caused me any excitement, never elicited in me any emotions. I can imagine myself standing at the foot of the Eiffel Tower; perhaps I would feel gleeful because I would have satisfied my curiosity, because I had seen a famous object. And that is all. But when flying at an altitude of about 200 meters and looking down at the Cai Lon River flowing into the Pacific Ocean at the Rach Gia estuary, I was not just seeing, taking it in: I was living it, I was losing myself in deep enchantment, I was overwhelmed by a dizzying sensation as when one finds oneself face to face with real beauty, as when one is witnessing a miracle. I imagined myself living the life of our forefathers in this grandiose scenery. I could see them, as I could see myself, steering a flimsy boat over the Tien Giang and the Hau Giang Rivers, armed with knives and sticks, looking up at the dark and mysterious vegetation of the U Minh forest on the banks of the rivers, and out toward the misty sea where a powerful tide was rushing in, filling the great expanse of the river with new life and new energy. This is where there is no clear limit between land and sea, where alluvial deposits flow out to sea and the sea reaches inland through the marshy forests planted deep in water along the coast, like in the beginning of times. I did not see only the Rach Gia estuary. I relived other times, at other times in history. I saw myself waking up in the middle of the night on the bank of the river, growing restless because of the lapping of the water among the reeds in the rising tide. Looking out the window of the helicopter at the sea 200 meters below, I saw not only the Pacific Ocean turning a saffron yellow along the coast because of the alluviums, I could also hear the heroic battle drums of troops under the command of Emperor Nguyen Hue chasing the Siamese through the foamy waves, and the flags flapping in the wind over the yellow sea. That is why it is so strange that I felt nothing when I was flying over the Ma River, or Ninh Binh province, or elsewhere in the North. Has there been some change inside me since yesterday? Why?

The helicopter circled over rice fields submerged under water, over the dikes, some willow trees, a misty scenery. I hadn't seen any bamboo trees, the national plant. Everything seemed so sluggish, compared to the liveliness of the South Vietnamese countryside. I continued to feel strangely calm. The plane was descending.

I opened my hand to try to catch the tiny droplets of rain. So this was the spring drizzle, the North Vietnamese drizzle. The droplets of water were so fine that it took a long time for me to get my hand wet. A group of people in drab brown and olive rainwater stood waiting for us at the airport. They silently watched us approach. I was walking behind Lieutenant Colonel Tuan Anh, the North Vietnamese officer who served as guide for the delegation of the Joint Military Commission. A nervous thought crossed my mind: what if those people rushed out and gave us a beating in return for the recent beating of North Vietnamese soldiers by the civilian population in Hue? The thought took on some credibility when I realized that some of the same North Vietnamese officers injured in the beating were aboard our plane and were being carried into the airport. Fuck! Why should I be afraid of them? I have brushed with death many times during my years as a combat soldier, and I have also gone alone into Loc Ninh and Minh Thanh; besides, I was telling myself, the Communists never did anything on the spur of the moment . . . their actions are always preceded by study sessions, criticism sessions, discussions . . . and this is the phase of reconciliation and concord . . . no, that cannot be . . .

In reviewing my own reactions and emotions, I found again, to my own astonishment, that I remained utterly calm. I remembered my return to Hue after a few years away: as soon as the plane approached the stormy waters of the Cau Hai estuary, I was seized with restlessness. It was a real emotional upheaval when I saw the misty waters of the Tam Giang confluent in the evening light, and the dark blue ribbons of the waterways curving through the Duong Nong and Niem Pho regions, and the old bamboo leaves floating on the water. . . . I had felt the same emotional disturbance when, standing in the Xa Cam rubber plantation, I looked out into An Loc crouching behind the smoke of artillery fire. But now that Hanoi was right here, before our eyes, as real as the drizzle that was cooling our faces, as tangible as the fine mist-like vapor that condensed on our eyelashes and wetted our clothes, my heart was strangely stilled. . . . It was an inexplicable strangeness, that absence of feelings. For the last few days up until last night, after the trip had been confirmed (after having been reassured that there would be no last-minute cancellation, as had happened with the trips scheduled for the 12th and 18th of February), I had been so restless, I couldn't stand still or sit still, I was suffocated with emotions that crescendoed as the minutes and the hours went by and I felt myself closer and closer to Hanoi, that vague place that had only existed in my imagination . . .

"This is the Tran Quoc Pagoda . . . O, ancient temple, weather-beaten and silent witness to so many upheavals, thou art pained with nostalgia . . ." proclaimed my friend Dang Giao. He pointed to the particulars on a map of Hanoi. "This is the former Governor's Mansion, this is the Hom Market . . . the Peace Hotel is here at this intersection, as Phuc said, and right behind there is the fountain with the toads spouting water . . . And be sure to remember to just have a glance into this house at number 102 on this street! I lived there until the last day before we were evacuated to the South. My aunt is supposed to be still living there. I wish you could look inside and see if there is anybody in the house. I am sure you will be able to walk through this street! My aunt and my mother resemble each other like two drops of water, so if you see her you will recognize her immediately!"

I tried to memorize almost a dozen addresses: number 102 and number 115 on X street, numbers 35 and 19 on Y street . . . the addresses and the recommendations given me in deeply moved tones of voice through which I could guess at the restrained sobs.

I had lived through two days of conflagration before setting foot in Hanoi. So this is the day, I thought—this is the day of the event, the day that I had hoped for. I can touch with my own hands the misty wetness in the air, I can actually feel the soothing coolness of the drizzle in the first days of spring in Hanoi—Hanoi, the cultural capital of the nation, the center of the civilized way of life. But I was unmoved. The restless anticipation of the last few days had vanished and in its place there was only cold and hard thinking. As I sat down, sipping the warm beer, the advice from my friends Pham Huan and Duong Phuc came back to my mind. I had to get myself ready for the confrontation. I would start with "a campaign of the smile," I thought. My heart flinched at the cold, almost rude, calculations taking shape in my mind, but I knew that was just a defensive reaction. I realized that I had to be wary. For more than a month, I had been the target of verbal attacks, always with a smile, always coming when least expected, lightning attacks right after a warm handshake, sudden thrusts during a chat, like poisonous needles lashed into your face out of nowhere.

"Where are you from? Are your parents still living?" a nice-looking Communist cadre civilly inquired.

-"Yes, I am from Quang Binh," I said.

-"Oh, this is heroic country, don't you know that? And then, that is the native province of Gen. Vo Nguyen Giap . . . however, it's all devasted . . . seven tons of bombs from the B-52's, yes, devastated."

That was the first verbal attack thrust out at me in that way. But I was also swift, being not so reluctant to invent stories when necessary: "Well, actually I am from Hue. I come from the Bai Dau area, you know, where you buried the corpses during the massacres of the Tet Offensive."

There were other incidents, while drinking beer on the north bank of the Thach Han River, or sipping coffee in Minh Thanh or Chon Thanh. More than a month working at the Joint Military Commission, the many hours in the conference room, aboard aircraft on field trips, and the encounters at the locations for prisoners' exchanges had taught me one thing: you always have to be on guard, you have to be constantly wary in talking with the Communists, never an unguarded word or phrase. . . because with them everything was calculated, everything was connected together into a system, and they would get at you whenever they could.

The reception was well coordinated: there was a welcoming party, the photographers took pictures at the chosen angles; the reporters asked pre-planned questions; answers to expected questions apparently had been rehearsed; everyone at his or her task, everything had been planned in advance. I refrained myself from saying anything more than was necessary. I remembered what happened in Quang Tri, on the north bank of the Thach Han River. I was talking and smiling and laughing, but right after the first swallow of beer, the Major who was political officer of Regiment 102 went to "work" right away. "Today we have this opportunity to sit down together and drink Truc Bach beer because of the Paris Agreement," the Major intoned. "It is truly in the spirit of national reconciliation, and it is also true that as Vietnamese we have the right to go anywhere we want in our own country!" The Communist officer wanted to talk about Article 1 of the Paris Agreement, which stipulates that Vietnam is a unified, indivisible country which means, in the Communist view, that North Vietnam has the right to move troops and war materiel into the South to help the South Vietnamese people, and that the official and sole representatives of the South Vietnamese people are the National Liberation Front! That was in Thach Han. I should expect even worse in Hanoi, the eagle's nest where all the plots are hatched, where there is all work and no . . . feelings. Indeed I was calm. Because I had to be wary.

My apologies to the North. My apologies to Hanoi. I came to you with my eyes wide open, my mind clear and alert, and my heart cold. But I just couldn't be otherwise, because I have learned that I have to be "highly vigilant" in dealing with the Communists.

The writer Hoang Hai Thuy had talked about the drizzle in Hanoi, and how beautiful it is when you see the fine droplets of water clinging like dew on the velvet robes that are worn by the women during the winter season. But this morning, at the Gia Lam airport there were no women or young ladies draped in velvet, there were only young ladies clad in white shirts, black pants, and plastic sandals, serving as guides to the East European correspondents who were rushing about on the tarmac.

Our cars crossed the Long Bien bridge. This was a steel bridge, paved with wood planks, with a railway running in the middle and two walkways about one meter wide for pedestrians. The steel structure was black and rusty and heavy. Apparently some repairs had been done to it and, to celebrate the completion of the work, the bridge was decorated with red flags all along the two kilometers of its length. There were strange-sounding slogans strung across the steel girders: "Bridge construction units . . . Performance up to standard. . . ." The cars moved at a crawling pace, sending up an ear-jangling tremor.

I looked out the car window into the river below. The water was low, and the riverbed looked immense in the fog. I felt uncomfortable and a little dizzy. I tried to get a sense of where I was: I was crossing the Long Bien bridge, passing over the Red River. I had come to a place shrouded in the mythical history of thousands of years . . . but I was not feeling as lightheaded, as drunken with emotions as when I was going down the Deo Ca Pass and looking up I saw looming above me Vong Phu mountain where, on top, outlining against the sky, a rock in the shape of a woman, the War Widow rock, made goose bumps appear on my skin. Outside the rain-spotted glass of the car window, the historic river appeared in patches through the heavy cover of fog extending to the horizon. It was a sluggish waterway. A dead scenery.

The novels of the writers Nhat Linh and Khai Hung had created in my mind the image of the Red River as a great and powerful waterway with rushing and tumbling waves at the foot of the dikes, and the foam and the spume swept by the gushes of wind across is flaming immensity. But the reality before me was quite different. The low level of the water in the dry season was as placid as the water of the Tra Khuc river in South Vietnam. It had none of the power of the Mekong River, especially where it flowed through Rach Mieu and My Thuan, where the rushing waters boiled up into a permanent cover of fine mist stirring in the sunlight.

But it was not the low level of the water flow in this season that destroyed the grandiose images of the Red River. It was some sluggishness in the air that weighed down on the river. It was the threatening intimidation of the forest of flags the color of blood. The presence of so many flags and so many slogans had infringed upon Nature and destroyed her beauty. The great historic river that I pictured in my mind this morning had been desecrated by the densely planted flags and the slogans calling for increased production.

The cars moved slowly, very slowly. There was a ringing in my ears, the air was stuffy inside the car, and the driver blew the horn uninterruptedly. Ahead of us, two men were trying to push to the side a cart laden with various tools and objects, and a soldier transporting a little girl on a bicycle had just stopped for fear of being crushed between the larger vehicles. He carried the little girl to the pedestrian walkway then rushed to retrieve his prized vehicle. After getting himself out of the way, the soldier stood there and looked at us. He was probably over forty years old, his face was emaciated, the cheekbones and the bridges over the eyes were prominent—a typical face of the North Vietnamese peasant, with buck teeth, hollow cheeks, eyes tainted with a sickly yellowish color, and a resigned look. The man, although dressed in combat fatigue with pith helmet, was quite the opposite of the common image of the North Vietnamese soldier, the vanguard elements in the task of building socialism as publicized in the Communist slogans and propaganda texts. I realized that in the Communist society, he was only differentiated from the power station cadre, he cooperator cadre, or the engineer cadre, etc., by his military uniform. But I had thought that the North Vietnamese soldier, since he was the principal portrayal of the regime, and directly bore the burden of the war, should enjoy many privileges from the regime and should receive great consideration from the people. The impatient horn blowing of the driver, the piteous and resigned look on the peasant's face, his standing there, confused and stolid in the drizzle and the rising mist, filled me with something like compassion. I remembered the Regional Force soldier one afternoon in Long An province. He had just come back from a routine patrol and was relaxing himself with a fishing rod at the foot of the bridge. He looked so peaceful, so contented, so unworried. The image of the prosperous and happy region of the South gradually emerged through the reflection of its soldier. What a difference!

I crossed the Red River with a drizzle hanging in the air feeling a complete absence of any tender emotions and instead a slow build-up of quiet resentment inside me. The little girl also had a kind of pith helmet on her head, the kind of helmet made of dry leaves often seen in the 1950s in the Northern part of Central Vietnam. This was the beginning of spring and it was still quite chilly, but I hadn't seen anybody with a sweater, including the little girl. My heart filled with sorrow as I imagined a scene in winter, a group of people walking in silence on the bridge under freezing rain and the river rising and the wind whipping against the girders. With the sense of being watched closely ever since we arrived at Gia Lam airport, I grew more and more depressed as we entered Hanoi, the cultural heart of Vietnam, the city of romance and of dreams. That depression still lingered within me until today, five days after we left Hanoi, when I took up my pen, or looked at the pictures I took there, and even when I took up my bowl of rice I could still feel the confused emotions I felt during my trip to Hanoi.

Depression it was—no other word could describe what I felt while I was there. After crossing the Long Bien bridge, the car ran down and then climbed up again, passing the street where the Central Station was, winding through other streets. I didn't care what their names were. I had lost interest. My friend Dang Giao had given me a map of Hanoi and I had it in my pocket. I knew I could follow the route on the map but I was too tired to care to take it out of my pocket. The anticipated excitement had completely gone and I only felt exhausted and wished to go back to the South immediately if I could. I actually had that wish when we reached an intersection where there was an arrow pointing one way north to Hanoi and the other way south to Ha Bac (possibly a combination of the former provinces of Ha Dong and Bac Ninh). Hanoi was still four kilometers away. The drizzle had turned into freezing rain. A bare-footed woman had dismounted from her bicycle and was trudging up a street going uphill.

A big slogan on the roof of the station said: "The People Are Forever Grateful to President Ho Chi Minh." I wondered if Kissinger and Le Duc Tho had also passed by this station during Kissinger's visit here last month? The people were grateful to Ho Chi Minh because the Americans had promised to bomb only from the Gia Lam airport to the Long Bien bridge, because after twenty years of socialist construction since the victory at Dien Bien Phu some people, such as the woman I just saw, had managed to procure for themselves a piece of nylon to use as rainwear. The road we were driving on was built since the colonial time. The lead car broke down and I took the opportunity to get out and snap a picture of a roadside coffee shop. The shop consisted of a single table of pine wood, about one foot high, surrounded by low stools. On the table were displayed a few packages wrapped carefully in white paper, probably tobacco and the like, with a big pot of tea in the middle. Next to the shop was the stall of a barber. The barber was a young girl who was trimming a child's hair. I couldn't believe my eyes. We are in 1973, the year when the Apollo Project was completed. Elsewhere in the world, Mrs. Indira Ghandi and Mrs. Golda Meir have proved that women can govern a nation as well as any man. And closer to us, Mrs. Nguyen Thi Binh, the NLF's "Minister for Foreign Affairs," attracted more and more admiration for her "civilized" way of going about with her proletarian revolution which apparently was not so bad in the trendy "City of Lights." But here, four kilometers from Hanoi, this young girl from the North, the symbol of "three qualities and the three readinesses" (note: a Communist slogan), looked so much like the Communist women cadres of the provinces of Binh Dinh and Quang Ngai in the years prior to 1954. Where are all the beautiful aristocratic "Hanoiennes"? Is this the way to progress as promised by Ho Chi Minh, I wondered? Is this why the people have to be forever grateful to Ho Chi Minh?

Our car went through the North Gate where (a hundred years ago) governor Hoang Dieu committee suicide before Hanoi fell to the French. A sign at the Gate said: "This is the place hit by an artillery shell of the French . . ." or something like that, because I was not able to read all of the inscription. It served to remind the Vietnamese people of the war against the French and to strengthen the spirit of independence. The Paris negotiations, which the Communists considered a great historic victory, had concluded, but working committees were still meeting to discuss the problem of reconstruction aid for North Vietnam. We were now in the center of the city. I seemed to hear the same kind of Chinese-sounding music I had heard before on the bank of the Thach Han River. Hanoi is no longer, I thought. I was probably saying it aloud because Captain Tuyen, who was sitting next to me, kept mumbling: "Nothing is changed. . . . Exactly as it was in yesteryear. . . ." In a sense this was so. Exactly the same. The same streets, the same houses, the same row of trees, the quiet and shadowy sidewalks, the same street corners hidden away in the hanging mist and the leafy shades. This was a spring morning and everything was calm and dreamy and Hanoi seemed largely intact, not a single tree was missing, not a single stone brick broken. The sidewalk on which the writer Thanh Tam Tuyen had stamped his foot twenty years ago must still be the same.

But there was such a depressive mood hanging in the air, and although the city was crowded with people I found it strangely deserted. Was it because there were so many people in uniforms, and the dominant olive drab color had driven the white, the gray, and the blue into the background? The paramount color of the fighting man, of the collective, of demonstrations and meetings, of cold discipline and regimentation. . . . Hanoi had broken up. I did not hear the clacking sounds of the wooden clogs on the sidewalks, only the stealthy and hurried steps of feet clad in plastic sandals. Even the streetcars rolled silently on without the clanging of the bells as described in the novels of Hoang Hai Thuy and Nguyen Dinh Toan. Was it because they ran on time and the riders and pedestrians were so disciplined that there was no use for the joyful ringing of the bells? Was it for reason of economy because the clanging of the bells would unnecessarily use up some more energy? I was walking in the drizzle in the heart of Hanoi without noticing the streets and seeing the people, conscious only of a suffocating depression. The writer Tran Dan[1] a long time ago had voiced his despair at seeing the beloved city being crushed under the overpowering red color of the flags. . . . As for me today, I was trudging along in the bosom of the city, feeling wary in the dreadful environment of a strange uniformity.

Hanoi, which had appeared in my mind as a mythical city, had remained outwardly intact but its heart was gone. "Is this really Hanoi?" I asked myself, and my head throbbed in pain with the resounding question. . . .

Hanoi Hilton. A gray stone structure. The meeting room. Strong tea and dry tobacco. The resounding and arrogant voice of the commanding Captain. His heavily accented speech of a native of Quang Nam province. The big and tall Lieutenant interpreter with his brutal eyes. Complete security. Everything under control. Even though a key had been conveniently misplaced, which helped cut short the time for meetings with the prisoners. The same tricks, the same stage acting, complete with plotting and denouement. I crossed the volleyball field and saw that the net stretched across the middle of the field was brand new and still dry in spite of the drizzle since morning. Glancing up, I saw lurking behind the steel bars of the windows the emaciated faces and the sad eyes of the American P.O.W.s. Repressing my emotions, I raised my hand and shouted to them: "Thank you, and we'll see you again." They looked back at us and their eyes were brimming with tears. Prisoners of war, the most miserable and consecrated creatures of war, mournful gifts of peace. "Hello, friends," I greeted them once more. My camera had run out of film No need to reload it. Hanoi Hilton. A good story. It is a pity I am not a real reporter.

In writing about Hanoi, I found I had two sets of completely opposite reactions. Did I look at Hanoi with an objective eye, or was it possible that my impression of Hanoi had been filtered through the "distorting" lens of my "nationalist" views? Could it be that my military uniform had prevented me from reaching out to the

1. Tran Dan was a dissident poet prominent for his participation in the 1955 movement of intellectuals, writers, and artists in North Vietnam to protest the Vietnamese Communist government and was among one of several thousand prisoners of conscience later incarcerated by the regime.

real Hanoi before my eyes and therefore only allowed me a selective view that would serve some propaganda purpose? Actually, up until the fifth and last day in Hanoi, I still remained overwhelmed with sadness and depression—and still dumb-struck with the nagging question: Is this really Hanoi? Could this sacred land of culture, only three hours distant from Saigon by air, be in reality such a strange, alien place? I tried to be calm, to use all my power of analysis while I wrote down these impressions and attempted to describe the troubled emotions that came to me during my visit to Hanoi. . . . I wanted to write truthfully about the destruction of the mythical image of Hanoi. . . . Dinner at the Hoa Binh (Peace) Hotel, renamed from the Metropole Hotel. There was a revolving door at the entrance to the hotel which, twenty years ago, was something like a symbol of civilization in Hanoi. The glass panes were translucent and the woodgrained frame was cold to the touch. Everywhere I went in Hanoi I saw that everything had remained unchanged.

The hotel was built in the French colonial style, with thick walls and many small, shuttered windows. The walls were newly repainted with a clean yellow that looked cold, neat, and uncluttered. There were blue gauze curtains on the windows of the dining room near the entrance way. The draperies at the doors were new and starched to a wooden stiffness. Two cases of Truc Bach beer were in the corner. The menu included well-known dishes from the North: boiled lean ham, cinnamon-flavored broiled ham, barbecued veal and perfumed rice. . . . There was nothing extraordinary, but it was a delicious meal, and the ham and the meat were quite tasty. I remembered in a gastronomic essay the writer Vu Bang had written with intense feeling about the chicken in the North whose flesh, since it is not confined in a cage and can range freely in the garden and pick and choose its own feed, tastes of the full flavor of the plants and flowers of the country. The savor of the meat on my tongue brought to my mind whole pastoral scenes: the swaying of the bamboo trees, the sweet, cool sounds echoing from the wells, the crowing of the rooster in the misty morning.

Socialism has dehumanized the people and the land, but it cannot destroy the millennial sentiments of the people. The people who raised the animals on the farm with such love and care, and the people who cooked such delicious meals must still have retained intact the subtle individualistic character of the inhabitants on this devastated land. There was a chill in the air. The waiters were fussing around, delicately handling each piece. I was besieged with confused thoughts and strange feelings. I was being offered some of the best dishes in the North and I suddenly had the idea that these were the end product of so many cumulative efforts and miseries of the people here in North Vietnam. I could hardly swallow, and it took me great effort to get myself a second helping. . . .

After dinner, I asked to have a picture taken of a waitress with me. Two North Vietnamese officers joined in immediately. There was a crowd looking in at us from across the street. The North Vietnamese political commissars certainly would not let slip away an opportunity to make a show of the "spirit of national reconciliation." "Strive to Perform Good," such was the motto. . . . Life is certainly complicated, I thought.

Back to the cars again for a sightseeing trip through the main streets of Hanoi: Trang Tien, Pho Hue, Hang Nang, Hang Gai, Hang Dao. We drove fast along the crowded streets and again the drivers were impatiently blowing horns without interruption. . . . The cameras clicked. A streetcar. The vast square before the Great Opera House. The main department store. A movie house. A tailor shop. I was thrilled by each foot of ground we covered, completely oblivious to all the bumping and shaking motions of the car. I am now in the heart of Hanoi, I was telling myself. These snapshots would have historical significance, the truth of the moment was being frozen through the lens of my camera and would be kept forever. The driver, by driving fast, seemed intent on preventing me from catching glimpses of the truth, but I had a Topcom camera and good telelens and I hoped they would not betray me.

At the end of Truong Thi Street, or Street of Imperial Examinations, the car swerved to the right and there before us we saw the smooth green surface of the Little Lake lying placidly under the wisps of white mist. The sight sent tremors up my spine and goose bumps to my skin. I could distinctly see patches of moss on the Turtle Tower in the middle of the lake, the young grass of the lawn, the steaks of blue-green on the water through the translucent mist, the Ngoc Son Pagoda partly hidden behind the leafy trees, the expertly drawn Chinese character, and the curving The Hu bridge with its reflection now vanishing, now reappearing on the surface of the water. These were the living images of national history. Today, I had the opportunity to inhale the soul-cooling vaporous air of this millennial lake. Today, I had the chance to see with my own eyes the crimson-red characters of the two verses inscribed in base-relief on the gate of the Xa-Tac temple. I saw the small hill in front of the temple . . . was that the Nung Hill? Probably not: the Nung Hill was supposed to be higher and I believed it was situated somewhere else. . . . But the first troubling emotions that flared up within me soon vanished and left me cold. . . . Why was that? I suddenly left a strange coldness in my ear, a sense of being lost and a certain dizziness. I didn't see many strollers around the lake, and the temple looked deserted.

There was an imposing, three-story building which used to be the City Hall. It was draped with huge banners and the street below was jammed with people but it seemed to me they were moving about silently. It was the absence of sounds in a city during the curfew or during the general strike; it was a stillness of an area that for some reason had been cordoned off—and it was then that you missed the familiar noises of the city. But here, in the daytime, and despite the crowds overflowing the sidewalks, the city was strangely and uncannily silent. It was like the wearied silence of a crowd at the end of a mass rally after all the slogans had been shouted, all the protests had been voiced. There was such a spookiness around the Little Lake. And where there were crowds, there was always the overwhelming presence of the olive drab uniforms, and the absence of the usual clamor of the crowd, the sign of life being lived. All the people that lolled on the bank of the Little Lake looked as if they had been drained of all vitality. I was shaking and suffocating. It was stuffy inside the car despite the draft that blew in through the car window and made me feel uncomfortable as if I was catching a cold. A verse from the poet Tran Dan came to mind: I walk in the city and I see neither streets nor crowds. . . . Today, that same line took on a brutal intensity with the lake right before my eyes. True, I did not find anybody in the heart of Hanoi, on the bank of the Little Lake. . . .

Hats off to the Communists in North Vietnam! You have certainly surpassed your comrades in the Soviet Union and in China! Within nineteen years, you have managed to turn a city which used to have such strong cultural life, such vigor, such sophistication, into a so thoroughly dehumanized conglomeration. You have succeeded in erasing all the contours of the human beings, equalizing the young and the old, men and women, intellectual workers and menial workers, children and grown men. You have achieved complete regimentation, systematization, quantification, and dehumanization. After nineteen years in the Communist furnace, the Hanoi man has been turned inside out, cleaned and drained. This must be truly beyond the imagination of Karl Marx and Lenin. What is even more terrifying is that, physically, Hanoi remain exactly the same—the same vegetation, the same building structures, the same sidewalks paved with bricks, the same antiquated street lights and electric poles, the same leafy trees, the same decrepit streetcars, the same placid surface of the Little Lake mirroring the trembling reflection of the mossy Turtle Tower. Everything was still there but Hanoi emanated a terrifying coldness that confused me. Is it possible that the city, the people, and the air they breath could be so dehumanized? That question has filled me with distress up until today, the fifth and last day of our stay.

At the ceremony for the release of American P.O.W.s there were two Thai soldiers who looked so lost, as if they were there by mistake. I thought of the character in the Gheorghiu novel . . . the eyes lit up with renewed hope, the confused footsteps in parade march, the hand raised in unsteady salute. . . . A moving spectacle that made your eyes burn. All strategies and politics aside, the soldier, regardless of his race and nationality, remains, first and last, the one who has to shoulder the most pain and suffering. To be a prisoner is to have come to the last phase of a stormy life. There was a nurse who walked a group of prisoners to the tail of the C-141 and there, before boarding, she gave a burning kiss to each and every one of them. I felt for them, I felt for life, and I thought of the Vietnamese P.O.W.s about to be released to the other side who had unfurled their flags and staged a riot. Is hatred because of ideological conflict a kind of basic human emotion? I was unwilling to engage in any discussions of verbal jousts but I could not get rid of the young East European reporters and therefore I had to invent some stories for them. "This man and I," I said, pointing to the North Vietnamese reporter assigned to accompany me, "we are former classmates." "Really?" they said. "Yes," I affirmed. "Captain, what do you think of the B-52s?" They asked me, "How old are you?" "Twenty-five," one of them said. I found a way to get rid of him: "You are still too young. You have to wait a few more years to be able to understand the situation in Vietnam. As long as you cannot differentiate between my accent (Central Vietnamese) and his accent (North Vietnamese), you cannot understand the politics here. It is not your fault. It is only because you are too young, and this war is older than you are."

I felt tired even by this short exchange. Why should I go into this? I got away and wandered on the tarmac, snapping pictures, waiting for the time to go by.

After the ceremony, the North Vietnamese reporter (I don't wish to mention his name) who had been sticking close to me since the morning pulled me over to a corner for a chat. I had a bitter smile inside me. For more than a month now, I had been "tested" so many times. They had tried everything on me, from "reconciliation" to "B-52s." All right, let's see what else, I thought. I felt that from now on there was nothing more they could use against me. We shook hands, sat down on the grass, and exchanged cigarettes. "Brother Nam, how old are you? And where are you from?" he began. I glanced behind his back and saw that his microphone was switched to the "on" position. That was funny! I was furious: "You see, here I also have a tape recorder and it is even more advanced than yours! It has a built-in microphone and I can put it in my pocket and I can record everything while talking to you by flipping this switch. . . . Although I am not a journalist I know how you operate and I would advise you to just put that thing away and I will talk about the South, in my capacity as a young soldier from the South. . . ."

Being caught red-handed, my "friend" had to do what I said, but he remained straight-faced and did not show the least sign of shame or embarrassment as a man with a sense of ethics would under the circumstances. I did not have any enthusiasm but I forced myself to lecture him about freedom of the press in South Vietnam. As evidence, I mentioned the *Song Than* paper, which on March 3 published a picture of the (anti-government?) demonstration of the Hue people at Bai Dau, and the serialized memoirs of returnee Nguyen Anh Tuan. I believed I had a good speech but I know it was a futile exercise. I was talking to the wall, impervious to the truth. And then I saw he had a second microphone. Fuck him! I wanted to say that to his face.

We were scheduled to board a propeller-driven plane for our return trip. I thought of the Nga Nams and Nga Sau neighborhoods in Saigon. I tried to figure out the street scene on Truong Minh Giang and Le Van Duyet streets at this minute. Must be rush hour in Saigon, I thought. I could smell the gas fumes, sense the heat waves, see the melting macadam. Oh the filthy "hell" of Saigon! Just one day away from you was enough to make me sick with longing. There was a depressing stillness at the Gia Lam airport. The day was coming to an end and the mist was rising and it began to feel chilly. I thought of the snack stalls on the sidewalks of Saigon where people would stop by to have a snack of dried cuttle-fish in the evening when, strung with lights, the stalls would look, from a distance, like strings of sparkling diamonds. I could feel the warm caress of the breeze in Saigon at night. I missed the bright sunlight in Saigon during the day. I even missed the fishy and mildew smell of the slum areas of Chuong Duong and Van Don, poor, but teeming with life. Saigon—messy, and hot, and prosaic—would be my last country, where I would have my body buried. I had no doubt about it. All through the many years living in the South I had always thought that all this is just temporary and that eventually I would be able to go back to live in my native province. I never had a good word for the South, for fear of being labeled the government's sycophant. But today I have to write, to sing praise, to shout out my mea culpa: Saigon, the land of freedom, forgive me for I have been so long indifferent to you! Forgive me, dear and generous South, forgive me warm and loving Saigon!

I smiled wryly at Lieutenant Colonel Bui Tin who continued to try to work on me even as the propeller of the plane started to whirl. "Did you see those MiGs? They have downed hundreds of air pirates!" he chuckled. Fortunately, the engine noise drowned out his speech as he was coming to the subject of the B-52s!

—

The plane taxied down the runway, then took off. Plane! Fly high, higher, for I don't need to look back at the Red River or the Duong River! Fly higher and faster, over the Ngang Pass, over Dong Hoi, and bring me back quickly to the South. . . . In the west, as the red circle of the sun was sinking slowly into the darkness, the aircraft swerved back overland and I saw dots of fire in Long Khanh burning like jolly bonfires. This is the South, I thought. A wave of warmth rose inside me. I am back in the South. I am back!

I reread an article I wrote last year to see, with the advantage of perspective, if I had composed it under some kind of pressure. But I had to admit to myself that I had written it truthfully, accurately, and that the article did not contains any exaggerations, was not overdramatized, or "biased" by a "nationalist" point of view, or over embellished, that I had depicted Hanoi as I saw it and as I felt it. . . . There were other trips, but they were only routine trips required by my duties, and they were boring, exhausting, and devoid of any excitement, anticipated or otherwise. There were a few interesting things, such as the visit to Van Mieu (the Temple of Letters) and to the Museum, which has a fairly complete collection of objects collected by the former French Ecole d'Extreme-Orient and a number of objects newly uncovered by the authorities in the North. But these only provided purely intellectual joys. I was happy to be able to see and learn a few more things for my own intellectual enjoyment but there were no more emotions than in the first trip.

I reread the year-old article on the occasion of watching an old movie with scenes of Hanoi and the North more than twenty years ago. The film was shot by a bad cameraman, but still it gave me a better idea of how beautiful Hanoi used to be. . . . The name of the movie was *Kiep Hoa* ("The Fateful Life of a Beautiful Lady"), and it included many scenes of Hanoi which, despite the lack of artistic and technical skills of the film-maker, did give a sense of the beauty and the spirit of the city. There was such freshness, such kindness and friendliness in the way of life then. The sidewalks in the cool shade echoed with the sounds of wooden clogs. The beautiful young ladies of Hanoi, proud and aristocratic, strolled on the bank of the Lake of the Returned Sword, along the winding footpaths in the cool shade of the willow trees, the sunlight drew patterns on the surface of the lake, and the cool and moving reflections played on the bark of the trees on the grassy banks: that was the cultural capital of Vietnam, the birth-place of our civilization. I watched the film on the screen and, taking out mentally all the actors and actresses who were only soap opera figures on the stage of Hanoi at the time, editing out all the discordant background music, I saw the real Hanoi appear dazzling in the sunlight, moody in the rain, meditative in the misty drizzle.

Hanoi, a most precious cultural legacy bequeathed to us by our forefathers. I saw that the Hanoi then was in stark contrast to the Hanoi that I had seen with my own eyes during my first trip there, a trip that was filled with depression and disappointment. I could still see in my mind the strangely silent crowd of that Sunday afternoon, March 4, in Hanoi. It is terrifying! Communism has struck down the deep-rooted Vietnameseness in the nation's cultural capital. Once again, I was gripped with distress at this terribly brutal reality—the same distress I felt a year ago. . .

The old movie also reminded me of one thing—that the war had gone on so long in this country. The scene depicting refugees fleeing on the dikes and in the rice fields, although badly staged, did strike at your heart as a dizzying, heart-rending blow as we saw little kids with bags of clothing on their shoulders, tattered hats on their heads, running bare-footed on the dirt road in a devastated countryside. The war indeed has gone on too long: almost thirty years of raging fire and spilling blood, of generation upon generation wasted away. The kid in the film must be a grown man by this time, reliving the same miserable life in the fire and smoke of war somewhere in our dear country. The film was made in 1952 or 1953; the pagodas hit by artillery shells as shown in the film probably still remain unrepaired, or have been razed to the ground by new fighting. How painful it is that our motherland, so sweet and so beautiful, had to endure thirty years of war without a single day of peace. . . . The only permanent presence is made up of bombs and shells, the permanent obsession was death, the only constant readiness was to flee. How bitter it all is! Peace, sacred, miraculous Peace, despite so many appeals is still nowhere in sight. Peace, the most cherished dream of the whole people for the last thirty years, has not come. Thirty years of war, war for thirty years. . . . Did the Communists ever give a thought to this heart-rending pain?

Five

A Time of Deception

THE DAY WAS COMING to an end. Down on the river, the setting sun was making moving patches of light. This was one of the first days of the year when a lingering chill from the past winter still made itself felt. I stood looking over to the south bank of the Thach Han River where the yellow flag of the Republic of Vietnam was flapping in the wind on a background of blue sky and low-flying white clouds. . . . I was hoping that I could return to the other side of the river early enough. I felt light-headed. The last batch of P.O.W.s had been turned over to the other side, and the last meeting of the day was about to begin. Talking and meeting are the two activities that always received elaborate preparations and coordination from the Communists and they take great delight in going about doing that work. I sat down on the hard bench, feeling utterly bored. A woman attendant quickly brought out a steaming hot cup of tea from nowhere. Everything was well planned.

Major Nguyen An Giang, commander of the area on the north side of the Thach Han River, stood up and announced the beginning of the meeting. He then proceeded to review the activities of the day, analyzing the achievements and the shortcomings, and concluded with an outline of the activities planned for the next day. Empty, useless, and discordant words being spit out. Face pallid, cold, hard, and solemn. The major summarized the activities of the day in the usual phrases:

-"Good progress has been achieved, reflecting the spirit of national reconciliation and concord. The two sides have completed the exchange of prisoners as scheduled in a spirit of goodwill and of urgency, in accordance with Article 8(a) of the Annex, in serious application of the Cease-Fire Agreement that has received whole-hearted support from the peace-loving progressive peoples in the world. . . ."

I sat distractedly watching a gray cloud moving over the river in the direction of Ngo-Xa-Dong, vaguely remembering in bits and pieces a heli-borne assault in the area in the winter of 1967. In my notebook, I jotted down a few numbers, and the number of prisoners released during the day. . . . Major Giang went on:

-"To conclude our review of activities today, I wish to raise a minor point for Captain Nam (he wouldn't use the appellation 'the Republic of Vietnam Side'!) to take note of and to correct in conformance with the spirit of the Annex and the Cease-Fire Agreement. This has to do with the Titles at the head of each list of military personnel of the Provisional Revolutionary Government that is returned by the Military Police (Note: again, they wouldn't specify 'Military Police of the Armed Forces of the Republic of Vietnam'). Because in our view, and according to the spirit of the Annex and the Cease-Fire Agreement, in order that the two sides in South Vietnam have opportunity to carry out the spirit of national reconciliation and concord, particularly through the exchanges of military and civilian personnel, the title 'North Vietnamese Communist Prisoner-of-War, Infiltrated' as written on top of each list of prisoners to be returned does not conform with the 'de jure reality' as understood in the spirit of the Annex. It is requested that Captain Nam take due note of this, and correction be made accordingly. . . ."

So this is a new attempt to cause us trouble, the result of the closed meeting that took place all afternoon between "the revolutionaries," I thought. I sat up straight, all distraction gone, getting myself ready to counter the enemy. Damn it, VC! I mumbled the expletives within myself. Today, Feb. 19, 1973, was the third day of the Second Phase of prisoner exchanges at this location on the north bank of the Thach Han River. From the first day of the prisoner exchanges, Feb. 12, at the other locations such as Loc Ninh, the Military Police had always used the same title on the lists of prisoners to be turned over to the other side and there wasn't any problem. So now, they want to play games, I thought. I tried to concentrate. After Major Giang sat down came the turn of Major Vay, team leader under the Prisoners Subcommittee of the NLF delegation on the Joint Military Commission:

-"First, let me express my thanks to the International Committee for Supervision and Control whose members have actively carried out their duties of supervising and controlling the exchanges of military personnel . . . realizing the spirit of national reconciliation and concord (!). Let me also thank the local authorities for their elaborate welcome offered to us. Finally, let me discuss the 'minor point' that has just been raised: According to Articles 1 and 2 of the Annex concerning the problem of exchanges of prisoners, prisoners are only classified into three categories: Civilian and military personnel of the U.S. and other countries, and civilian and military personnel of the U.S. and other countries, and civilian and military personnel of the two other sides in South Vietnam. Therefore the proposal of Major Giang realistically reflects the spirit of the Annex and Captain Nam is requested to take due note and to make appropriate correction."

Major Vay sat down, flickered his Thang Long lighter to light his Dien Bien cigarette, blew a cloud of acrid smoke, and balancing his leg, listened with avid interest to the next speaker—because it was now the turn of Captain Lan of the North Vietnamese Army: "Thank you, . . . thank you. The spirit of reconciliation . . . the minor point raised by Major Giang . . . Articles 1 and 2 of the Annex. . . ."

A third repetition from a third speaker! A proposal that was repeated three times with such solemnity, and translated three times with difficulty into broken English. The men sat in a circle, nodding gravely, especially the Hungarian and the Polish delegates who also pulled out their little notebooks to look up Articles 1 and 2 of the Annex. . . . They glanced at the text with severity and whispered to each other about the "realities" of the prisoners according to the terms of the Annex. The whole deceptive comedy was played out to the maximum. While Captain Lan and his interpreter were still discoursing on Articles 1 and 2 or the Annex, I did some quick calculations in my head. . . . It is true that there is no mention of Communist North Vietnamese P.O.W.s in Articles 1 and 2, neither is there any mention of the People's Army of the Democratic Republic of Vietnam (North Vietnam) anywhere in the text of the Cease-Fire Agreement. . . . So, what would be the appropriate response? And on what basis? . . . The Agreement was a bag of lies applauded by the whole world!!! Colonel Thompson of the U.S. delegation was smoothing it out with an expression of thanks, reviewing the number of flights during the day and concluding with even more thanks. I realized that our unique ally was not in a position to give any help because today, Feb. 18, North Vietnam had just released the second batch of American P.O.W.s at Gia Lam airport—and the issue of the P.O.W.s was the last great issue of the war that had to be given top priority.

I stood up. The last sunlight on this day at the beginning of a new year had died away in the hills west of La Vang, whose outline was now indistinct behind a veil of gray mist. The yellow flag of the Republic of Vietnam planted at the other end of the Quang Tri bridge was still snapping in the wind but I could see columns of smoke rising from the paratroopers' base camps in Tich Truong and Nhu Le. We were being shelled by North Vietnamese artillery. . . . The fighting was taking place far away but I felt as if the echo of each explosion was being magnified inside me, causing me the greatest pain. I was engaged in combat. . . .

-"Gentlemen, let me pass over the detailing on the number of P.O.W.s that we have returned to you today. That, you know. I also think it is unnecessary to pass in review again all the accomplishments that you have already confirmed. I want to go directly to the 'minor point' that Major Giang has just raised. . . . That is the issue of the prisoners. Gentlemen, the classification of P.O.W.s into North Vietnamese Communist infiltrators or National Liberation Front guerillas has been made realistically by the Military Police of the Republic of Vietnam on the basis of biographic information furnished by the individual P.O.W. The biographical information has been compiled from answers given by each prisoner to specific questions concerning his birthplace, his unit, and his base area. For example, a prisoner's birthplace may be either Bac Lieu, Soc Trang, Quang Ngai (South Vietnam), or Thanh Hoa, Ninh Binh, Nghe An (North Vietnam). Concerning his unit, the prisoner may have belonged to a guerilla team operating in Tan Binh district, Gia Dinh province, or he may have come from the 5th, or the 7th, or the 9th Division of the armed forces of the National Liberation Front, or he may be a soldier of Division 308, or 320, or 324B, or 325 of the People's Army of the Democratic Republic of Vietnam (North Vietnam). The prisoner's testimony also served to define the base operating area of his unit. For example, a guerilla operating in the village of Xuan Thoi Thuong, of the district of Tan Binh, province of Gia Dinh may have been detached from the Ly Van Manh secret zone between the three provinces of Long An, Hau Nghia, and Gia Dinh. Or a prisoner from the 7th Division may have come from the Parrot's Beak area, crossing the Cambodian border to attack Loc Ninh and move on to An Loc. . . . And the classification of 'Communist North Vietnam, infiltrated' is given to those issued from such places as Nghe An province in North Vietnam and sent down the Ho Chi Minh Trails to Tchepone in lower Laos where they would take Route 9 to cross the Laotian border to join battles in the Tri-Thien zone in Central Vietnam, as for example the prisoners captured from Division 325 of the General Reserve of the People's Army that is now present here in Quang Tri province of the Republic of Vietnam. . . ."

I glanced around at Major Giang, Major Vay, Lieutenant Colonel Marin (Hungary), Colonel Garrick (Canada), and I could detect either embarrassed or angry looks on their faces. They all wanted to look away from the facts, they all wanted to close their eyes to the fact of a North Vietnamese invasion of South Vietnam. They were all willing actors in the drama of lies and deceit that was the Cease-Fire Agreement, the text of which had been hailed by the whole world, and whose real value was just a piece of paper to cover up the greatest deception of the century and the real bitterness and suffering of the people of Vietnam.

I half-closed my eyes, trying to repress the rancor and rage that threatened to break out of control. On the other side of the river, to the left, the rubble of Quang Tri city would remain forever a symbol of pain; the ghosts of what was the Citadel, the City Hall, the hospital that now lay among those mounds of broken bricks and stones were raising a hellfire of hatred within me. I continued, stressing each word:

-"And you know, more than anybody else, yes, you know too well the realities, as clear as daylight, that I just exposed. Articles 1 and Article 2 of the Annex amount to a play on words, designed to cover up the truth. And the truth is that there is an aggression, an invasion by North Vietnam against South Vietnam. If you will recall, in 1966 we released a number of prisoners of war belonging to the regular forces of North Vietnam. And the list of those prisoners, who were returned to you on the north bank of the Ben Hai River, had the same heading. The classification of that type of prisoners, based on their own declarations, has not changed since 1966. Consequently, there is no reason for us to change the titles on those lists. Let me affirm, therefore, that we will continue to maintain the same designation 'Communist North Vietnam, infiltrated . . .' on our lists of P.O.W.s to be returned to you, and we will do so until the last prisoner is sent back to you."

Again, there were whispers of disagreement and an exchange of angry looks. I stood defiantly, waiting for the reactions to explode. I saw that Le Thanh Lan of North Vietnam was leaning forward. Vay, of the National Liberation Front, was nodding and winking his eyes as he listened to the latter. After a brief moment, Vay stood up:

-"Captain Nam has presented his ideas in an impertinent manner, despite the fact that he is the youngest in age and lowest in rank among us. . . ."

I had a wry smile and I shouted to his face:

-"We are meeting here to carry out the tasks of history (!), not to make distinctions of rank and to analyze the morality of each individual. . . ."

The interpreter, named Chi, mumbled: "How should I translate? And do I have to translate at all?" "No need." I sat down, feeling ridiculously gratified. Sooner or later, we would be ignored by all of them. . . . The thought drained me of all energy. I didn't feel like putting up any more noisy defense. I let out a sigh. . . .

Back in the South, as the plane took off from the airstrip into the dense fog, returning the International Committee members and the Joint Military Commission team to Hue, I stayed behind amid the broken bricks and tiles, watching the Marines consolidating their defense perimeter against any enemy attack from the north. I wandered toward the Long Hung intersection, finding my way around the mounds of broken rocks along the slippery road. I was walking in the center of what used to be the city of Quang Tri, a town that had indomitably survived through so many trials of history ever since the first days of the Nguyen dynasty. . . . I stood uncertainly before the carcasses of a house, its steel-reinforced concrete roof collapsed to the ground, the iron shutters in the front crushed into scraps. I wondered what it used to be: a bookstore at the corner of Gia Long street? I looked toward the Old Citadel to get a sense of direction. During the year 1967 I would often drop by that bookstore to browse through the books but it was utterly unidentifiable now. I made a great effort searching my memory for familiar landmarks, but I was largely unsuccessful in correlating the places where I had been during my lengthy stay in this city with what I saw now.

The arguments I had just had on the other side of the river, five hundred yards across, had become an immensely insulting joke. I wondered what had become of human integrity. I wondered if Kissinger and Le Du Tho, when they went about analyzing each word, polishing each phrase of the Cease-Fire Agreement, realized that they were jointly working out a disgusting deception against the 15 million people of South Vietnam. I wondered if political analysts, when they studied the Agreement to make sense of it, would not be amused by the thoughtlessness, the nonsense, the brutality even, of those words which had no other purpose than to serve to cover-up the immense crimes that had been committed—crimes that were high as the mountains, as bottomless as a sea of blood, as dense as the bodies strewn along the nine kilometers of the Highway of Terror, and crumpled at the foot of each rubber tree in the plantations along Route 13. . . . The whole world closed their eyes and applauded. The whole world welcomed the Cease-Fire Agreement and peace in Indochina, with ticker tapes, with the ringing of bells and toasts, and Mr. Kissinger would be given the Nobel Peace Prize and the North Vietnamese Communists acknowledged for their own active contribution to world peace. Oh, how painful it all is!

The words of the Cease-Fire Agreement restoring peace to Vietnam took the shape of taunting little devils in my mind and, as in a nightmare, I could see them dancing in the rain, sauntering among the broken tiles and bricks and on the streets that had been plowed up by artillery shells and turned into roads of red clay, slippery under the rain. From the beginning to the end, there was absolutely no mention of the invasion of North Vietnam against South Vietnam, no stipulation that the People's Army of the Democratic Republic of Vietnam should be pulled back to the North, except for Article 5 which stated vaguely about the withdrawal of foreign troops not belonging to the two contending sides in Vietnam. . . . That was pure wickedness, because the North Vietnamese troops could be reconditioned into troops of the National Liberation Front after one session of political indoctrination. A soldier from North Vietnam could easily claim himself to be a native from Quang Tri province[1] who had gone into the hills to join the armed forces of the Provisional Revolutionary Government of South Vietnam! And then who in the world would suffer the consequences of this gross and brutal deception? How could there be peace when troops of the 324th Division, the 325th Division, the 308th Division, and others, all North Vietnamese, all under 20, all of them obstinate, fanatical, determined to kill and to get killed, became "natives of Quang Tri" and after laying the roads, cleaning their rifles, repairing the airstrips, setting up the rocket batteries, marched right through, crossing the Thach Han River into South Vietnam? This would be a crime for which the whole world should be held accountable, from the eggheads in the West to the bunch of peaceniks swarming in the South, from the last surviving colonists in Paris to the weak-kneed politicians hoping for an opportunity to be used like a piece in a chess game in trouble times. . . . The whole world had readily agreed to put on masks and go to the ball, dancing over the bodies of the Vietnamese people. . . .

1. Quang Tri is the northernmost province of South Vietnam, where the demarcation line of North and South Vietnam is drawn.

It is strange how deception, when pushed to the highest degree, can take on such a convincing appearance of truth, how crime, when perpetuated with subtlety, can be seen as an act of humanity, of salvation. The Chinese writer Kim Dung, when he created the character of Vi-Tieu-Bao in the role of a Fool, must have realized the total disruption of this time when the world is ruled by violence and deception. What is most disgusting is that crimes are being glorified by most of the world. . . .

I traced my steps amid the rubble of Quang Tri, in the drizzle, on a slippery road that led nowhere. The pain, the anger, and the rage swelling within me made me oblivious to the rain and the gusting winds. The storm that was wreaking havoc within me had knocked out all my senses. . . . What could I do now?

[QUANG TRI, MARCH 1973]

Six

Communist Prisoners, Nationalist Prisoners

THE LANDING STRIP traced a dark red line in the heart of the green rubber plantations. The helicopter descended in a spiral and the airstrip rose quickly into view. I stepped out on the tarmac of the Minh Thanh airbase, situated less than 15 kilometers from Route 13. I was in enemy territory.

Standing in the stilled shadows of the trees, in the quiet forest, I slowly inhaled the smoke of my cigarette, listening to the wind blowing through the thick leaves. . . . I enjoyed to the full all the tranquility before a day that promised to be tense. The Communist cadres who had come up from Saigon were holding a meeting with their local comrades. This was the only pure moment to live for oneself. In half an hour, I would have to assume a different role.

Today, I was to attend the release of four hundred prisoners to the Communists and the reception of two hundred of our prisoners. I had been here once, and I knew how the Communists in the South would behave under the direction and control of the Communists from the North. And this time, I came better prepared. Minh Thanh airbase was in Tay Ninh province. It would take the Communists only one day and one night to move in from the Bathu secret zone across the border in Cambodia. The cadres from the NLF's Central Office had lately begun to carry out their activities openly. The vast rubber plantations spread out of sight. The Americans were talking to each other in low voices. I found myself surrounded by a complete stillness, the calm before the storm.

-"In order to avoid causing psychological shock to the people who are about to be released, in order to express our true love for people in the spirit of national reconciliation and concord we request the Captain to instruct the Military Police not to carry weapons into the prisoners exchange location and to leave all weapons on the plane," the National Liberation Front cadre began.

I bowed my head, looking to the ground, trying to analyze the Communist request and to find a response in an orderly way. No weapons! Another difficulty they wanted to cause us! There had been successive requests: helicopters should not circle the airstrip, the Military Police should call each prisoner "brother" during the roll calls, and the Military Police should not call out the names of the prisoners when the prisoners were being returned to the Communists (even before the final certification of the lists of prisoners). And the delegates on the International Committee would nod in agreement, and so would the North Vietnamese and the National Liberation Front members on the Joint Commission. And there was that Lieutenant Colonel Tue, an aging man of over fifty, with a pale face, a distended belly, and the characteristic accent of the peasantry in North Vietnam. And the commander of the Minh Thanh airbase was a Lt. Col. Hue, the man with the famous remark, exposing all his knowledge about the operations of an airbase: "Tell your C-130 to land! Our cadres at the airport have said it's OK!!!" And the cadre who was the so-called airport engineer of Minh Thanh, a man with buck teeth and bad eyes, would nod repeatedly to express his agreement in a most demonstrative way. Who said there is no class in a Communist society?

The plane was coming. I had to stop my play-acting and to work seriously. The Lieutenant-Colonel commanding the Minh Thanh airbase rode out majestically in a jeep with an airborne marking. So, the Communists also knew how to play tricks on you (they did that—using a jeep captured from paratroopers—because they saw that I wore a camouflaged uniform).

The release of the prisoners began with the usual annoying difficulties. The prisoners went through the routine of shedding their prison uniforms, discarding the cans of meat and fruit, raising their hands and shouting the slogans without much enthusiasm, with handshakes that proposed to be warm, and with unfocused eyes. A well-rehearsed tragicomedy that was painfully played out without real enthusiasm. The brown garb and the bags of clothing newly issued to the prisoners were discarded for flimsy sweat scarves and hastily dyed green uniforms with light and dark spots. Nobody was sure where this "revolutionary" comedy came from. It was not performed during the first releases of prisoners in Loc Ninh and Thach Han. It certainly did not come from the initiative of the prisoners themselves. Because after the ceremony was over, they would have no more opportunities to make use of such good, strong stuff. Understandably, the brown prison uniforms marked with the initials T.B. ("Tu Binh," prisoner of war) had to be discarded, but the other items, such as underwear, mosquito nets, blankets, etc., once discarded would be lost forever. That was not a frivolous argument: a look at the "soldiers of the revolution" would give us a clear idea of how miserably equipped they were and that was true for the North Vietnamese as well as the South Vietnamese Communist soldiers. They were clad in badly frayed uniforms and sandals with used-out soles—and that was only for important occasions. The miserable uniforms, coupled with the childish arrogance of the "awakened revolutionary people" ready to sacrifice themselves for Freedom and for the Revolution: there evidently was something wrong with these Communists. These men used a system of dialectic materialism as a guide for their actions, but at the same time, more than anybody else, they were aiming toward purely abstract objectives: Freedom, Communism, the Motherland, the Revolution, words infused with passion and excitement to push generation upon generation of young men into committing fanatical acts. The year was 1973, the year of great scientific advances that not so long ago could only be dreamed of, but the Vietnamese Communists still had to struggle hard for each piece of manioc, for each can of rice, each hand-rolled cigarette, each cookie on their path of sacred struggle for the realization of Socialism. That was indeed pitiful. An entire transportation unit had to meet and discuss for four long hours, from 5 pm to 9 pm, on the Ho Chi Minh Trail, to decide on the standard issuance of five cigarettes for each man. And they included many engineers and doctors and cadres with the ranks of Major and Lieutenant Colonel. The liberation and proletarian revolution waged in South Vietnam was certainly wasteful in manpower. But then again, manpower was probably a minor factor in the Communist calculations, a resource that could easily be replenished and therefore did not deserve serious discussion.

The poverty of the Communists was not something to be held in contempt, but it would be something unacceptable for the normal mind to conceive of that poverty as a strong point that had to be achieved through struggle. And what did the Vietnamese Communists achieve after thirty years of struggle covering immense fields with bodies: a bicycle for a high cadre in Hanoi, the baggy uniform of the "Minh Thanh airport commander," the meatless meals during eighteen years of the inhabitance of the Tuyen Quang province in North Vietnam, two cigarettes solemnly received by the mechanical engineer on the Ho Chi Minh Trail . . . the other side of all the splendid words, that sounded as unreal as echoes from a confused dream. So miserable and so pathetic, but the Communist prisoners, as soon as they stepped out of the plane and set their foot on the "liberated" ground before their release had to behave like automatons. They would clap their hands and would sing in their hoarse voice . . . "We are strong if we are united . . . We would rather die than retreat, and we will kill all the traitors. . . ." If they want to kill off all "the traitors" then they would be absolutely contrary to the "spirit of reconciliation and concord" that they, the "South Vietnam" Communist soldiers coming from the Xuan Mai military training camp in Ha Dong and speaking the accent of Son Tay or Thai Binh provinces in North Vietnam, never tired of repeating as if that were a new motto to guide their release, would only raise their clenched fists, chanting slogans: "Long live President Ho," "Long live the anti-American national salvation struggle." President Ho certainly was not the President of the National Liberation Front and the "anti-American" spirit had actually gone out of fashion. I thought I would remind them of that. But there they were, like a bunch of automatons, stripping themselves of their prison uniforms and discarding their bags of clothing. The underwear, an expensive item under Communism, was thrown away with a look of obvious regret while they pinched their mouths and, frowning, swung their arms, chanting slogans.

The hatred cultivated in men during wartime was something awful, but all the encouragement to hatred at this time of "cease-fire according to the Paris Agreement" sounded like violence that had gone out of date. Whom do you want to convert? Whom do you want to hate? Who are the traitors? Oh, wasn't it true that this country was brought to ruin by your active contribution, you, the Vietnamese Communists? Hatred, traitors, killing of the cruel and corrupt cliques, the fall of 1945, the winter of 1946, the late 50s, the early 60s, so many songs to urge you on, so many clapping hands. The French, Mr. Diem, the Americans, so many targets of struggle that had come and gone but the struggle still went on with a content that had become so frayed with time. It was strange that some of the elementary principles that seemingly should be no more than interesting subjects for leisure discussions had been turned into basic motives for struggle—like the issue of hatred, which the Communists used as a condiment in their bloody feast over the Vietnamese people, and they never seemed to have enough of it. What would they become without that dope? The dog of Pavlov would not have the saliva come to his mouth without the ringing of the bell. Hatred, that short and nerve-wracking word, that cold ringing of the bell, had a whole mass of people under its spell, men who, although their senses remained intact, had lost their basic humanity and become pure automatons, men without souls, men who do not live for men but for the Revolution, for the "Motherland," for "Peace," for "Progress," for Socialism. . . .

This was not just an extreme reaction from a radical "anti-Communist." I was just trying to rationalize the existence of such men who had become so wedded to a set of unnatural principles, men who could be pressed and trained to such fanaticism. I would imagine that when a man is released from captivity he should feel, well, so light as if he could jump off this earth, he should swing out his arms and fill his lungs with all the refreshing breeze blowing high in the sky. . . . But the Communist prisoners were not allowed to express that happiness, instead they had to express their "unyielding determination to fight and to win," they had to demonstrate their "undiminishing hatred and anger." They had to erase out of their minds the humiliation of the past years, the day when they had to raise their arms to surrender before the point of the South Vietnamese guns, they had to forget the humane treatment they received after they had been disarmed, they had to forget the cigarettes that had been offered them in all sincerity even though they were only prisoners. . . . They even had to forget the realities—they had to ignore their strengthened bodies, their developed chest, the muscles that tightened on their arms, their shoulders under the prison uniforms after their stay in the Phu Quoc prison camp favored with the invigorating air of the seaside. Their health so contrasted with the sick pallor and wispy condition of the comrades that turned out to welcome them.

The Communist prisoners had to ignore even the realities on their bodies to stand up and denounce: "They have starved us, they have brutalized us in prison. . . ." As the Polish and the Hungarian officers solemnly took notes, I felt anger rise in me like a storm. The truth had been blatantly ignored and distorted in the coldest and most shameless way.

Because the realities did not rest on the bodies of the Communist prisoners. The realities were also at the end of the airstrip, about five hundred meters from where the prisoners were to be released, where about two hundred South Vietnamese prisoners sat silently with blank stares in their eyes.

-"Are you sure we are going to be released, Captain? Are we coming home, Captain?"

-"Absolutely. We have more helicopters coming, never mind the last one that just flew away. I am here to receive you."

-"Captain, am I going to be returned to our side?"

Hundreds of squatted forms were whispering to each other in fearful voices. Their fear and worry could be seen in the trembling fingers they held out for the cigarettes I offered them, the anxious look in their tired eyes toward the Communist cadres. I wanted to say something that would definitely reassure them. I wanted to give a warm hug to every one of them, and grab at once two hundred of them and carry all of them to the waiting aircraft and then we would take off very fast away from the dark and dense rubber plantations, away from the watchful, taciturn Communist guards whose cruelty and wickedness were imprinted as the dark red veins in their faces. I wanted to push the Hungarian, the Polish, and the Canadian officers toward the prisoners and have them confront face to face each and every one of the prisoners so that they could see, right before their eyes, the hollow cheeks, the festering wounds, the pale and transparent skin, and the sunken eyes of the South Vietnamese prisoners. I wanted to shout into the forest, for the whole world to know where the truth lay, where brutality resided. The Communist prisoners, standing about five hundred meters away, were strong and healthy and their denunciations were like white hot spikes poking into my eyes while the South Vietnamese prisoners did not have any more force even to give an oral signal of their presence when their names were called, as they stumbled past the desk of the officers supervising the exchange of prisoners.

The truth was there, in the contrast between these two bodies, but then why did millions of people in the world still looked so favorably on the Communists—including the truly religious peoples and the "sages" of the world? They tended to look from a particular point of view: the Communist point of view. I wished they could come here and find the truth in the eyes of those prisoners. One prisoner stood up and it was seen that the bottom of his pants was all wet: in his anxious wait, the prisoner had pissed his pants! But no, that was not true! We must listen to his explanation: "I am very afraid of them. They are very brutal. Their treatment is not of the kind we can expect from man to man. I was afraid that if I asked for permission to go for a leak, they would hold me back and not release me, then I would die." Tears were welling up in my eyes. I wanted to cry out in anger. Where was that Polish officer? I wished he could hear what the prisoner just said, the voice of a man who had been in a Communist prison. But everybody seemed to have turned away.

People have lost their conscience. Nobody took a picture of the pool of urine on the ground strewn with dead leaves. Nobody cared to take pictures of the two hundred human beings squatting on the ground, looking as eerie as two hundred enshrouded corpses. Why didn't the Hungarian officer rush to take a picture of the South Vietnamese prisoner who collapsed on the tarmac, saliva bubbling out of his mouth, because of exhaustion after long days being fed a starvation diet? We have expressed so much sympathy for the Hungarian people during the days of bloody uprisings for freedom in Budapest. But of course the Hungarians who cherish freedom and who live for the truth did not come here. There was only the presence of the Communist cadres who happened to have Hungarian nationality. I realized that the relationship between human beings in a human community, but was mostly defined by the state, the group, the Party. As "Hungarians" then, they would have to give support to the Vietnamese Communists and to create difficulties for the Republic of Vietnam. Because the instructions had so decided, the denunciations about the brutal prison policy of the South Vietnamese government by the healthy, even athletic Communist prisoners were more reliable than the plain and obvious truth as personified in the Nationalist prisoner who squatted there, in frozen immobility, still fearful even then that he would never regain freedom, and too exhausted even to respond when his name was called. Because of the instructions, the Hungarian had to forget his conscience, to turn his back to the truth. He only took pictures of the North Vietnamese prisoners raising arms and shouting slogans, and ignored the festering wounds over the bodies of the South Vietnamese prisoners. It amounted to absolute alienation when such behavior was commended as in conformance with truth and justice. How outrageous it was! It was not only the behavior of Colonel Martin of the Hungarian delegation that was deplorable. It seemed that the whole world—including the progressive and peaceful people in the world—was afflicted with a case of moral cruelty toward the Vietnamese people.

[MARCH 1973]

Seven

The Castaway

IT WAS ONE O'CLOCK in the afternoon of July 24, 1973. The exchange of prisoners at Loc Ninh had reached an impasse. The Communists had mobilized a great number of civilians, and cadres, who were massing around the tent where the exchange was to take place in order to create pressure. These people would crash into the tent to create confusion according to a scenario that had been seen in Quang Tri and Quang Ngai. I had become so very familiar with this tactic, and I had received clear instructions to postpone the release of prisoners if the Communists should commit some procedural violations. So the release of prisoners would have to be canceled. My friend Noi and I were getting ready to announce a suspension of the prisoners' exchange because of the obstruction instigated by the Communists. The International Committee would have to be formally notified of the reasons for the suspension, and our position would have to be clearly explained. This was also the last day of the Canadian delegation, and after six months of team work, the various members on the International Committee had come to a thorough understanding of the ways and positions of each other on the Committee. The terms of the Agreement and the Annex in effect had been neutralized by the realities of the situation in Vietnam, not to say of the blatant obstruction by the Hungarian and Polish delegates. They had made small change of the "impartiality" demanded of the International Committee and had freely acted in collusion with the Vietnamese Communists. After dozens of trips for prisoners' exchanges during the past six months, I had become so fed up with the work of the International Committee, but I would still have to play the game and make the solemn announcement, as formally required of "a delegate":

-"Gentlemen, first of all I wish to express, in the name of the government of the Republic of Vietnam, our warmest thanks to you, delegates on the International

Commission, who have come here to supervise and to witness the release of prisoners. At the same time, I would like to explain to you the reasons why we have to suspend this release of prisoners. . . ."

Lieutenant Noi struggled with the translation into English. I pretended to squint my eyes in the sun while discreetly watching the reactions of Major Vay of the National Liberation Front, trying to guess his intentions. Somebody was strumming a guitar and singing along somewhere in the distance, bits of tune carried over on the breeze. It was one of those songs by Pham The My or Trinh Con Son, about the motherland, peace, the end of the war, and, although the singer was not a professional singer, it was sung with such enthusiasm and sincerity. The students in the "struggle movements," returned to the Communists the previous day, July 23, were gathering in a tent next to ours waiting to come and express their aspirations to members of the International Committee and to present their request, through the Vietcong Major, that I sign an affidavit so that they could return to Saigon and be what they had always been: simple students working for peace.

The group of students consisted of about twenty people, including such well-known student leaders as Vo Nhu Lanh, Trinh Dinh Ban, Cao Thi Que Huong, Tran Thi Lan, Tran Thi Hue, Nguyen Thanh Cong, etc. All of them had been charged with disturbing the peace by staging street demonstrations protesting militarization of the university, the Americans, the government of President Thieu, calling for peace and demanding the right to live.

I said, partly in response to Major Vay, of the National Liberation Front:

-"These people have been returned to you on the seventh and the eighth exchanges of prisoners that took place yesterday, July 23, at this location. Now they are demanding that the Government of the Republic of Vietnam should take them back, should grant them unconditional freedom, and guarantee that they will not be arrested again. In my capacity as a member of the Saigon delegation on the Joint Military Commission, I refuse to accept these demands because, through their acts, they have committed crimes as noted clearly in court documents. I could not accept them as 'exclusive students arrested for having participated in struggle movements,' since that would be an indirect refutation of the principle of prisoners' exchange. This, I repeat, is an exchange of civilian prisoners between the two sides in South Vietnam. It is also not in my authority to give guarantees that go beyond my capacity as a mid-level military officer. Besides, these people were definitely returned to your yesterday, and the Government of the

Republic of Vietnam does not have any more responsibility concerning them. According to the accepted procedures, any wish from the prisoners could only be considered during the exchange. . . ."

I believed I was quite articulate in presenting my arguments. The officers on the International Committee were nodding in agreement, including even the Hungarian and the Polish delegates who, had no choice but to agree to our position although normally they would give unqualified support to the Vietcong. I continued:

-"In short, those twenty students no longer fall within our authority. And the International Committee likewise does not have any more responsibility over them, because your duties are limited to supervising the exchanges of civilian prisoners between the two sides in South Vietnam. Now, the students are saying that they belong to neither of the two sides, that they are part of a 'Third Force.' But even so, I believe this is outside Article 7 of the Annex which only stipulates the exchanges of civilian prisoners between the two sides. . . ."

I concluded with slavish quotes from the Cease-Fire Agreement and the Annex to the Agreement. The Polish and the Hungarian delegates showed obvious sign of weariness. They turned to each other for a brief exchange of views trying to find some way to help their comrades and finally could not find anything more to say than to state vaguely: "We take note of the problem concerning the students. . . ."

So I had won. A big outside obstacle to the exchanges of prisoners had been overcome. But that was the part of me that was official, that had certain duties to be carried out because of the uniform on my body, and the badge of rank on my collar. There was another part of me that was wandering in another sphere of sadness and loneliness, the part of me that was under the influence of the siren song for peace, the part of me that had caught the pure and altruistic look of the twenty young men and women. Their problem would never be solved.

Actually, I never had any faith in the character and ability of the students in the "struggle movements," those who would stage frequent street demonstrations for such short-term objectives as anti-militarization of the schools, protest against the government, the Americans, the war, etc. I had great doubts about those students, either inside the country, such as Huynh Tan Mam, or outside the country, such as Doan Hong Hai and Nguyen Thai Binh.[1] As a combat soldier,

1. Phan Nhat Nam's suspicion proved to be correct. All these students were Vietcong agents working in the student body. They were appointed to be members of the Communist rubber-stamped National Assembly after the 1975 takeover.

one who suffered the most from the war, who was exposed to the most immediate and direct impact of this absurd and brutal conflict, with all the pain and misery, I had done my best to survive and at the same time to find justification for my acts. That is why I believed that, however "anti-war" you could be, it would be extremely absurd to assign total responsibility for this war on the government and the soldier of the Republic of Vietnam, the latter being the person who suffered most in the war. I could never accept the argument that we should lay down our arms unconditionally, and the praise lavished on the "justified" fighting undertaken by the Communist soldiers of especially the fashionable anti-war movements carried out under the most odious and sickly forms.

In July of 1972, I wrote an article criticizing these students in the *Dieu Hau* newspaper, a very strong article, as I recalled, full of rage and anger during a furlough from combat duty in the "city" of Quang Tri that was strewn with bodies. I remember I wrote it with my hand shaking, my eyes blurred with visions of clothing still burning on charred bodies coiled on the gray sand—the bodies of civilians killed by a Communist artillery barrage on May 1 of 1972. I remained constantly obsessed by these visions of terror. That is why, when I afterward had to confront, across the negotiating table, the enemies, who were so new to me because I had just confronted them in battle, I could not help being tormented every minute, every hour, with the questions of the hows and whys of the war, and of the capacity of the Communists to kill people in such a cold way. In that state of mind, I had looked upon people such as Mrs. Ngo Ba Thanh, deputy Tran Ngoc Chau, student Huynh Tan Mam as people who were affected with mental disorders of a debilitating nature, who acted under the guidance of some satanic power, and I would even identify them with plain murderers. This is a time when great masses of human beings have fallen victims to Pavlovian reflex conditioning and dupes to all the beautiful words such as liberation, freedom, peace. . . . That is why I looked with rage and certainly intolerant eyes on those "anti-war" people who were clamoring for peace in the streets of Saigon or in the parks of America, blindly following the hot pants of the strip-actress Jane Fonda, and joyfully insulting our dead.

But today, I had heard that song brought to me by the wind, I had seen the intelligent and candid though wearied look on the face of student Nguyen Thanh Cong as he was talking to the Hungarian colonel, I had discovered something new and exhilarating in them. I believed I found the explanation to the anti-war movement and discovery made me feel dizzy with anger: It is true that the Communists have been destroying so many generations of good people with a very elementary tactic: They have used lies and repetitions of a number of slogans with many meanings couched in a seemingly logical system of thought to lure people to the call of blood. The discovery caused me anger and pity at the same time. Now, I knew.

I had come to the realization that these students squatting under those trees and singing their songs with so much enthusiasm and sincerity were not, could not be Communists. They could never be turned into Communist zones, even if they had been sent back into the cities to work as underground agents among the students according to the instructions they had received from the Communist central headquarters and under the control of the Commissar in charge of Youth in the Saigon-Cholon sector. They were not, could not be Communists even if they had been given membership cards by the Labor Party, or by the National Liberation Front's Youth Groups. Because their song, their tune, their look truly reflected the real aspirations of the youth of all times: the aspiration to get out of the present tragic situation and to devote their efforts to the building of a bright future for the country. And the Communists had taken advantage of those aspirations, those dreams, to further their own tactical aims of the moment. And these students had unwittingly become efficient vanguard elements working for the Communists in the streets of Saigon, in university auditoriums, among our youth.

In trying to make use of these young people, the Communists never unveiled their true face. They only taught them a number of tricks to work on the masses, some methods and means to stage demonstrations and to carry on the struggle, to start with "reasonable" or even rightist objectives. In these, the Communists are experts and they can draw on unlimited resources of people of goodwill. Gradually, the Communists would have them try some "tactical" objectives: protest against the drafting of people into the army, anti-militarization of the university, etc., which would be of important interest to the students themselves. And so on, with more infiltration into the "struggle movements" they would help build up mass movements against the war and for immediate peace. The objective became more and more open with widespread movements in the world. From unwitting actors, these people became truly involved after seeing that their own interests conformed with the objectives of the Front, and, starting out as draft dodgers and anti-American protesters, they became, in one short step, real fighters in the "anti-American national-salvation struggle" of the National Liberation Front. At the end of the road, the government of South Vietnam, and the whole South Vietnamese community became real enemies after they had thoroughly absorbed the lesson: "The Vietnam war is a revolutionary war against the reactionary war instigated by the Americans. The Vietnam war is undertaken by the peace-loving, class-conscious people of Vietnam, with the support of all peace-loving peoples in the world." After all the good-sounding words such as peace, consciousness, revolution, etc., inserted in a seemingly logical system of thought had been absorbed, the students would have lost all independent judgment and clear-mindedness and become simply Pavlovian animals led by the Communists.

But, as I said, these young people could never become real, hard-core Communist cadres because they did not come from the peasantry or the worker class. Neither were they members of the bourgeoisie that had been "awakened and enlightened" to the cause of Communism. They were only the Communists' "advance elements in the streets of Saigon, at press conferences of students" headquarters, agitators in street demonstrations armed with a nylon bag of water and lemon to protect themselves against the tear gas, the bodies to fill the government's detention centers to provide support for the Communist claim that the Saigon government has arrested many patriotic students. And especially because, as "patriotic students," they were still students and patriots, they could never become pure Communists, and there would be no exception.

Therefore, by gathering a number of civilians and soldiers to come and listen to the songs and music by "the patriotic students," the Communist cadres had drawn a line between the "students and intellectuals" and the class of peasants and workers. There was a clear distinction between the white-shirted representatives of the urban class and the crowd of ragged, underfed civilian and soldiers rounded up to listen to the songs and dances of the urban people. By the same stroke, the students had been cast away from real collectivity, and wedded to the struggle of the NLF. The students had played their part. There was nothing more they could do in Loc Ninh within the Communist world. Let the opposition students sing even louder in Saigon—like the singer Pham Duy, who once had brought his romantic and heroic music to the Fourth Combat Zone, to the hills and valleys of Yen Bay, had the rivers of Central Vietnam resound with echoes of his songs, with the vigor and the passion of those "national salvation" days after the autumn of 1946The songs of the students today also had some of the same romanticism and heroism. But that was all. The rules of the war had come to an end and at the same time the streets of Saigon, and the schools, had receded into the distance. In your passion, you had become outcasts while the Communists were still feasting on the warm blood that you had provided.

That was my initial reaction—a feeling of compassion and regret. But I had another contrary reaction, and that was one of anger. I was angry because I thought that these young people, having been nurtured in the South, and being aware of the painful realities of the country, should have seen more clearly than anybody else the true nature of the war—the natural outcome of the conflict among the world powers trying to reach a resolution, a situation of equilibrium between the contenders. These students should have been more acutely aware than anybody else of the danger of total destruction of the Vietnamese society which had survived and prospered through more than two thousand years in an orderly and harmonious way, a society in which all social conflict, including class segregation, had been neutralized and channeled toward the common national objectives.

Of course, I would not be so foolish as to affirm that Vietnam had always been a perfect society through its more than two thousand years of history, but it should be evident that Vietnam had always been a stable society and that was an outstanding achievement in the dynamic process of our history. And therefore these young men, with their fresh generosity, their open-mindedness, their aspirations and their patriotism, should have realized that this war was only the last in a series of conflicts between two ideologies issued from the West which, though nominally in conflict, were, basically, but facets of the same situation of collapse and deterioration of a social structure built on materialism. Communism, capitalism, freedom, democracy, liberation, dictatorship, colonialism are all products imported from the West and should have remained with the West. But disaster had befallen us when these conflicting ideologies came and used our country for their battlefield, and to try to reach an equilibrium, to achieve reconciliation and concord over the dead bodies of the Vietnamese people. These young people should have known this before they engaged themselves in the game, because there would never be a second chance, because once they were in the game, the only alternative was only between life and death for themselves and for the whole people. But these young people could only see in one direction, held only one point of view, and resolutely believed that they had chosen the right way, and that led them to disaster.

These young people in the struggle movements also committed another serious mistake, a basic mistake that seemed to be quite common elsewhere in the world. That mistake is the hopeless complex of the intellectual. Indeed, everywhere in the world from the East to the West, from Paris, the City of Lights, to the dark and remote corners of an undeveloped country in Asia, there is a class of intellectuals full of humanistic aspirations and moved by great aspirations and, arrayed against them, and choking them off, there is a whole inhuman structure of society. The intellectual, while conscious of his own value, is also hopelessly, and tragically, aware of his limits. Because this is no longer the time of the individual but the time of the collectives. There are no longer poets, there are only the workers. This is no longer the time of the intellectual in his ivory tower, but the time of the man engaged in the world, accepting the trials by fire that life will reserve to him. This is also a time of conflict between the Essence and the Existence, where the depreciation of spiritual values is a by-product. In this era of the dethroned intellectual, the struggling young man has not hesitated to try to follow in the footsteps of Sartre, of Gide, of Malraux, who tried to contend with Communism, armed with their intellectual capital. And the outcome in Vietnam, was that these engaged young men, like Hoang Phu Ngoc Tuong, Nguyen Van Xuan, Nguyen Van Trung, and Le Hieu Dang, had dipped their hands in blood, and in doing so they probably felt the exhilaration of those who had succeeded in getting rid of their complex of incapability and in transforming themselves into a new class of patriotic, "enlightened" intellectuals. Such was the disaster that befell them, such was their perdition. The young intellectual, if he is now somewhere in the hills and jungles of the secret zone, must be reviewing his accomplishments in order to have a clear judgment of his own value. . . . But he is lost among other "comrades," who are separate from him because they come from a different class, the class of peasants or workers, with their own values, their own achievements, their own class consciousness. Hoang Phu Ngoc Tuong, the brilliant student in the Hue student struggle movement, is now an officer on the district education board of Gio Linh district, meager reward for a life of struggle. And Trinh Dinh Ban and Tran Thi Hue, what are they going to do in the hills of Loc Ninh? I saw them being ordered around by that fellow

Nam Tich, the lieutenant colonel who used to be a blacksmith, that morning of July 24 in Loc Ninh and I felt so bitter about it. . . . That was the end result of their "struggle"—that was the end of the road: a picture-taking session with Lieutenant Colonel Nam Tich, the former blacksmith and whose "revolutionary achievements" Ban could never hope to equal. I wondered if that was just a process of self-destruction of the young man who had hoped to find a way out of the dormant environment of the family and the school. . . . Young man, what did you find in the dark green shadows of the Loc Ninh rubber plantations?

[LOC NINH, JULY 24, 1973]

Eight

The Prisoner of War Issue

Issue:

ON JAN. 27, 1973, the Paris Agreement was signed to put an end to the war in Vietnam. The Agreement consists of nine Chapters containing all the basic Articles to realize the cease-fire and to solve the problems of peace. The exchanges of prisoners between the warring sides are a main feature of the Agreement, and are governed by Article 8 of Chapter III, which gives a general outline, and an Annex consisting of 14 Articles stipulating the duties and responsibilities of each side as well as a number of basic operating procedures. The exchanges of military and civilian personnel between the two South Vietnamese sides were carried out in accordance with Article 9 of the Agreement and the terms of the Annex. We will leave aside the problem of the return of military and civilian personnel of the United States and other foreign countries (countries participating in the war on the side of the United States and within the framework of the Free World military assistance program to the Republic of Vietnam) captured by the National Liberation Front and the Democratic Republic of Vietnam. We will dwell mainly on the issue of military and civilian prisoners of the two South Vietnamese sides as stipulated in Article 8 (a to c). Basic principles to resolve the issue are provided in Articles 1 and 7 of the Annex.

Article 8 of the Agreement and the Annex defined the terms under which the exchange of prisoners could be efficiently carried out. But on the whole, the entire Agreement and the Annex are built on certain vaguely defined principles which could lend themselves to various interpretations. For example, the Agreement calls on all sides to resolve their problems "in a spirit of unanimity, of reconciliation, and concord between the warring sides, particularly the spirit of national reconciliation between the two South Vietnamese sides." An agreement that is so emotionally based has therefore created right from the start an atmosphere of indecisiveness and confusion, with each side coming to a different and sometimes opposite understanding of the text of the Agreement. Thus, Article 8 of the Agreement and the other Articles in the Annex failed to mention the fact that there are South Vietnamese military and civilian personnel captured and detained by the regular forces of the North Vietnamese Army, that there are soldiers of the Republic of Vietnam Armed Forces captured outside South Vietnamese territory, and that there are South Vietnamese civilians abducted by Communist forces and kept under detention ever since the beginning of the war, and even as far back as the time of the partition of the country after the Geneva Agreement of July 20, 1954. Articles 1 and 7 of the Annex did provide a framework for the exchange of prisoners between the two South Vietnamese sides. The Articles say that all the prisoners captured during the war should be released, and give a time frame for the completion of the exchange of prisoners—"in the spirit of national reconciliation and concord, dissolving all hatred, and relieving the sufferings of the prisoners detained on either side." But it was just a framework, and it was not enough for a satisfactory solution of the problem of Vietnamese P.O.W.s. Article 1 of the Annex stated simply: "All captured Vietnamese military personnel, belonging to the regular armed forces or to the irregular forces will be returned to each South Vietnamese side, those who served under the command of either one of the South Vietnamese sides being returned to their side."

There is the gap. The problem of the North Vietnamese prisoners of war will be solved satisfactorily after they have been turned over to the armed forces of the National Liberation Front. The confusion about their operating areas would be resolved without much problem since their receiving units, even though nominally belonging to the NLF, are ultimately under the political leadership of the Politburo of the Labor Party in North Vietnam. In other words, a Communist P.O.W. who was a soldier with the North Vietnamese 324B division, for example, and who was returned to the National Liberation Front in Loc Ninh, would have no problem in continuing to carry out his duties with his new unit. The gap that caused great disadvantage for the Saigon government in Article 1 of the Annex has to do with the almost complete lack of clarity concerning the problem of the South Vietnamese (Saigon's) P.O.W.s captured by the North Vietnamese Army, those captured outside the territory of South Vietnam, Laos, or Cambodia. This gap also revealed a most dangerous trap in the Agreement: the participation of the North Vietnamese regular forces in the battlefield of South Vietnam is either ignored or completely negated. In this way, the Communist slogan "Born in the North to Die in the South" is not just used for propaganda purpose to heighten the morale of the Communist troops, it also points to a guiding concept of the strategy that the North Vietnamese Communist party is determined to carry out.

There is another gap in Article 7 of the Annex. The Article does not clearly and definitely specify the problem of the South Vietnamese civilians captured during the nineteen years of the war. Article 7 reasserts "the spirit of national reconciliation and concord," but this is not enough to resolve the tragic problems of the South Vietnamese civilians caught in a local conflict of the two opposing ideologies in the world. That spirit of national reconciliation as proclaimed in Article 7 was of no help to the 67,501 civilians and administrative cadres of South Vietnam abducted between 1954 and Jan. 1973. The National Liberation Front has stuck to those gaps in Article 7 in order to ignore the fate of those people.

Development:

Jan. 27, 1973, was also the first day to begin the practical steps to restore peace. The United States suspended all bombardment over the entire territory of North Vietnam. The warring parties in South Vietnam put an end to all military operations and troops were ordered to remain in their positions. On the same day in Paris, the Republic of Vietnam handed over to the representatives of the National Liberation Front a list of 26,734 prisoners and received from them a list of 4,285 prisoners. The NLF representative also promised to forward a supplementary list of South Vietnamese prisoners "in order to show goodwill," in accordance with the "spirit of national reconciliation and concord." The Committee in charge of the problems of P.O.W.s of the 4-Party Joint Military Commission held its first meeting in Saigon on Feb. 3, 1973. The problem of prisoner exchanges according to the lists that had been made available to each side was now put on the negotiation table.

During the period of 60 days, starting from Jan. 28, 1973, in accordance with Article 8a of the Agreement and Article 4a of the Annex, the Committee held 50 meetings to complete the release of 26,508 military personnel of the National Liberation Front, 585 military personnel of the U.S. and other foreign countries, and 4,956 military personnel of the Republic of Vietnam. The prisoners were released in four groups at the following points:

- The Republic of Vietnam returned 26,508 Communist prisoners at Loc Ninh (Binh Long province), Minh Thanh (Binh Long), north of the Thach Han River (Quang Tri province), and Bong Son (Binh Dinh province).
- The Republic of Vietnam received 4,956 prisoners from seven locations: Loc Ninh, Quang Tri, Minh Than, Thien Ngon (Tay Ninh province), Bong Son (Binh Dinh province), Duc Pho (Quang Ngai province), and Tam Ky. In particular, at the Duc Nghiep location, in Pleiku province, despite three inspections, 410 South Vietnamese P.O.W.s continued to be held by the National Liberation Front and they would have to wait until the following year to be finally be released, in three batches within one month, from Feb. 8, 1974 to March 7, 1974, with 31 of them still unaccounted for.
- The National Liberation Front and North Vietnam returned 585 military and civilian personnel of the United States and other foreign countries at Loc Ninh and Gia Lam airport (Ha Noi). There was one Korean soldier released at Duc Pho (Quang Ngai province) and two Thai soldiers released at Gia Lam airport.

In total, the two South Vietnamese sides used seven locations to return and receive their P.O.W.s within the period stipulated by the Agreement. March 28, 1973 was the last day in the 60-day period. The problem of military prisoners concluded with 26,508 National Liberation Front P.O.W.s released and with the Saigon side receiving in return 4,956 of their military personnel captured by the Communists. Until then, there were still two remaining problems: 410 military personnel of the Republic of Vietnam were still waiting to be released from Duc Nghiep, and 210 Communist prisoners who had been classified as "returnees" and 28 others who were considered as defectors. In addition, a significant number of military personnel of the Republic of Vietnam continued to be detained by the Communists despite the promise of the NLF that they would provide supplementary lists and the efforts of the Commission to get them released. This problem would drag on past the 60-day period, and the subsequent 90-day period that was prescribed especially for the civilian prisoners, and had to wait until March 3, 1974, before the case could be considered closed after the NLF had released the last of the 410 prisoners at Duc Nghiep.

In accordance with the stipulation of Article 7b of the Annex, within 15 days after the signing of the Agreement on Jan. 27, 1973, the two sides would have to provide lists of civilian prisoners held on each side, and within ninety days from Jan. 27 the two sides would have to complete the exchanges of prisoners as listed. In order to seriously carry out that Article, the Republic of Vietnam, during the session of Feb. 12, had prepared a complete list of 5,081 civilian prisoners, but since the front had only a list of barely 140 people, the exchange of prisoners' list did not take place. According to the Saigon side, up to 67,501 people had been abducted by the Communists between 1954 and 1973 and the Saigon government had a complete list of their names, their biographical data, and the dates and places of their capture. Confronted with the logical demand of the Saigon side, the National Liberation Front came up with what they described as their definitive list of 637 civilian prisoners, adding that there could be more but not many.

This was still far from the demand of the Saigon side, but in order to show goodwill and to observe the time frame as prescribed in the Agreement, the Saigon side proposed a schedule for the exchanges of civilian prisoners to start on April 28, 1973. According to the plan, 750 prisoners would be released to the National Liberation Front at Loc Ninh and on the north bank of the Thach Han River between April 28 and May 11, 1973, and at the same time 385 prisoners would be returned to the Republic of Vietnam from three locations in Loc Ninh, Quang Tri, and Binh Dinh. But as had been suspected, the other side inserted 128 military prisoners into the group of 385 prisoners to be returned to the Saigon side, an impertinent shuffling in serious violation of the terms of the agreement stipulating exclusively the exchanges of civilian prisoners between the two sides. This, and other deceptive tricks of the Communist resulted in much delay in the exchanges of prisoners. For example, during the exchange of prisoners in Quang Tri on May 9, 1973, when 10 of the first group of 25 prisoners wanted to declare their decision to defect on the spot and refused to go back to the Communist side, the NLF's delegate insisted that the Saigon side first return to them the remaining 225 prisoners before the group of 10 would be allowed to express their wishes, in violation of the agreement had been reached in principle at the Joint Military Commission. The exchange of prisoners then was delayed until May 11, 1973. Because of these and similar problems, the Saigon side announced a suspension of the exchanges of prisoners until the two sides agreed on a basic document regulating the exchanges of civilian prisoners at all locations where prisoners were received or returned.

On June 13, 1973, a Joint Communique was signed in Paris in an attempt to get the Cease-Fire Agreement out of the impasse. The problem of the exchanges of military and civilian personnel also received more elaborate treatment in Article 8 of the Joint Communique. According to the new time frame, all military personnel should be released within thirty days and civilian personnel released within forty-five days starting from June 13.

But, as with the Cease-Fire Agreement, the Joint Communique, despite all the apparent goodwill and the strict specifications, could not be truly carried out because of Communist obduracy. Moreover, there were still gaps, whether intentional or unintentional, and the Communists were quick to take advantage of them to resist all the logical demands of the South Vietnamese side. As a result, even after the Joint Communique, the National Liberation Front continued to insist that they would not have more than 637 civilian prisoners to be returned to the Government of the Republic of Vietnam, and since 385 had already been released, there remained only 252 civilian prisoners to be returned to the Saigon side. Once again, in order to prove to the world its earnest aspirations for peace, the Republic of Vietnam proposed another schedule for prisoner exchanges so that, between July 23 and Aug. 28, 1973, all the remaining 4,331 civilian prisoners would be released at the two locations of Loc Ninh and Thien Ngon, at the same time the Saigon side expected to receive 410 military and 252 civilian prisoners from Duc Nghiep. But this plan was not to be carried out.

Before the Lunar New Year, the Year of the Tiger, the Saigon side tried to get the situation out of the impasse with the hope that the exchanges of prisoners could be resumed and completed before the New Year Celebration. But the two sides remained at odds. The Republic of Vietnam wanted to treat the issue as part of an overall solution of the problem of prisoners of war that would include the release of all remaining prisoners on the lists, the military personnel captured by the Communists in Lower Laos in Cambodia and during the Communist Tet Offensive of 1968, as well as civilians abducted by the Communists since 1954. However, the National Liberation Front only wanted to resume the exchanges that had been suspended since July 1973, insisting that the prisoner problem could be considered as solved with the completion of that schedule. They also claimed that the Saigon government was still holding about 200,000 political prisoners belonging to the Third Force and demanded that these prisoners should be released in return for 410 military and 252 civilian prisoners that they still detained. That was a most wicked joke. Who said that the Communists are humorless people?

The New Year rolled by, and there was still no movement. The exchanges of prisoners only resumed on Feb. 8, 1974, and were completed on March 7. In the end, the Republic of Vietnam released all of the 5,081 civilian prisoners and 76 additional military prisoners to the Communists, and received 410 prisoners from Duc Nghiep (less 31 unaccounted for) and 252 civilian prisoners. It was a long tug-of-war before the rest of the prisoners were released.

According to Article 8a of the Cease-Fire Agreement, the warring parties were required to immediately exchange complete lists of prisoners and to release all military and civilian prisoners within a period of sixty days from the day of the signing of the Agreement, Jan. 27, 1973.

A ninety-day period was fixed for the release of all Vietnamese civilian prisoners who were defined according to Article 21b of the Geneva Agreement as civilians who, as a result of their participation in the armed or political struggle of one side, were captured and detained by the other side. In other words, their participation may be under various forms so long as they are not soldiers in uniform. The Articles specified naturally that the exchange of prisoners should be carried out in a spirit of national reconciliation and concord!

One of the most painful and concrete issues of the war, one of the most complicated and destructive wars in history, a war of liberation that was waged with such totality and intensity, is dispatched with 11 lines consisting of 195 words in Article 8 of the Agreement and four pages of the Annex which attempt to outline the practical steps to carry out the agreement the prisoners problem. Because of the lack of clarity, the gaps, and the traps in the Agreement, the Saigon side gradually saw itself as the loser in the exchanges of prisoners, while the other side was enjoying the pain and suffering of the prisoners, the former soldiers of the Republic of Vietnam Armed Forces.

I wonder if, during the days when they bargained each word and polished each phrase of the Agreement, in order to negate the presence of the North Vietnamese Army, the negotiators of the Agreement realized that they were sacrificing the blood shed by the South Vietnamese soldiers captured by the North Vietnamese Army during the fighting. From a close reading of Articles 1 and 2 of the Annex, it would seem that there are four different categories of prisoners: Prisoners of the United States and other foreign countries (which participated in the war on the side of the Republic of Vietnam), civilian prisoners who are foreign nationals (U.S. or others), and military and civilian prisoners in South Vietnam, that is, prisoners held by the National Liberation Front.

There was absolutely no mention of the soldiers of the regular forces that came down the Ho Chi Minh Trails from North Vietnam to participate in the fighting at what the Communists called the B-Front (covering the Quang Tri and Thua Thien provinces), or the tri-border area designated as the B-3 Front. There was absolutely no mention of those soldiers captured on the field, on whose bodies was tattooed the slogan "Born in the North to Die in the South," even though they would not hesitate to make such declarations as this one: "I belong to Division 304b, under the command of Senior Colonel Nguyen Son. My unit was formed in 1965 in Thanh Hoa. We came to the South on Oct. 9, 1967, and were engaged in fighting at Khe Sanh starting from Jan. 19, 1968, etc." There was not one word in the Agreement to describe this category of prisoners—the captured soldiers of the North Vietnamese Army (sent to B, meaning to the South, in the Communist jargon), and naturally it was deemed superfluous to mention specifically that 304b Division. That is terrifying, that scene of the whole world, including many figures well-known for their works for peace, acting as accomplices to the robbers.

The tragic and painful consequences of this state of affairs was that the fact of the South Vietnamese soldiers captured and detained by the North Vietnamese Army was tacitly rejected as nonexistent! In other words, the existence of the men who were captured by the enemy during the 1972 offensive and the Tet Offensive in 1968, of the men who were sent to fight the enemy in Cambodia and across the border into Laos was completely denied, negated, nullified. There was no such category of prisoners in the Agreement for Cease-Fire and for the Restoration of Peace in Vietnam. And, it was said, the prisoners problem would be solved on the basis of the "spirit of national reconciliation and concord," free from hatred and with a view to alleviate the suffering and to allow the prisoners to be reunited with their families. The whole world lauded the neatness and the humanity of the Agreement. The South Vietnamese soldier captured by the North Vietnamese Army, where art thou? The whole world has agreed in unanimity to nullify your existence. While the whole world is celebrating the advent of peace, is there anyone who thinks of the South Vietnamese soldier who, at that very minute, lies prostrate in shackles deep in the hills and jungles of North Vietnam? They are the men discarded from the game of peace.

In the exchange of lists, while the Republic of Vietnam made public a list of up to 26,750 Communist P.O.W.s, the National Liberation Front handed over a list of only 5,018 military prisoners. The 26,750 Communist P.O.W.s were divided into several categories: Regular soldiers of the North Vietnamese Army, elements that were regrouped to the North after the 1954 Geneva Agreement and returned to the South to participate in the fighting in later years (from 1959), and prisoners who were former soldiers or guerrillas of the National Liberation Front. For their part, the National Liberation Front only indicated that the 5,018 prisoners were captured by the liberation forces during the ten years of war in South Vietnam. Most of the prisoners were captured during the 1972 offensive. Only a few were captured in the earlier years 1968, 1969, 1970, and 1971. Prisoners captured prior to 1968 were not mentioned and their names were not included in the lists.

Most wicked of all, the Communists would not return the South Vietnamese soldiers captured during the cross-border operations, arguing that they were really prisoners of the Pathet Lao and the Khmer Rouge.

The Republic of Vietnam could not accept that 5,018 represented the total number of prisoners held by the other side during the more than 10 years of war. To agree to that assertion would be to act as accomplice to a crime. After the exchanges of prisoners had been completed a serious discrepancy was discovered in comparing the list of 5,018 prisoners actually released with the names on the list received from the other side of Paris: There were 29 officers and 1,033 non-commissioned officers and privates whose names were on the list but who had not been released! There are two ways to interpret that discrepancy: either 29 officers and 1,033 non-commissioned officers and privates had died and had been supplanted by other prisoners, or perhaps they were subsequently added after the Communists, for some reason, were not able to come up with the 5,018 prisoners as they had announced in Paris.

Either way, a conclusion seemed unavoidable: many more soldiers of the Republic of Vietnam Armed Forces were still being detained in Communist prison camps. This is an instance: the 101st Artillery Battalion based at Gia Linh came under attack by the Communists at the start of the offensive in March 1972. The base was overrun and Lieutenant Thanh was captured and taken to North Vietnam to be detained there. Some time later, Thanh was seen with a group of other prisoners in a picture published in the North Vietnamese *Doan Ket* (Unity) paper that was circulated in Paris. Thanh's family also heard a message from him over Radio Hanoi. The existence of Lieutenant Thanh was irrefutable and could not possibly be covered up, but he had not been released. The case of Lieutenant Thanh was bought up at the Joint Military Commission. The NLF's delegates duly took note and the whole issue quickly lapsed into oblivion "in the spirit of national reconciliation and concord."

The case of Thanh was only one example of the thousands of other cases of ARVN Army, Republic of Vietnam) prisoners still being held in the sixty prison camps in Vietnam, Cambodia, and Laos. Among the prisoner detention centers, there was one code-named T-2 located between the two villages of Viet Hong and Viet Cuong, in the district of Tran Yen, Yen Bay province. Camp T-2 was set up in April 1971, about two months after the campaign into lower Laos to hold the South Vietnamese soldiers captured during the cross-border operation. Among the prisoners, there were Colonel Nguyen Van Tho, Commander of the Third Airborne Brigade, Major Tran Van Duc, Operations officer, Major Phuong and Captain Phuong, artillery officers of the 3rd Artillery Battalion on Hill 31. The existence of these prisoners had been confirmed by other prisoners who had been released, by the disclosures of four returnees who used to work at the prison camps, and by the prisoners themselves who had been brought out to talk on the Radio Hanoi. Despite all the clear and concrete evidence, including taped evidence, the Communists remained totally unresponsive. The National Liberation Front took notes of the cases but at the same time they asserted that prisoners such as Colonel Tho, Majors Phuong and Duc, etc., fought in Laos and were captured by the Pathet Lao Forces and, as such, were not under their responsibility. And they would end with a promise, never kept, that "based on the compassion toward fellow-compatriots, they would try to intervene with the Pathet Lao forces to seek their release because, in any case, these prisoners are also Vietnamese." (!!)

That was convenient. The National Liberation Front and North Vietnam unconcernedly passed over the issue, the more so because the Paris Agreement and the Annex did not contain any mention of this category of prisoners. Also according to the Agreement, the North Vietnamese Army did not go into Laos, did not fight in South Vietnam, and that country and that government stood outside of the war in South Vietnam. That was indeed monstrous and painful especially when you heard so many voices shout words of welcome for peace, for goodwill. There are so many causes for war, and cries, and among them is use, or abuse, or names. The Communists for example, fight for certain names, certain slogans, and use them to cover up the traces of their killings. Many people do not see the real face of the Communists behind such names as Peace, Goodwill, Reconciliation.

That was the problem of the military prisoners, which had run into serious difficulties when confronted with Communist obduracy. The problem of the civilian prisoners also presented us with tragic aspects. After Jan. 27, 1973, the Ministry for Civic Actions made public a list of all civilians and administrative cadres abducted by the Communists since 1954, totaling 67,501 people, including 50,747 civilians and 16,754 government officials. That list, however lengthy, was complete with well-checked details. That did not include a significant number of civilians abducted by the Communists in remote areas who would have to remain unaccounted for. Confronted with the list, complete with names, birthplaces and birthdates, family status, official positions as well as the dates and places of their capture, the Communists responded with a straight face: since the armed liberation movement was only launched in 1959, and since the National Liberation Front was only officially set up on Dec. 20, 1960, it is absurd to say that the NLF is involved in the capture of civilians and government officials during the period between 1954 and 1960! And after 1960, they went on, the NLF did arrest and detain a number of government cadres and civilians, those who did not have "progressive revolutionary consciousness," but since the policy of the NLF is to reform people by re-education and not to hold people in prisons, these people after a period of re-education have understood the NLF's policy and have been released or have willingly joined in the liberation movement! In the end, "to prove their goodwill and their respect of the Agreement and the Annex," the Provisional Government handed over to the Saigon side a list of 140 people being detained by the NLF with the promise—again, to demonstrate their love for peace—that there would be additional lists as the case arises!

That was a blatant insult to common sense: only 140 prisoners during the whole period of the protracted war! It may be true that the Communists do not have a policy of holding prisoners because they have killed a great number of civilians and government officials. They have indeed murdered numerous innocent people, and when the world applauds the goodwill for peace of those pale-faced people coming out of their secret zones to the Paris Conference, they are really rooting for murderers. Those wicked and fanatic butchers have had their enthusiasm fueled by the warm blood of the South Vietnamese people—the people in Hue massacred during the Tet Offensive, the inhabitant of Quang Tri pulverized by shelling along the Highway of Terror, the refugees from Binh Long cut down along Route 13. The superman theory of Nietzsche pushed the Nazis to a frenzy of killing, and Mao's thoughts unleashed the Red Guards to unthinking destruction, while in South Vietnam, land of miseries and disasters, a gross Marxism refitted and updated, has turned lose the cadres of the Labor Party on innocent people, "with full consciousness." It is disgusting that in this second half of the twentieth century, there are still so many people in the world so affected with intellectual sadism that they would gladly act in collusion with the murderers.

So, in the end, that was the blatant response by the Communists even after the Saigon government had made public full details about prisoners detained at the Ba Sao prison camp in Nam Ha (a province that combines the two provinces of Nam Dinh and Ha Nam) where there were detained among others, Bao Loc, the former deputy province chief of Thua Thien, Nguyen Van Dai, government delegate for the 1 Corps, Ha Thuc Tu, chief of the railway service in Da Nang, Nguyen Dinh Ba, student, and newspaper woman Nguyen De, former Public Health Chief in Bong Son, captured by the Communists in May 1972. The detention of Dr. De was discovered by a journalist of the Japanese newspaper *Asahi Shimbun*. "The case of Dr. De, who was forced to stay with the Communists, is a blot on the liberation movement," he wrote. All these prisoners were not on the list of 637 civilian prisoners.

The first exchange of prisoners took place on Feb. 12, 1973. North Vietnam released prisoners in Gia Lam, the Republic of Vietnam turned over prisoners to the Communists on the north bank of the Thach Han River, and the National Liberation Front returned their prisoners to the Saigon side from Loc Ninh. The release of prisoners in Gia Lam took place without a hitch. In addition to the number of prisoners scheduled for release that day the Hanoi government also released a Lieutenant-Colonel because his mother was seriously ill. In Quang Tri, the release of prisoners had to be delayed because the North Vietnamese cadres on the north bank of the river said they had not yet completed all the preparations to receive their prisoners. In Loc Ninh, NLF's representatives wanted to play games: the exchange was scheduled to take place at 8:30 in the morning, but they procrastinated and only released the prisoners late in the evening. General

Woodward reacted immediately by rushing a protest note to the Chairman of the International Committee and a warning to General Tra of the NLF, reasserting that the American withdrawal would be directly related to the progress of the release of American P.O.W.s.

All 556 American P.O.W.s were released on time in March 1973. After some initial procrastination, both North Vietnam and the National Liberation Front stuck faithfully to the schedule for the release of American prisoners of war, wisely retreating in the face of strength. ". . . We do not come here for fun. Mr. Kissinger is now (Feb. 1973) in Hanoi with precise instructions from our President to request you to release the prisoners on schedule. . . ." The firmness, and the authority, with which General Woodward and Colonel Russell warned the Communists contributed to making the releases of American prisoners take place smoothly. The Republic of Vietnam also completed the return of 26,508 military prisoners (except for the 210 who had declared their wish not to return to the Communists).

The NLF, in an about-face, refused to release the remaining 410 South Vietnamese P.O.W.s at Duc Nghiep without giving any justification. While proclaiming their respect for the Agreement and the Annex and their "spirit of national reconciliation and concord," the Communists continued to hold on to the 410 prisoners, past the 60-day period, and then past the 90-day period until the problem of military prisoners had to be temporarily suspended in May 1973 (by then 30 had died in prison camp), and the exchanges of civilian prisoners began. The Republic of Vietnam returned to the NLF 750 prisoners and received back 385 prisoners. The exchanges of civilian prisoners came to a stop when delegates of the International Committee refused to travel to the locations for prisoners' exchanges because the NLF refused to guarantee the safety of the air corridors. Also, the Communists had insisted on receiving their prisoners on the north bank of the river instead of the south bank as initially proposed for fear that it would then be easier for the prisoners to refuse to go back to them and to stay back as defectors with the Saigon government. There were 36 such cases in the first phase during which 750 prisoners were returned to the Communists, and there would have been even more. . . . On the other hand, the National Liberation Front also prepared another tactic aimed at exploiting such people as Mrs. Ngo Ba Thanh, student Huynh Tan Mam, lawyer Nguyen Long, etc., to use them in the Third Force and to create trouble at the locations for the exchanges of prisoners in the presence of the media.

In the protracted negotiations from May to July 1973, the Saigon side worked hard to get the Communists to release all the prisoners on the list, especially the 410 prisoners still stranded at Due Nighiep, along with the remaining civilian prisoners. Particular emphasis was put on the issue of the prisoners still detained in various prison camps in Cambodia, Laos, and in North Vietnam, including especially the 7,061 military and civilian prisoners held in 34 prison camps in North and South Vietnam. The Communists remained obdurate in the face of precise numbers, clear evidence, and exact locations of the prison camps put forward by the Saigon side. Their argument ran as follows:

-"We have at most one or two more prisoners. You fought in Laos and in Cambodia so you were captured by the Pathet Lao forces and the Khmer Rouge, not us. . . ."

The most unusual arguments, the most nebulous reasons were repeated again and again without the slightest embarrassment and in a most serious tone. The most reasonable demands of the Saigon side were met with stark indifference and obduracy. Many ARVN P.O.W.s remained shackled in the remote hills and darkest forests in Tuyen Quang, Vinh Phu, Yen Bay, and Son Tay, and former administrative cadres of the Saigon government continued in forced labor until they succumbed in various labor camps in Thanh Can, Thanh Hoa, and the former concentration camp of Ly Ba So, the reputed hell on earth in the Communist Gulag. Toward the end of the new forty-five-day period prescribed in the Joint Communique of June 13, 1973, the Rangers and paratroopers of the ARVN 3rd Brigade detained in camp T-371 continued to be taken out of camp in their daily forage "for supplemental rations" in the hills and jungles of Lang Son province in North Vietnam. Other ARVN P.O.W.s continued to be held in Tra Bong, Tra Mi, Ba To, A Shau, A Luoi, in South Vietnam, for re-education and reform, and in the meantime trying to survive with a meager ration of about two mouthfuls of rice with salt daily. When the end of the forty-five-day period arrived and all prisoners had been returned to the Communists, the Saigon side would have nothing left to bargain with the Communists for the release of these prisoners. And then the cries of rage of the thousands of their comrades-in-arms would never reach them beyond the hills and the forests. Oh, what would you become, soldiers who fought on Hill 31 in Laos, on firebases A-1 and A-2 in Gio Linh, who fought to the last bullet in Tan Canh and Hoai An—what would you become, you fought for peace, for humanity, for the world.

The NLF also used another tactic to evade the problem of the Saigon prisoners by raising the counter-demand that the Republic of Vietnam should immediately and unconditionally release 200,000 political prisoners still detained in government prisons. They argued that these prisoners were people who had struggled for Peace and National Reconciliation, and therefore belonged to the Third Force, which was indispensable for the formation of the Council for National Reconciliation and Concord. The NLF asserted that these 200,000 people were prisoners of common law detained in prisons of the Government of the Republic of Vietnam.

That was a new issue raised by the NLF's delegates at the Joint Commission after May 1973. There are two reasons why this issue was brought up so late in the negotiations at the Joint Military Commission.

In the months of March and April 1974, the National Liberation Front concentrated all their efforts on receiving the 26,750 military prisoners returned by the Saigon side and at the same time they had to make preparations for the reception of 5,081 civilian prisoners that would be released in the next phase. That was very important to them because they needed to use these prisoners to fill in the depleted ranks in their infrastructure that was weakened and sometimes neutralized after the Tet Offensive, or as a result of the cross-border operations of the Republic of Vietnam Armed Forces in 1970 and 1971. During the years from 1969 to 1972, the communication lines between their headquarters and the local organizations, their logistics, and their grassroots support had been badly damaged or destroyed. The NLF also needed that source of manpower to relieve the North Vietnamese pressure by the presence of political officers from North Vietnam everywhere in the South to support the 1972 Summer Offensive, spearheaded by the North Vietnamese main force divisions. But after the first phase of prisoner exchange from April 28 to May 11, 1973, during which 750 civilian prisoners were returned to the Communists, the NLF realized that these prisoners had become useless either because they had lost the will to continue the struggle or because they had proved unable to counter the influence of the cadres from North Vietnam. That explained why the NLF had lost their initial enthusiasm and turned their attention toward the issue of the political prisoners.

A second reason to explain that belated change of direction was that only after May 1973 did they gather enough documents and facts to start the fight.

After they had equipped themselves with all the documents concerning the Con Son prisons, the Tam Hiep prisons, and the books and magazines of such leftist intellectuals as Ngoc Nhuan, the National Liberation Front tried their utmost to exploit the situation, in conjunction with the anti-government activities of the various left-leaning or pro-Communist organizations whose main target of criticism was the prison system in South Vietnam. The political prisoners in South Vietnam thus became a big issue, with probing attacks from outside and criticism from within. After getting hold of the movement, the NLF exploited to the hilt the issue of civilians charged with "disturbing the peace and security" of South Vietnam. Moving with the current, the NLF helped turn such people as lawyer Nguyen Long, Mrs. Ngo Ba Thanh, student Mam, student Ban, Father Lan, Father Hue, etc., into symbols of the "patriotic" Third Force, condemned by the government for their activities for the cause of peace. The Third Force adopted a Communist line of thought, and Communist strategy and tactics. Their activities were stepped up in the month of June 1973. The Communists included the above people in the 200,000 political prisoners and clamored for their release.

With such an objective in mind, the National Liberation Front gathered all the facts from the "White Paper" by deputy Ho Ngoc Nhuan, exploited a statement by a government official about the problem of political prisoners, press articles by the group of left-leaning Catholic priests, and a letter of student leader Huynh Tan Mam. Their activities were well coordinated with the support of the anti-war intellectuals in the West. The point of fixation of the movement was the accusation that the Government of the Republic of Vietnam was detaining hundreds of thousands of political prisoners in the prison camps in Con Son, Tam Hiep, Phu Quoc, at the national Police Headquarters, and at the various detention centers in the provinces all over South Vietnam. They also demanded that the Government should immediately and unconditionally release all opposition students, and anti-government figures such as Chau, Long, Trong, and Thanh, and pledge that they would not be arrested again. This was also implicitly included in a Communist proposed schedule for the release of prisoners in which there was a separate article requesting the release by the Government of all elements "belonging to neither side in South Vietnam." These demands also served as an evasive tactic for the Communists when the Saigon side requested the other side to provide additional lists of civilian prisoners as they had promised.

This was clearly revealed when the Saigon side released twenty civilian prisoners, most of them students, to the Communists at Loc Ninh on July 23, 1973. From the time they disembarked till the time they completed all the formalities for release, these students had revealed their true identities as real Communist cadres well trained in the Communist methods of struggle. The NLF had made elaborate preparations to provide these students with an opportunity to denounce before the International Committee delegates the Saigon Government's policy of arresting and detaining people, including themselves, without charges. That would be part of their long and continuous struggle on the issue of "political prisoners." But despite all the tricks and dark plots of the Communists, truth and justice still prevailed. Article 7a of the Annex specified that there were only two categories of civilian personnel to be exchanged between the two sides in South Vietnam. They were the people who participated in the armed or political struggle on either side and as a result were captured by the opposing side. The definition, as it was, was based on Article 21b of the 1954 Geneva Agreement. Consequently, twenty-four hours after they received that group of students, the National Liberation Front had to come to the conclusion that they had failed completely in their desperate attempts to create any commotion out of a false issue.

Nine

Prisoner, Where Are You Going?

AS THE TITLE INDICATES, most of this memoir has to do with the prisoner, his situation, and the destruction and tragedy of his life. In the previous chapters, I have described some principal aspects about the South Vietnamese prisoners captured and detained by the Communists, the most miserable prisoners in the world. These prisoners had been subjected to humiliation, had their names vilified, had been deprived of their rights, their dignity. Being a prisoner is the most painful and miserable human condition. But the Communists do not even call them prisoners. They put a label on them. They call them pirates, puppets, traitors, and the prison camps, re-education camps. The prisoners are organized into units to build roads over mountains, to plant corn and cassava to supplement their daily rations, and to "pay their debts toward the people." The Saigon prisoner is not left alone in his miserable condition. Even in prison, he has to try to fight through every minute, every hour, for his spoiled bowl of rice, for every drop of water in order to survive. All his strength, all his energy is directed toward one single objective: survival. That is why, having lived through hell on earth, the Saigon prisoner, at his release, will run, stumble, crawl, and clamber on the helicopter that will take him away, very far away from the terrifying nightmare that he left behind and that he would try to forget forever and as quickly as possible, in order to start a new life that had seemed to be irremediably lost.

For the Saigon prisoners, to be released is to be returned to the paradise on earth in the government-controlled area—because they have lived with death. But in this chapter, I am not going to dwell further on these "miserably happy" men. I am going to write about the Communists captured by government forces and returned to the other side. They are men who had been captured with their arms in hand on the battlefields, or caught in the cities and towns for their subversive activities after the government had collected enough evidence and documents to incriminate them. It is not my intention to defend the prison system in South Vietnam, and it is not going to receive my praise since I abhor all prisons in general. I am going to describe only the situation of the Communist prisoner of the Government of the Republic of Vietnam, from the time he surrenders himself before the barrel of a gun on the battlefield or is handcuffed by the security police.

As I have many times stressed, the Communists would never give up their struggle under any circumstances. They would take advantage of any opportunity, any moment, however brief, to engage in struggle. There is no respite, there is no separate situation, no exception. From the time he joins in the struggle launched and conducted by the Party, he is embarked upon a continuous, relentless race until the realization of the Communist utopia. That is the general behavior demanded by the doctrine. In this particular situation, the Communists have moved beyond the phase of "anti-American, national salvation" struggle and have now come to the new phase of "struggle against neo-colonialism of the Americans and for correct and serious realization of the Paris Agreement." The Communist prisoner, even while in prison will have to continue to study the line of the Party, to discuss the current issues, and to strictly carry out the orders of the Party, so that he will be ready to resume the struggle as soon as he is released.

After being taken prisoner on the battlefield, the Communist P.O.W. will be interrogated on the spot by intelligence officers of the unit in the field. The interrogation will serve to classify the prisoner and to collect battlefield information. Since the combat unit in the field does have the necessary experts to conduct a thorough investigation, the on-the-spot interrogation is usually brief. After having given his biographical data and his unit identification, the prisoner would be moved immediately to temporary detention at the Regimental headquarters, or at the forward headquarters of the Division. Even there, with more time available and with the presence of specialists in prisoner investigation, the interrogation is still limited to such information as the prisoner's biographical data, battlefield activities, information concerning his unit, his base area, his routes of approach, and future plans.

The prisoner is moved on to a P.O.W. detention center. There can be no conflict between the prisoner and his captor. The branch of the Army charged with the detention of the P.O.W.s is the Military Police, whose duties and responsibilities are clearly defined. The prison guards are assigned very specific and limited duties. It is simply a matter of management and control. There is no further effort to exploit the prisoners, to get more information out of them. There is no political propaganda aimed at them, so this relationship is not conducive to the development of serious conflicts between the prison population and the unit responsible for guarding them. Neither does it bring about a situation where pain and suffering are inflicted on the prisoners, as the Communists have always claimed in their propaganda distorting the policy of the government. However, a merciless and determined struggle will be waged between the Communist prisoners themselves. That struggle will result in certain death for some of them, the death sentences being carried out by their own fellow prisoners. Those who want to stay alive will have to adhere firmly, tirelessly, and unflinchingly the Communist position and to faithfully carryout all the orders from their representatives. The struggle, fraught with dangers, between the men on the same front begins in the prisoners in Vietnam.

At this point, we need to shift our view to another aspect of the problem in order to further our understanding of the situation of the Communist prisoners in the South Vietnamese prisons: the returnees. The returnees are those who willingly lay down their arms, leave the ranks of the Communists, and go over to the side of the Republic of Vietnam, under any circumstances, and on any battlefield. A prisoner can also be changed to the status of a returnee if, after having been taken prisoner on the battlefield, he is willing to cooperate actively with the Saigon government. In fact, there are many such returnees "of the last resort": those who decide to go over to the government's side after his unit has been destroyed, dispersed, or under siege, or under heavy and repeated attacks by government forces. But even if he had to lay down his arms in that passive situation, he would still be taken to a Returnees Center, instead of a prison camp, if, by his own will and through his own consent, he provides the information, reveals the arms caches, and asks to defect. These returnees, whether willing or "in the last resort," are only common returnees, returnees to safety, so to speak. But there is another category or returnees, those who choose to defect while in prison. Those are "returnees of the first order," men who have overcome death at a hair's breadth. The Communist prisoner, as soon as he sets foot in a prison camp, is immediately put through a thorough investigation by the representatives of the prisoners. He has to give not only his name, his age, the name of his parents, his birth date and birth place as with the prison management, but his full biographical data, his past struggle going back twenty, thirty years, detailed description of his family relationship, his relatives, his friends, his unit, his skills, his preferences. He will have to repeat his declarations five times, seven times, under close and horrid scrutiny. The purpose of this scrutiny is to help the representatives of the Communist prisoners detect the "traitors," that is, the returnees inserted by the prison management to keep watch on the prison population. It also helps the prisoners' representatives to judge his morale and his abilities so as to assign him appropriate duties. The representatives of the prisoners will also be able to discover, through interrogation of the prisoner, if he surrendered to the government forces because he had a morale problem or because of combat exhaustion after having really put up a determined fight against the government forces.

In short, after a period of close interrogation and scrutiny, the Communist prisoner is categorized and given a place in the prison system by his own representatives. If he is a stool pigeon, or if he had surrendered without a fight to the government, his fate is sealed. His case will be solved by one solution, one last and unique solution: death. He will be killed in various ways: a chopstick pierced through his head from one ear to the other, scalping, throat slitting, strangling. The execution will be carried out in plain view of the other prisoners, as a threat, and a warning to those who are giving signs of wavering, discouragement, or of wanting to give up. The representatives will assign the new prisoners to the various groups who will work together and watch over each other. Those who appear to be tired, discouraged, or planning to defect and cooperate with the prison management will be reported immediately to the prisoners' representatives. The suspects will be summarily executed.

In this terrible situation, the Communist prisoner always has to remain vigilant, to demonstrate his unwavering faith in the position of the Party, to maintain firmly his revolutionary resolve to struggle for the liberation of South Vietnam and the reunification of the country under the leadership of Uncle Ho and of the Party. He will have to firmly grasp his position, to study the documents sent in from outside, in order to have a firm grasp of the situation and to direct his efforts toward the objectives presented by the Party. In order to ensure success in these difficult endeavors, the Communists would not hesitate to infiltrate hardcore political commissars into the prisons by having them pretend to surrender on the battlefield and then try to get themselves moved to the prison camp of their assignment. One instance is the case of the soldiers in the Communist Quyet Thang (Determined to Win) Regiment whose morale was seriously shaken after their attacks in the Cay Thi area in the province of Gia Dinh during the Tet Offensive of 1968. A number of them were taken prisoner by governmental forces. Seeing the need to firm up the morale of these prisoners, the command of the National Liberation Front's armed forces had a number of political commissars pretend to surrender to the Republic of Vietnam Armed Forces during some fighting in Binh Duong and Tay Ninh. After being taken prisoners, these political commissars were transferred to the prison camp in Tan Hiep, Bien Hoa province. At Tan Hiep, after being informed that the prisoners from the Quyet Thang Regiment had been moved to Phu Quoc, they created disturbances in the prison, were punished by the prison management, and were subsequently transferred to the prison camp in Phu Quoc. At Phu Quoc, they continued to create troubles until they were moved to the same cells as the prisoners from the Quyet Thang Regiment, the target of their assignment.

The Communist prisoner lives in this oppressive situation of close supervision and control, and under constant threat of harsh punishment by his fellow inmates. Anything can lead him to instant death: an insufficient show of hatred toward the military policemen who bring his meals to him, a lack of consciousness about "the corruption and impotence" of the Government of the Republic of Vietnam, doubts about the achievements of the National Liberation Front, which claimed to have extended control over three-quarters of the territory and four-fifths of the total population, or perhaps even a discreet sigh in the night. A prisoner that is called to the prison supervisor's office is asked a few details concerning his biography and returned untouched to his cell, may be sure that his life as virtually ended. That is why a prisoner who asks to defect in this situation is a first-class returnee, an outstanding returnee, a man who made a choice at the risk of his own life. That is the tragic situation of the Communist prisoners.

In the prisons, beside the fanatical young cadres of the North Vietnamese regular divisions, there are also many former soldiers of the Communist local forces, and former guerillas at the district or village level. Beside the young North Vietnamese with their "steel-and-blood" faith in the future of the revolution, their constantly built-up hatred against the South Vietnamese people and government, the latter are prisoners of circumstances, the failed revolutionary combatants, the former peasants who found themselves caught in the "liberated" area, or abducted from a disputed area and forced to join the Communists. At first, they would be assigned to "production" units, then they would be used in digging roads, building up obstacles, distributing anti-government leaflets, and collecting information. After he has been judged to have performed his duties well and to have "awakened" to the cause of the revolution, he will become a village militia. Then again, if he does well, he will be promoted to become a guerrilla at the district level, and eventually he would advance to the status of a full soldier in the reserve force operating in the province.

When there is need for big operations such as the Binh Gia operation in 1964, or the Dong Xoai operation in 1965, and if the Communist regional forces are under strength the guerillas from villages and districts will be gathered to the Communist Secret Zone C in Tay Ninh and Binh Long where they would be assigned to the various Regiments belonging to the 5th, the 7th, or the 9th Division of the Liberation armed forces of the National Liberation Front. These guerillas from South Vietnam, including even the veteran cadres regrouped to North Vietnam in 1954 and later returned to the South after 1959, are very different from the young soldiers, whose average age is about 20, from the North Vietnamese Divisions infiltrated to the South. The latter are more active, more fanatic, more blindly and strictly overzealous, more completely loyal to the instructions and policy of the Party and President Ho. A small number would be discouraged after the tough trials of the Trails, or after they have seen with their own eyes the real situation in South Vietnam and the real achievements of the NLF, and would defect to the government soon after they reached the South. But the rest, if they have overcome the Trails, and if the real situation in the South was still not enough to open their eyes, would become even more fanatic. In their fanaticism, it is natural that they believe that it is an important and urgent task to destroy those who are known to be planning to defect.

Surrounded by these fanatical elements, a prisoner who plans to defect is really engaged in a race with Death. The Government of the Republic of Vietnam, before handing over a definite list of prisoners to the National Liberation Front, in accordance with the Paris Agreement, launched a campaign called the New Life Movement in all the prison camps housing Communist prisoners. On the surface, the purpose of the campaign was to train the prisoners and help them acquire a professional skill, to create conditions to give them meaningful work during their stay in prison; but the real purpose was to present to them the real situation in South Vietnam so that they could make a choice between Freedom and Communism. The campaign was overwhelmingly successful; more than 10,000 prisoners chose to defect on the occasion of the New Year celebration, in the beginning of 1973, prior to the exchange of prisoner lists with the National Liberation Front in Paris. While this was a significant number compared with the 30,000 Communist prisoners that the Government had planned to return to the other side, there would have been a great deal more if the prisoners had complete freedom to make a choice before they were released, or if they had known more clearly the procedures at the prisoners' release locations where the prisoners are allowed to make known for the last time their wish to remain or to go back to the other side. The case of prisoner Thach Phen, released at Loc Ninh on Feb. 14, 1973, and the case of prisoner Ho Van Cong, released in Quang Tri on March 17, were concrete examples of the silent tragedies of the Communist cadres native from South Vietnam. Thach Phen, a Vietnamese of Cambodian descent, was forced to join the National Liberation Front because he lived in a disputed area between a secret Communist zone across the border in Cambodia and the government-controlled area in Chau Doc. On Feb. 14, 1973, he was brought to Loc Ninh to be turned over to the Communists.

Stepping down from the helicopter, he looked around with terror in his eyes at the row of thatched cottages, the display of red flags, the forest of banners with harsh-sounding slogans, the pale faces and the watchful and vaguely hateful eyes of the Communist cadres coming out to welcome the prisoners. He was not reassured by the well-rehearsed smiles curling on the ugly mouths, and he was even more confused by the obviously Chinese-sounding tunes blaring out of the loudspeakers. Although he had borne arms to fight on the side of the Communists, on that day he found that he had been taken to a place that seemed utterly strange to him: the dark green rubber plantations tightly hugging the hills of red clay, the cadres with their olive-drab uniforms, their eyes yellowed by malaria, the rehearsed smiles on unsmiling faces—the faces of harsh and austere inquisitors.

Thach Phen had never fought with such fellow combatants and in such an environment of threatening hills and dark inscrutable forests. He felt even more miserable and lonely because the prisoners in his group were all North Vietnamese, and they seemed to enjoy expressing their hatred and their rock-hard beliefs in the strength and invulnerability of the revolution by raising their clenched firsts, shouting slogans, and singing at full throat. Thach Phen felt that he was utterly alien in that atmosphere full of hatred and fanaticism. He backed out, retreated to the rear of the group, then ran toward the officers of the Military Police who had accompanied the prisoners from Phu Quoc to Loc Ninh and asked to defect. Captain Loc, leader of the South Vietnamese team on the Joint Military Commission, reported the fact to the three other members of the Commission (the National Liberation Front, North Vietnam, and the United States) and delegates of the International Committee and requested that the defection of prisoner Thach Phen be formally acknowledged. But the two officers representing the National Liberation Front and North Vietnam rejected the request on the ground that Thach Phen had not made known his decision to defect in conformance with the agreed procedures—in other words, Thach Phen should have announced his decision either during the roll call or during the exchange of prisoners. The Hungarian and Polish members on the International Commission immediately voiced the same argument.

Finally, the South Vietnamese Military Police, with the intention of setting a precedent for similar cases that could happen in the future, escorted Thach Phen to the tent used for reception of prisoners, where he could repeat his decision to defect before everybody. But the prisoners in the same group rushed in to snatch Thach Phen and jumped on the Military Police, who were overwhelmed and had to release Phen to them and retreat for fear that Phen could be beaten to death in the scuffle. The Hungarian and the Polish delegates again intervened and declared that, while they took note of what happened, they had no other responsibility than to supervise the exchange of prisoners inside the tent and that prisoner Thach Phen, since his name had not yet been called, had not been actually released, according to the procedures. In the meantime, Thach Phen had been pulled away and returned a moment later with a smashed face. Right then, the "local authorities" of the National Liberation Front at Loc Ninh requested a meeting the presence of all four members of the International Committee to hear Thach Phen "freely" express his wishes. In the end, instead of announcing his decision to defect, Thach Phen announced that the Saigon government had plotted to "insert" him as a returnee among the group of prisoners and declared that, having regained his "clear-mindedness" and "consciousness," he now wished to return to the side of the Provisional Government of the National Liberation Front! The Hungarian and the Polish delegates again duly took note of the fact—that prisoner Thach Phen had expressed his true aspirations, free from any coercion or restraint!

The case of Ho Van Cong was a little better. Cong was in the first group of prisoners to be returned to the Communists in Quang Tri on March 17, 1973. Like Thach Phen, Cong was a guerilla in the village of Phung Hiep in Can Tho province and was captured by the Republic of Vietnam Armed Forces during a patrol. As a simple and straightforward peasant in the Mekong Delta, he was caught between the two sides and was led by the circumstances to join in the Communist armed struggle. On the bank of the Thach Han River, he looked across and saw the big red flag with a yellow star in the middle on a background of stillness and oppressive silence. He could probably imagine in his mind a whole world ruled by inhumanity and tight organization. The wind brought to his ears snatches of song inciting people to hatred, somewhere in the distance. Cong felt that his legs were giving under him. He asked himself, Where am I? Is this the Ben Hai River he sometimes heard about? It always seemed to be a million miles from his native province of Can Tho in the Mekong Delta. He had never thought that he would one day go that far, although the village party secretary had often repeated to him that Vietnam is one, that the Vietnamese motherland is indivisible, that the people can go anywhere, fight the enemy in any place. The representatives of the prisoners in the prison camp had also informed the prisoners a month in advance that they would be released in Quang Tri, that cadres of the local people's administration would receive them and then, afterward, depending on the practical requirements, they would be attached to the various units and organs and assigned different duties.

Quang Tri? Cong could not remember having heard of that name before. But this must be the Ben Hai River, Cong thought, and after everything is over I will be taken straight to the North! Cong wanted to shrink back when the time came for everybody to board the ferry to cross the river. He glanced to his right and to his left and he saw the marines and the paratroopers with their camouflaged uniforms and even the yellow flag with the three red stripes that had become so familiar to him . . . although once, a long time ago, he had fought against them. Those Saigon soldiers with their accents, their easy-going manners seemed much closer to him than the prisoners in his group, who were secretly whispering to each other, planning perhaps to shout their slogans when the exchange of prisoners would really take place. He had actually known the South Vietnamese flag ever since he was a kid, each day passing the militia outpost and the village office in Phung Hiep and seeing it snapping in the wind.

Cong had goose flesh when he thought of the land and the sky in the distant North where he would be taken, and of his native village at the other end of the land which he would probably never see again. He stepped on the boat and it rolled a little, bobbing lightly and the Marines on the shore were talking and laughing loudly, the accent of the South, the dear South. The engine chugged and the boat turned toward the north bank of the river where Cong saw the flag. A decision flashed in his mind. Cong stood up, pushed away somebody's hand trying to grasp him and pull him back, and jumped into the water. Cong tried to swim to the bank but the water was numbly cold and he soon found that he could hardly make any movement with his limbs, and his vision was blurred because of the water in his eyes, but he could still hear somebody shouting "Returnee! There is a returnee! Hoi Chanh!" The sounds were ringing in his ears—they came from the bank—and then, great waves lapping, an arm heaving him up. He touched his belt where he hid a picture of his wife and children in the South. He wanted to make sure it would not slip away.

The Marine physician gave him a shot of some invigorating liquid. His first question was: Where is the picture of my wife and children? Here, here. . . . And he touched the picture with his hand, running his trembling fingers along the rim.

On the north bank of the Thach Han River, I asked the International Committee members to serve as witnesses and to confirm the case of Cong in order to preempt the argument from the Hungarian and the Polish delegates that the defection could not be accepted because Cong had not reached the location where the release of prisoners was to take place (that is, on the north bank of the River). I informed them that Cong had jumped into the water while on the way to the prisoners' release location and that he was still too much in shock to be taken across the river on board the helicopter for Gio Linh. I was all alone, against the two Communist delegations on the International Committee, and the local Communist cadres, and their two interpreters—more than ten men, whispering, discussing, exchanging ideas, taking pictures, serving tea. The two Communist delegates on the International Committee again tried some delaying tactic by refusing to recross the river to witness the case of Cong. I only managed to get the Canadian and the Indonesian delegates back to the South bank.

On the ferry, I fell into a pensive mood. There was a drizzle and the water was blue and quite cold. I looked into the distance and thought a moment about the people who would commit suicide in order to die free. How noble and painful it is, I thought. Among the people who applauded the Paris Agreement, was there anyone who would think of the practical situations that would result from it? In the end, despite the absence of the Hungarian and the Pole, Cong was still classified as a returnee in the presence of the Indonesian delegate who was then Chairman of the International Committee for the current month. Thach Phen and Cong were the two cases that became known because of the circumstances, but there should be many more prisoners who wanted to defect but who could not do so either because they were unable to join the New Life Movement, or because they could not get away from their fellow prisoners on the way to the prisoners' exchange locations. How many people wanted to imitate the act of Ho Van Cong on March 17, 1973? How many prisoners wanted to raise their hands to declare their decision to defect? How many prisoners who actually felt miserable when they walked into the tent to wait for their names to be called and to be returned to "the people"? The people? The people in the image of a heavy, repulsive woman cadre with the strange Northern accent? I remembered the prisoners who without enthusiasm relieved themselves of the prison uniforms on their bodies and threw them into the river on the way to the north bank of the Thach Han, in obeisance to the order from their representatives although they were freezing with cold. I could still see them, gray-haired aging men, with wrinkled skin on their naked bodies, shaking and trembling in the cold drizzle and the chilly and dismal wind of Central Vietnam. Where to? The question, painful and miserable, reverberated in my mind.

It was far from my intention to dramatize the two cases as related above but there was in fact a great number, a very great number of prisoners who looked so hesitant, so depressed when they were going to be returned to the other side, beside other prisoners who made such a show of burning hatred. The former brought to mind the story of the Soviet prisoners who committed mass suicide by jumping out into the abyss from the train that took them back to the Soviet Union. They had the same look as the prisoners taken during the operations Atlante and Castor of the last war and returned to the Viet Minh by the French at the time of the Geneva Agreement. My own father, who had fought with the Viet Minh's 308th Division in Dien Bien Phu, who had given up a peaceful life beside his wife and his children to sacrifice his whole life to the revolution and the people, wrote to my mother from French prison camp No. 51 in Hai Phong, before he was returned to the People's Army in a prisoners' exchange, ". . . I am now very tired. But I can do anything: I can chop wood, I can cook rice. . . . I can do everything. I only wish that I could take you and our children to some place far away, very far away, out of this country, out of Vietnam. . . ." In 1954, even after this great victory the Communist prisoner, looking back on the road that he had traveled, and ahead of him seeing nothing but a utopian future, could not help having such bitter words. What would they feel now, the Communist prisoners of today, in this year 1973, when the border between Communism and Freedom had been blurred by the rice wine in Peking, or temporarily forgotten when Nixon observed a minute of silence in commemoration of the heroes of the Soviet Union in Red Square? "Anti-American, national salvation" had become an empty slogan. The "wicked and piratical troops of the puppet government" were only yellow-skinned soldiers who accepted their fate with quiet resignation. An achievement of the revolutionary struggle in South Vietnam was the nine kilometers strewn with bodies of innocent people along the Highway of Terror. Liberation, Freedom, People, Independence, ear-jarring words which only served to reveal all the inhumanity mankind is capable of, deceptive words for which the prisoner has offered his whole life as sacrifice. At the location for the release of prisoners, the Communist saw again looming before his eyes the prospect of long days surviving with a handful of rice with water, deep in the jungles and the hills, to build a paradise that had lost all its luster. The family, the village, the journey that never ends. Oh, you, Communist prisoner, where are you heading at this time of day when the light is dying and when your own life is also crumbling?

One more thing needs to be said. The Communist soldier, even though he has proved to be firm in his political position while in prison, still has to make an even greater show of hatred and indomitable morale at the location for prisoner exchange. Otherwise, after the welcoming ceremony is over and the first cup of tea has been cordially served, those found to be tired or unenthusiastic would be isolated, questioned, criticized, demoted, and even assassinated if necessary. This has been proved by what happened to the prisoners released according to the Geneva Agreement in 1954. The prisoners captured during the frightening battles of the First Indochina War were, after their release by the French, dispersed, isolated, abandoned, and left to rot until this day, nearly twenty years after they regained their freedom from captivity.

The Communists seek to think that it is a crime to let oneself be captured by the enemy. Their big propaganda machine did not mention, or barely made use of, the prisoners just released by the Republic of Vietnam. There were only sketchy reports about the releases of prisoners in the *People's Army Daily* or the *Liberation Army Daily*. There was no applause, no heaping of praises on the "heroes" who had spent time in enemy prison camps, as was the case with the "production heroes," or "heroes of the Ham Rong Bridge building unit," etc. It might be said that the fates of the Communist prisoners released in 1973 would not be much different from the fate of the prisoners of twenty years ago.

That was the fate reserved for the prisoners who have remained more or less unwavering from the beginning to the end. What would be the treatment awaiting those prisoners who looked at the red flag with eyes where all those sparkles of enthusiasm had gone, who had become so distracted that they would not even respond when their names were called, who walked hesitantly and indifferently amid the applause and the smiles of the welcoming cadres, who, their hair all white, did not care to hide their sighs? What would become of the Communist prisoners, natives of South Vietnam, the prisoners who were simple guerillas, and the prisoners who were near retirement? Where could they go? Where could they find a place to lie down to rest their tired bodies? Where was their native town or village? Home? The picture of Ho Chi Minh and the slogan "Nothing is more precious than independence and freedom" also had become blurred. The Communist prisoner, without a shirt on his back, his head bowed, his steps hesitant, walked into the unknown, into oblivion.

The fate of the civilian prisoners was even worse. They were called civilian personnel of the Communists and the definition was given in Article 21(b) of the 1954 Geneva Agreement: "Civilian personnel are people who have contributed to the armed or political struggle of one side and are captured by the other side." That is a large but also strict definition, and it does not leave out anybody between the two South Vietnamese sides. Anybody who has chosen to live on one side, has, by the same act, chosen one regime, adopted a political attitude, and his "contribution" could be deduced from that attitude without much error. According to that definition, there is no more place for the "innocent civilian" in this war, a "pure, independent" civilian no longer exists between the two opposing forces, everybody is drawn to either one of the two sides, without any coercion, so to speak, and everybody has to contribute something to either side, as a matter of course. There are no professionals earning their living independently, there are no independent traders, there are only the likes of Nguyen Van Tam, civilian personnel, forty years old, residing in the village of Dong Yen, district of An Bien, Rach Gia, and therefore arrested by the Provisional Government and released to the Government of the Republic of Vietnam at a location in U Minh Forest on March 2, 1974. Here is a dialogue:

-"Who is Tam Co?"

-"He lives in Rach Gia."

-"What did he tell you to do?"

-"He told me to spy."

-"Spy on what? What did you do?"

Nguyen Van Tam stood there, staring at me. He was not sure what kinds of work he did that could be called "spying," which seemed to denote something fraught with risks. Tam Co was probably a policeman in the district of Rach Gia, and what did he tell Nguyen Van Tam to do was perhaps something along this line: "Go and see if there is anything unusual." Every day, Nguyen Van Tam has to go to work on his ricefield in the U Minh forest. But spying? Tam, the miserable civilian, did not realize that, if so charged, he has committed a crime that is punishable by death during wartime. He has committed a crime as naturally as he had been born. Could it be that being Vietnamese in this worst of times is already a crime?

The case of Mrs. Le Thi Tam is just the opposite. Mrs. Tam is fifty-two years old. Her hair is dry and her shriveled body speaks of an extreme capacity for resignation. Mrs. Tam makes an effort to raise her eyes, which are heavy-lidded, tinted yellow, and veiled with a thin film of liquid, and says, in a tone full of sorrow:

-"My name is Tam, I am fifty-two years old, and a native of the village of La Chu, out toward Hue."

-"You have to tell us fully: your place of birth, which would include the village, the district, the province."

The Major of the National Liberation Front who has the duty to question the old lady seems equally depressed by the miserable aspect of the woman.

-"Ha? What?"

-"Tell me what is the district?"

-"But I just told you! I am from La Chu, Thua Thien."

-"You were arrested by the Republic of Vietnam Government for what crime?"

-"How could I know?"

-"You don't know the reason why you were arrested? Then why did you ask to stay back with the Republic of Vietnam government?"

-"If I go with the 'Bo Doi' then when will I be able to go back out there? I only asked to go home, if I can't go home, I'd rather remain in prison."

At this point, I feel I have to intervene. If I let the Major continue his questioning, Mrs. Tam will talk wildly, and all this can lead to some general confusion or embarrassment. I intercede into the conversation without much enthusiasm. [What is the point of "struggling" with the Communists to "gain?"] So I cut in and put a clear and definite question:

-"Now, do you want to go with the Provisional Government or to stay with the side of the Republic of Vietnam?"

-"I will stay," was the answer.

-"That's it. Thank you. Now please go with the Military Police and wait for the helicopter to take you back to Bien Hoa."

The Major of the National Liberation Front takes off his hat. I see strands of white hair wet with sweat. I suspect that even though he is a Communist, he is also stricken with a sense of despair. Mrs. Tam hastens after the military policeman, making small but brisk steps, sunlight shining through her shaggy dry hair. How can this woman realize that she has just made a momentous decision, a choice of government, an option between Nationalism and Communism? She has come, by no choice of her own, from the village of La Chu, district of Huong Tra, Thua Thien province. Every day, she would go to gather wood in the foothills west of Highway 1 in the Nam Hoc area of Hue. One day she was stopped by a stranger who gave her a package of tobacco and he told her to display it and sell it on the sidewalk when she came back to town. He also gave her money to buy cigarettes, soap, etc., for him. Wood gathering became secondary, street vending became her main source of income. Finally, her secret dealings were discovered by a hamlet security officer, and she was arrested. During the interrogation, she declared truthfully the amount of tobacco that she had sold, the money she earned, and she also sincerely disclosed that, after learning that these "strangers" were "Bo Doi" (Communist troops), she had tried to inquire about her husband who had disappeared into the hills in 1952, or 1953.

The relationship between Mrs. Tam and the "Bo Doi" fell within the article 21(b) coined by the many eminences at the 1954 Geneva Talks, and since they were men of such profound knowledge and such accumulated experience, they had committed no mistakes and left no omissions: the case of Mrs. Tam had been long foreseen. Mrs. Tam had engaged in trade with the Communists, she had built an economic relationship with the enemy and hence, had sold herself politically to the Communists. After all, the great conflict in the world today between Communist forces and the forces for Freedom is also a corollary of a fight to the death between the two opposing economic forces: Capitalism versus the Proletariat. Therefore Mrs. Tam had contributed to one side of the armed and political struggle between the two sides in South Vietnam. Mrs. Tam, in short, was a civilian personnel of one South Vietnamese side according to Article 7 of the Annex of the Paris Agreement that deals with the problem of prisoners! Her name was then put on the list of prisoners to be returned to the National Liberation Front at Loc Ninh on Feb. 21, 1974.

The case of Mrs. Tam was pathetic, but the case of Mr. Phan Van Hoat was even more tragic. Hoat was a man of over forty, small, and resigned-looking. He used to be a government employee in Hue, and was arrested in 1966 because he participated in the Buddhist struggle movement. Hoat was taken to Saigon where he was interrogated and it was found that he had indeed committed subversive activities for the benefit of the Communists; his activities in the struggle movement also bore some similarity to the Communist tactics; he was even found to have received instructions from the Communist underground in Hue, etc. On the day of his release, Feb. 18, 1974, at Loc Ninh, Hoat walked quietly between the two lines of welcoming Communist cadres, his face wet with tears and his lips tight, to the astonishment of the Communist cadres. That was the first time the Communists had seen such a phenomenon. Usually, most prisoners returned to the National Liberation Front would make a great show of joy, of hatred, of enthusiasm, and they would clap their hands, etc. But this was the first time after more than a year of prisoner exchanges that a prisoner was seen in such a miserable shape: tears of sorrow and of rage were streaming down his face, and the face was sad and drawn and expressionless, or perhaps his was of a man who had decided to give up everything, to abandon everything that would come his way from either side of the conflict, a totally passive man.

Hoat was a lonely man, a weak man in the conflict, and the only thing he could do was to cry his tears of sorrow, of pain, of a man who felt that he had been so very unjustly treated but there was nothing he could do. But Hoat actually was not alone. He was only a typical example. There were many others who somehow found themselves at the bottom of despair, who saw that their lives were completely blocked and torn to pieces in the conflict between Nationalists and Communists. Hoat could at least cry. But a great many others did not find any more courage to let their sorrowful tears run down their faces. I know there were many people who couldn't even weep or didn't dare to while they were being returned to the Communists.

The prisoners in Gheorghiu's novels were crushed under the inhuman machines of government acting in the name of Freedom and Humanity. The Vietnamese prisoner, crucified between two conflicting ideologies did not even have a period of life before and after the time he spent in jail. Because it is already a crime to live in this country. And every man is sentenced to life.

[MARCH 1974]

Ten

Peace, Oh What a Dream It Seems!

TODAY, WE ARE NEARING the fifth month of peace of the "Second Indochina War." The Americans have pulled out, and, with them, their giant war machine: a half million-man army, hundreds of fighter planes, innumerable insuperable flights of helicopters, and a network of airbases which have been gradually closed down. The Americans have washed their hands. 1960–1973. Thirteen years in the swamp of Indochina. The United States certainly needs a respite. Watergate has been like a high fever draining out the poison in the body of America. The burden of the war has been cleaned up. America had taken strong medicine to get rid of the sickness that has been plaguing it. The launching of Skylab, after some minor problems with a faulty cooling system, was accomplished on time and the astronauts, after circling the earth for twenty-eight days, made a perfect touchdown in the Pacific.

Golda Meir, Prime Minister of Israel, welcoming the Chancellor of the Federal Republic of Germany at Tel Aviv, made a historical statement: "Mankind would not exist if we did not have the courage to start anew."

In Paris, Kissinger declared forcefully: "I shall not return here again for the Indochina problem." That's it! The game is over! The world heaves a sigh of relief before a promising prospect that is taking shape.

But, in reality, not a single problem was solved in South Vietnam. On Jan. 27, 1973, when the ink had barely dried on the document "restoring the peace in Vietnam," the Marines pushed on with their objective code-named Tango to roundup the Cua Viet Operation. From Dong Ha and Khe Sanh, 130mm artillery gunfire rained down on Nhu Le and Tan Le to displace South Vietnamese paratroopers. On Sunday, Jan. 28, all routes leading to Saigon were cut. There was a roadblock on Route 15 south of Long Thanh, another one on Highway 1 near

Xuan Loc in Long Khanh province, the road to Tay Ninh was blocked, so was the road to Da Lat. The Vietnamese people welcomed peace with a wait-and-see attitude. They read about it in their newspapers while ducking artillery fire in their trenches, or fleeing from the war with their families. The Agreement for the Cease-Fire and for the Restoration of Peace in Vietnam—a brutal joke over the pain and sorrow of the Vietnamese people. Peace, that dream of a whole people, is but an illusion. Today, one of the last days of the fifth month of the cease-fire, all the components of peace have remained unfulfilled, except for the fact that the Americans have gone, leaving a sense of malaise where they have been in Tan Son Nhat, in Long Binh, in Cam Ranh Bay, etc. People realize that a "concrete" step has been taken on the road to "Peace": the retreat of American troops to the other side of the Pacific. That was the only thing that happened. Everything else has remained unchanged. Where is peace for the Vietnamese people?

There is indeed a sense of insecurity, of anxiety lurking in the air. What is going to happen next? Secession of territory for the formation of a third state? A true cease-fire in place to work toward a Council for National Reconciliation and a new political environment? Or, perhaps, a renewal of the fighting is in the offing? These nerve-wracking questions persist with the rumbling of artillery fire in the night.

What is going to happen next? The question has a corollary: What is the National Liberation Front planning to do next? Naturally, there can be no clear-cut answer to questions about the likely development of the situation, which, in its main lines, can be viewed in light of the grand strategy devised by the Vietnam Labor Party whose ultimate objective has remained unchanged: the communization of the whole of Indochina.

Such is the aim of the North's political strategy. But there is no instant answer as to the question of what is likely to happen next. Since in their long march, they have encountered thousands of obstacles due to the resistance of the Nationalists or to the unfavorable international situation, the Vietnam Labor Party, in the execution of chairman Ho's testament, has always proved to be flexible while never losing sight of their ultimate objective. They would make detours, or they would take shortcuts, depending on the situation, but their main lines of action, like the lines of force of a magnet, will not deviate from the instructions left behind by their deceased leader. Knowing the enemy strategic objective, we can perhaps trace a road for our own survival—we can find a way to save ourselves. The enemy has moved a bullet to the chamber of their rifle. We have to know the position and the direction of their fire so as to counter their attack. This will be our last battle. The outcome will be our continued survival—or a total collapse. Let us pose the question again: What is the National Liberation Front up to? That question leads to another: What are the Communists intentions behind their attempt to encroach upon territories which seem to have certain common characteristics?

Several factors emerge from an analysis of the zones under temporary enemy occupation. These will help us recognize the true enemy intentions.

On March 29, 1972, launching their Summer Offensive against the South, the North Vietnamese Communists pushed thirteen infantry divisions and three armored Regiments along the two axes East-West and North-South in an overpowering attack directed at Quang Tri province, with Dong Ha as their first objective, after pulverizing the string of fire-bases from Lang Vei, Huong Ha on the Laos border, to Caroll, Sarge, C-1, C-2, A-2 on the coast with 130mm artillery fire from their three artillery Regiments. The 3rd ARVN Infantry Division and a Brigade of Vietnamese marines was unable to sustain attacks on a line of defense spread out to 30km and providing no depth of maneuver. The front at Dong Ha broke.

Quang Tri fell on May 1st. Refugees fled to the South by any means they could lay their hands on. It may seem strange to the outside observers that the Vietnamese people, normally so calm, so used to the facts of war, would so readily flee at the approach of the People's Army. The 147th Marine Brigade, taking up rear guard action, provided security until the last refugee got out of Quang Tri and set up a second line of defense at My Chanh.

On June 29, two South Vietnamese main force divisions, the paratroopers on the left and the Marines on the right, moved up in two-pronged counterattack to retake Quang Tri.

The battle raged from the June 29 until the end of July when Quang Tri city was virtually liberated by South Vietnamese troops. Three Marine battalions completed sweeping up the Dinh Cong Trang citadel, the last point in the city still in enemy hands at noon on Sept. 15. The front line was now clearly demarcated by the Thach Han River.

The war dragged on, as anticipated, with no winners and losers.

The conclusion was the Agreement for the Establishment of a Cease-Fire and for the Restoration of Peace, a strange and tricky document which any party can interpret to their own advantage. For the first time people conjured up that sacred word—Peace.

In terms of territorial gains, the Communists have seized the areas from Lao Bao Valley to Cua Viet and from the Ben Hai River to the Thach Han River in their theater of operation in the northern part of the country. Did they originally aim to seize Hue? That was a question that was constantly on the minds of the South Vietnamese during the first phase of the Communist Offensive. The answer can be based on two unequivocal premises. From a tactical point of view, Hue was also a target, but it had a strategic value for the Communist 324B Division only. The enemy division had tried its utmost to move its units in a comb-like disposition deep into the area of operation of the 1st ARVN Division in its attempt to force South Vietnamese troops out of firebases King, Birmingham, Bastogne, and Checkmate southwest of Hue. If this attempt had been successful, the enemy would have pushed up Route 547, the same line of approach they used during the 1968 Tet Offensive, to advance toward Hue. But Hue remained a tactical target, not a strategic target for the North Vietnamese 1972 Offensive.

That was indicated by the sudden stop by the Communists on the north bank of the My Chanh River after taking Dong Ha and Quang Tri. The enemy advance was slowed down by logistics problems. In other words, the Communists had not made adequate preparations for a further advance southward. It is known that the Communists always gave top priority to elaborate and painstaking preparation before any attack in the past, as evidenced in their Tet Offensive, their counterattacks in Lower Laos, and their attacks against Dong Ha, Loc Ninh, and Dak To in April 1972. Despite the repeated pounding against ARVN 1st Infantry Division in the hills southwest of Hue, that city was not the primary objective of the Communist 1972 Offensive.

This leads to a corollary—a conclusion as unavoidable as a result churned out by a computer after all available data have been fed into its electronic brain—that one of the objectives of the Communist 1972 Offensive was limited to the arena north of the Thach Han River, 150 square kilometers of terrain with no economic value and barren of population since 90 percent of the inhabitants have crossed the river, leaving behind their devastated homes and villages to flee to the south. Such an area, without economic and human resources, could not be a valuable objective in a conventional war where the seizure of terrain, the capture of population and resources are prime considerations. But, from a map of Indochina, we can see, without any sophisticated knowledge of geopolitical science, that te area on both sides of Route 9 from Dong Ha to Tchepone constitutes the center of gravity controlling both the east and the west sides of the Annamese Cordillera stretching over three countries: Laos, Vietnam, and Cambodia. A comparison with Route 12 connecting Thankkhet and the Mu Gia Valley and Route 19 connecting Stung Treng, Duc Co, and Pleiku would serve to underline the importance of Route 9 which, while relatively shorter (longer than Route 12 but shorter than Route 19), is at the center of the Indochinese peninsula and which, in conjunction with the Ho Chi Minh Trails, forms a crossroad connecting north to south and east to west of the whole peninsula. Control of Route 9 would secrete Lower Laos, open to the North and enable an unrestricted southward advance to seize the whole of Indochina. This conclusion is reinforced by a look at the other fronts: the battles of An Loc and Dak To.

From Attopeu, the Ho Chi Minh Trails branch out to the east. This is a network of well-constructed roads running through high terrains and often easily observable by plane or even by naked eye from various base camps such as Ben Het, base camp No. 5, or the other base camps manned by airborne troops along the Poko River. The war in the tri-border area has always consisted of attacks against base camp No. 5, base camp No. 6, and the support base at Dak Song. The Communist Yellow Star Division (main force of the Communists in Kon Tum, Phu Yen, and Binh Din provinces) carried on a war of maneuver in the high hills and at the same time was responsible for the protection of the trails leading into the Central Highlands. In the highpoints of their 1972 Offensive, the Communists used the 320th Division (also called the Steel Division or the Dien Bien Division for their participation in the battle of Dien Bien Phu) to mount concentrated attacks against base camps Delta, Charlie, and Vo Dinh but, despite repeated attacks by units of the 320th division and FLO division under the overall command of the Communist B-3 Front, no final attack was launched against Kon Tum in an attempt to capture the city, except for penetration by a few sapper units with the support of some tanks in the month of May.

For a brief moment, the city of Kon Tum was severely threated, but it held. Communist attackers were stopped south of Vo Dinh, at a vaguely defined point with no geographic characteristics. Kon Tum, which many people feared would fall into enemy hands, had seen the war recede completely as early as June of that year when President Thieu came by helicopter to pin the first stars on Colonel Ba, commander of the 23rd Infantry Division.

Kon Tum has never been subjected to the fire of the enemy 130mm guns. Why has the enemy not moved their big guns that far south?

In An Loc, the Communists certainly committed a mistake by failing to achieve appropriate coordination between their tank and infantry units in their concentrated attacks in the first weeks of April, when general Hung had yet to complete deployment of the 5th Infantry Division and when the reinforcement units were still not ready to join the battle. The enemy as a result missed a big chance to capture An Loc while they were enjoying a position of strength. The battle of An Loc took place as it did because the enemy, instead of moving on to attack and seize the city, opted for a siege strategy, with choke points established on Route 13, hoping for opportunities to destroy reinforcements brought up for the defense of the beleaguered town. The seizure of An Loc would have enabled them to pose a serious threat to Lai Khe and Binh Duong and, connecting with units of the C30B Division in Dau Tieng and Tri Tam (the 5th, after taking Loc Ninh on April 5, moved in two separate detachments to attack Phuoc Binh and Dau Tieng), could have pushed close to Saigon and attempted even an attack against the South Vietnamese capital. It became obvious that the objective of the Communist attacks was the control of the areas near the border and on both sides of Route 13 where they could set up a command headquarters targeting Saigon and with a dominant position with regard to the vast areas in the Central highlands toward the north and the Mekong Delta toward the south. It would also be a good location to set up a capital for the National Liberation Front if indeed that was their intention.

After an analysis of the three areas of operations in the Communist 1972 Offensive, as well as the recent political developments and the results of the Paris Peace Conference, we can now arrive at some general conclusions. Two points stand out:

First, the Communist General Offensive in the summer of 1972 in the three border areas of the Republic of Vietnam was not aimed only at gaining political advantages. They chose these targets not solely because the targets happened to be close to their lines of supplies and logistics and because they would have facility in tactical maneuvers in mounting attacks. The General Offensive was not carried out with such a simple conception. The fighting raged at the three fronts, smaller but no less intense fighting also erupted in populated areas, in approaches to the capital, and in the coastal areas such as Hoai An, Bong Son, Ba Ria, Long An, Chuong Thien, Tay Ninh, Binh Duong, and Log Khan. These should not be viewed as purely military operations in support of the main targets of the Communist Offensive in the border areas.

It would be a mistake to think that the Dat Do district headquarters (in Phuoc Tuy province), or the Hoai An district headquarters and the De Duc base camp (in Binh Dinh province), or such other points on the map constituted the main targets of the company- or battalion-size forces. We can come to the conclusion that the Offensive had important strategic objectives: in mounting the Offensive, North Vietnam aimed at re-establishing a strong infrastructure for the National Liberation Front in the whole of South Vietnam, especially in the populated areas, along the axes of communications, and areas around zones firmly under government control. These would serve as springboards for future struggles in the days of "peace," the days after successful attacks against Quang Tri, Kon Tum, Pleiku, and Loc Ninh, would secure vast areas all along the border which would then serve as staging areas to move on to take over the whole of South Vietnam. In that scenario, enemy troops from Quang Tri would thrust down to Hue, capturing the Imperial city and seizing the Hai Van pass; another thrust from Kon Tum to the central lowlands would turn Route 19 into a beltway cutting the country in half along the Kon Tum–Binh Dinh axis; and from An Loc enemy troops would push down to capture Saigon. The Mekong Delta would easily fall into Communist control through concentrated actions between local guerilla forces and the victorious units in the North. In that situation, the Communists would leave the Paris Peace talks, establish a Communist government, and reunify the country. Naturally, that aim has not been achieved.

By the fall of 1972, the Offensive had sputtered to a halt, South Vietnamese troops had retaken some of the areas that had fallen to the Communists in the first days of the offensive, and cities and towns were no longer subjected to enemy artillery fire. But the enemy succeeded in re-establishing their main lines of communications, which had been disrupted by big allied operations such as the one code-named Johnson City in 1967 and after the Tet Offensive, or rendered inoperative in the years of 1969 and 1970. From the Ho Chi Minh Trail to Attopeu, Communist cadres can now move freely to Ben Het and Dak To and from there travel along Route 14 to the Thu Bon River flowing out to the lowland of Quang Nam province, or turning east from Dak To on Route 5 to Gia Vuc Valley, the open door to Quang Ngai or Binh Dinh.

The offensive also served to consolidate the enemy lines of communication on the other side of the border in Cambodia. These are also lines of approach leading to the secret zones of Ba Thu, Ly Van Manh, Rung Cham, and Bavu, convenient staging areas for an eventual attack against Saigon, and close enough to put the center of the capital within range of their 82mm mortars. The enemy lines of communication were firmed up. The disputed areas were expanded. Incidents of roadblocks and mining became more frequent. The hamlets of My Nhon and My Yen, to cite just one instance, right on Route 4 between Binh Chanh district (in Gia Dinh province) and Ben Luc district (in Long An province) were downgraded to “C” in the Hamlet Evaluation Program. It became difficult for government tax collectors to enter these two hamlets.

The overall situation had reverted to the same situation we knew in the year 1960, except that we now had to deal with a new generation of grassroots Communist cadres. These are younger, more capable political cadres sent in from the North and they had become quite active in most rural areas of South Vietnam. While a new political battle was taking shape, the beginning of 1973 also brought a new event: an agreement was completed at the Paris Peace talks.

During the six months of the Offensive, people feared that Communist sappers could at any time emerge from their deep cover to carry out acts of sabotage and violence in the cities. People also expected imminent collapse in Hanoi under relentless attacks from the air, especially after the 12-hour, dawn-to-dusk bombing and strafing by 100 B-52s and 300 fighter aircraft on Dec. 5, 1972. But none of these fears or expectations materialized, and in the end, people still came to a Cease-Fire Agreement, greeted as a most welcome event. The Agreement contains terms that are to be carried out with certain fixed time frames. There are others that are more concrete and more easily identified and they are taken up first. The game of peace has begun.

At the top of the agenda is the release, and reception, of prisoners of war. Elaborate schedules have been drafted for transport flights from Phu Quoc, Bien Hoa, and from Gia Lam (in Hanoi) and Loc Ninh (in Binh Long). As the clearest results of nine months of intense fighting, locations for the release of prisoners of war have been set up.

Two months after the signing of the Paris Agreement, 26,000 Communist prisoners of war and 5,018 South Vietnamese prisoners of war have been released from six principal locations: the north bank of the Thach Han River, Duc Pho (in Quang Ngai province), Hoai An (in Binh Dinh province), Loc Ninh and Minh Thanh (in Binh Long province), and Tien Ngon (in Tay Ninh province). The exchanges of prisoners have served to implicitly legalize the "reality" of areas under the control of the National Liberation Front. These areas are interspersed with areas under government control, so that, on a map, they look like dots on a leopard skin. Clearly the Offensive was only one aspect of the struggle, clearly its real conclusion can only be found in the Paris Peace Accord, and in order that this objective could be reached, the Paris Peace talks could not possibly be allowed to collapse.

But when it comes to the execution of the Agreement, the Communists have refused to accept the principle of a cease-fire in place. They have rejected temporary demarcation lines, which would serve to delineate provisional zones of occupation between local commanders to pledge peace and to discuss cease-fire problems as proposed by the Saigon government in articles, 2, 3, and 7. The Communists have not accepted the designation of "provisional zones of stationing of armed forces." They claimed that these are "de facto" ones of control of the National Liberation Front, that their areas of control extend to wherever are present Communist troops. They insist that they would only agree to meetings between local commanders if individual soldiers on both sides were also allowed to meet. Naturally, these demands are not acceptable. After the Paris Conference in May and July of 1973, and the last days of talks before the issuance of the Joint Communique of June 13, we detected a dark plot of the other side; the Communists want to legalize their temporary zones of control so as to establish a separate "state" with a separate government and army. That became obvious as early as June 1973 at the opening meetings of the Joint military Commission, as well as at La Celle-Saint-Cloud.

Another observation is in order. A common concern of both the Saigon government and the National Liberation Front is the presence of the so-called Third

Force in the Council for National Reconciliation as stipulated in Article 12a of the Paris Agreement. That Third Force, although without as much force as the other two components, is nevertheless viewed as the essential element conducive to peace, according to the Paris Agreement.

The establishment of a "third" state is hardly a feasible possibility in view of the dispersion of the armed forces of the National Liberation Front. Their forces are spread out in a spotty pattern all over South Vietnam, from Quang Tri and Quang Nam in the north to Chuong Thien and Kien Phong in the South. In certain areas, the Communists have managed to secure control of a whole district, or even larger ones, such as the one zone north of Quang Tri encompassing the districts of Gio Linh, Huong Hoa, Cam Lo and part of the district of Trieu Phong or the area north of Kon Tum, which includes the Tan Canh district. Another instance is the area north of Binh Long province where the Communists extend their control over the district of Loc Ninh and parts of the districts of Chon Thanh and An Loc. However, there are instances where Communist control is limited to a small hamlet within a large area under the control of the government, such as the case of the Van Ly hamlet in Quang Ngai (Duc Pho district). In many other areas, such as in Chuong Thien and Dinh Tuong, the Communists only have some underground cadres and perhaps some armed guerillas whose intermittent presence is clearly not enough for them to claim control of the locality.

We can come to certain conclusions based on a study of the general situation as it has evolved from the start of the Offensive in April 1972 to the issuance of the Joint Communique of June 13, the results of the fighting, the progress of the peace talks, the sterile meetings of the Joint Military Commission in April and May of 1973, the total impasse of the bipartisan talks in Paris, and the text of the Joint Communique between Kissinger and Le Duc Tho.

Although there are clear pointers to what we can expect to happen in the future, we cannot claim to predict with any certainty the precise course of future events. For one thing, the political and military calculations of the North have remained secret, buried in the brains of Le Duan, Pham Van Dong, Vo Nguyen Giap, and Le Duc Tho, or in the secret files restricted to the Politburo of the Vietnam Labor Party. The Communist Resolution of Feb. 10, 1973, does not necessarily reflect the real thinking of the Party Central Committee. It may be only an official document without any connection to the future strategy of the Communists and it may not have the complete agreement of all Committee members.

The following conclusions, therefore, should only be considered as an attempt to detect certain outlines in a confusing and ambiguous situation:

a) The 1972 Offensive was a high point in the war. North Vietnamese main force divisions were launched in all-out attacks, with intention to capture several cities and towns in South Vietnam such as Hue, Kon Tum, Binh Duong, and possibly Saigon (as originally planned after the battle of An Loc). In case of complete victory, the Offensive would put the big cities in the South under the control of the Communists, the political administrative machinery of the South would be dismantled, and the Paris Peace Talks would collapse. But, as we have seen, the Communists have not been able to achieve the complete victory which would have been predicated upon the hypothesis of a very low morale and fighting capability of the South Vietnamese armed forces as well as a weak level of reaction from the United States. As a result, negotiators in Paris concluded their talks on Jan. 27, 1973, with an Agreement, albeit a document that can easily lend itself to various interpretations.
b) Although denied a complete victory, the Communists still managed to gain control of certain border areas and to have a Peace Agreement which they can interpret to their own advantage. They clearly indicated their intentions when they rejected the Saigon government's proposals on the problem of cease-fire in place, the meetings of local commanders, and the zones of temporary troops stationed prior to the formation of a Council for National Reconciliation and the general elections. The NLF delegation has continued to insist on the prior condition that the Saigon government should recognize the reality of two armies, two zones of control, and two separate governments in the South before they would agree to the discussion of other problems such as cease-fire, the stationing of troops, general elections, etc.

In connection with this pre-condition set forth by the Communist delegation, we might want to have another discussion to further our understanding of another possibility—a projection beyond Articles 9 and 12 of the Peace Agreement concerning the right for self-determination of the South and the spirit of reconciliation between various parties. A clearer and more concrete understanding of the situation would necessitate a closer look at the zones under temporary enemy occupation. There is an area adjacent to the south of Quang Tri province, and there is a hilly terrain south of Khe Sanh and Huong Hoa stretching southward toward the coastline. Starting from Van Xa, the mountains are only about 10 km from Highway 1. As the chain reaches the points of Truoi and Cau Hai, the Annamese Cordillera runs parallel to the coastline and finally looms high over the ocean at Hai Van Pass, which is the natural border post between Thua Thien and Quang Nam provinces. In this hilly area, the Communists have positioned units of their 325th Division all the way from Khe Sanh to Co Bi and Hien Si (close to An Lo district and Hue city) and from there we come into contact with the enemy 324B division whose presence in the area has been known for a long time and whose area of operations extends far south in the direction of A Shau, and Thua Thien. Parallel to Highway 1 from Quang Tri to A Shau, there is a whole network of hundreds of kilometers of trails—routes 518, 547, and 561. These were originally simple dirt tracks usable only for infantry movement, but after Jan. 27, 1973, the Communists have mobilized all efforts in enlarging and clearing the road trails, especially Route T-7 leading to A Shau or Base Area 611, and these newly paved roads are now good even for their Molotova truck convoys. From A Luoi, about 10 km from the Laos border, Route T-7 branches out westward to connect with Route 922 in Laos. Route 922 itself is a branch of Route 92, also called strategic Route 36, which is part of Route 559 in the Ho Chi Minh Trails.

In the valleys of A Luoi and A Shau, there are already in existence three airbases, including the Ta Bat airbase which could accommodate C-130s with proper guidance. The new roadwork provided easy access from the mountainous region to the coastal cities as well as to the deeper interior of the Indochinese peninsula. This area lies on the same parallel as Da Nang (about 100 km north of the 16th parallel) and is situated right at the center between Da Nang on the Pacific coast and the border between Laos and Thailand. The Ta Bat airbase is also an all-weather airbase. A new road leading south from A Shau valley is also being built. The road connecting Khe Sanh and A Shau follows the line of crest in Trieu Phong (Quang Tri Province) and Nam Hoa (Thua Thien province) but the construction work here must have been easy because the Annamese Cordillera tapers down to about 1,000 meters high, especially in the hills upstream of the My Chanh river at the border of Quang Tri and Thua Thien provinces.

South of A Shau valley, where the terrain consists of a series of high mountains and deep valleys one after another all the way from the Hai Van Pass to the Laos border and beyond, road construction can pose serious problems. But here again the Communists have exploited to the full the labor of their troops and of the civilian construction units made up mostly of South Vietnamese P.O.W.s to improve the network of roads connecting Khe Sanh, A Luoi, A Shau, Dai Loc, and Dak To. These consist of routes 458, and 547, north of National Highway No. 14. Incidentally, one of the locations chosen by the Communists for the release of South Vietnamese P.O.W.s is situated south of the Vu Gia River (a branch of the Thu Bon River) about 10 km east of Ha Tan (Quang Nam province) and the Ha Tan valley is the intersection between Route 458 and the northern extremity of Route 14 reaching down to Kon Tum.

The network of roads run smoothly from Ta Lon, Ha Tan in Quang Nam province to the delta of Thu Bon river to the north of Kon Tum province. Route 14 runs along the Cai River, which flows in a valley almost barren of vegetation. This road requires minor repair to become serviceable.

We have just reviewed the configuration of the terrain in a geographical area covering the provinces of Quang Tri, Thua Thien, Quang Nam, Quang Tin, Quang Ngai, Kon Tum, and Binh Dinh and a network of roads consisting of routes 518, 516, 547, 548 (in Khe Sanh), 458 (Thua Thien and Quang Nam provinces), 14 and Interprovincial Route No. 5 (connecting Kon Tum and Quang Ngai), and Route 514 (connecting Quang Ngai and Binh Dinh from Gia Vuc Valley to upstream of An Lao River). The Communists used these roads to move their tanks from the tri-border area to participate in the fighting in Hoai An in May 1972. The Communists have continued to improve this network of roads, which generally run parallel to Highway 1 and pass through the hilly regions of the five northernmost provinces of South Vietnam. Returnee Tran Duong Cuong had this to say about the northern portions of the roads: "They are building new roads in the Annamese Cordillera, from Quang Tri to Quang Nam. Three battalions of civilian construction workers are used for this road improvement effort and for the repairs at the A Luoi airbase. For the last four months (since Jan. 27), heavy tanks have been moving south on this road."

This is evidence in support of our earlier observation: that the Communists are not so much interested in the cities. The cities may be main targets for enemy divisions on tactical maneuvers for a limited period of time. And the last Offensive was not aimed at achieving the final objective. In fact, both sides could claim victory with their own interpretation of the results that each side has achieved on the battlefields. Similarly, both sides can claim victory with their own version of the Peace Agreement.

We come to a conclusion that may not be too far from the truth. The Communists cannot and will not give up the area east of the Annamese Cordillera running through five provinces in the north. This chain of mountains is only a natural border. It cannot be a geographical or political border because the people moving on either side of the mountains belong to the same force and harbor the same political intentions. The Ho Chi Minh Trails are but natural roads in a hilly country.

The Communist plot to establish a second state within South Vietnam has been uncovered by their intention to attack the targets as indicated. The plot has also emerged in the way they have tried to consolidate and to improve the areas under their temporary control, although at the negotiating table they have consistently denied that intention with the most passionate arguments: "Vietnam is one, the people of Vietnam are one. There is no North or South Vietnam. The 17th parallel is only a temporary military demarcation line. The country will be reunited through general elections and talks will be held to normalize relations between the two regions. How can there be a third or a fourth state?" All of this is just rhetoric, words that they have committed to memory to use in a certain period. While the Communists at the negotiating table continue to talk, in their areas of temporary control they continue to build to consolidate and to carry out struggles on all aspects to win recognition of the reality of their "liberated zones."

—

In the meantime, the roads continue to be lengthened to reach Tay Ninh, Binh Long, and Phuoc Long, passing through Quang Duc (we will return to this issue toward the end of this article).

The Communists continued to consolidate their "liberated zones." They set up administrative committees to represent "people's local government" at areas captured during the Offensive such as Cam Lo, Gio Linh, Dong Ha, Tan Canh (Kon Tum province), Xa Mat, Thien Ngon (Tay Ninh province), and Duc Co (Pleiku province). Ceremonial appellations and designations were strictly observed. At the Duc Nghiep prisoner release point, about 30 km southwest of Plieku, a

Major, his face green with malaria, declared after emerging from a corner of Duc Co forest: "I, Major Tran Canh, representing the local administration of Pleiku province." The same play-acting was observed through all the rank and file. There was a uniform repetition: "The provisional government with its effective zones of control. . . ." In their attempt to set up a second state in the South for the Provisional Government of South Vietnam, North Vietnam has effected a forced migration of tens of thousands of civilians from provinces north of Central Vietnam to settle in the Highlands, in the north of Quang Tri province, and in the east of the Mekong Delta in the South. The motto of the program was "New Country Life," and the core of the program was made up of a number of youths, particularly young women whose duty was to get married to young soldiers wo had been sent to the South before and who had become "Southerners." ("Southerners" with a purely Northern accent!) There could be no mistake about it: the Communist motto, "Born in the North to Die in the South," was not just a propaganda line to boost the morale of the troops sent to combat in the South, but had become a true "strategic order" in the Communist long-range plan to communize the whole of South Vietnam through human settlements! In such a scenario, the National Liberation Front and the Provisional Government of South Vietnam would gradually play out their tactical roles until the day when the real and final battles would be a direct conflict between the South and the North. It appeared that most people in the world were not fully aware of this wicked plan—although it has been openly carried out.

In order to reinforce the presence of the second state, the Communists have set up industrial and power plants at the "cities" of Xa Mat and Duc Co. Diplomatic activities were also stepped up in order to complete the trappings of a state for the NLF's Provisional Government. Elaborate ceremonies were organized for the presentation of credentials from the Ambassador of the U.S.S.R., the Ambassador from the People's Republic of China, and the Ambassador of Algeria to Nguyen Huu Tho. An international press conference held by Chairman Tho was announced. "The People's Republic of South Vietnam" was being set up piece by piece in the jungles and hills of the Annamese Cordillera.

If the Communists had wanted to discard the Peace Agreement and revert to war, then the period of June 1973 would be a good start for them to move on to tactical preparations for a renewal of the war. But the Communists still refrained from staging big battles. This is not out of their love for peace or their respect of the spirit of the Peace Agreement, but is probably in accordance with the directives of Resolution of Feb. 10, 1973, in which Hanoi presented its view of the current situation and outlined the new struggle—not to be conducted through the barrel of a gun. This seems to accord with the observation of Professor P. J. Honey after his recent visit to Hanoi: "While Communist North Vietnam sill persists in their aim to communize the whole of Indochina, their strategy to achieve that aim has been changed" (March 27, 1973).

In this new strategy—now that it has secured a "safe" country straddling three central zones of the Indochinese peninsula—North Vietnam is but a short strategic distance away from achieving its ultimate aim.

We are fully aware of the Communist preparations on the other side of the Thach Han River, in the Ba Long Valley, and from west of Hue all the way down the Annamese Cordillera to Loc Ninh, Binh Long, Phuoc Long, into the secret zones of the Iron Triangle, Duong Minh Chau, Ho Bo, Boi Loi, etc. We received reports of the Communist attempt to seize complete control of the Seven Mountains in Chaudoc, particularly Dai mountain and Cam mountain where the caves have provided Communist troops with natural bunkers in the past. We learned of the inconclusive fighting in the swamp of Chuong Thien, where the objects of dispute were deserted villages and hamlets and fallow land. The Communist tactic was to deny any respite to the enemy, or even to their own troops. It would certainly mean trouble for the Communist leaders, whose minds have been desensitized by dozens of years of hard struggle, if their troops are given time to think, to pose questions, to weigh and compare.

Reports from zones under temporary Communist control told of feverish activities. There were preparations for the next phase of struggle to be waged through a combination of means in order to achieve the ultimate objective at any price—although apparently they were still waiting for definite decisions to be taken in the days and months ahead. Indoctrination and study sessions were held for Communist cadres while the armed cadres were instructed to get ready to wage political struggle in combination with armed struggle to win control of the people. The Communists also put great emphasis on the training and indoctrination of the civilian population in their zones of temporary occupation. Through propaganda and terror, they have forced the people into production units, self-defense units, and construction units. Tax collection was stepped up. They are paying particular attention to the youth, easily excited and easily exploited. The Communists see a lasting political and military asset in this mass of young population.

They are studying the experiences gathered during the 1972 Offensive and other military operations in previous years. They are reorganizing their manpower resources, stocking up on supplies. They are being re-equipped and reinforced with new, modern weapons, with tanks, artillery, anti-aircraft guns, and rockets secretly moved in from the North. The Paris Agreement has provided them with a period of recuperation before embarking on a new phase of struggle. In the next period, their strategy will basically remain the same. We probably will not see an open invasion of the North against the South. North Vietnam will try hard to avoid that. They will try hard to create the impression, among the people in South Vietnam as well as among the people in the world at large, that any armed struggle in the future, with all its attendant horrors and disruptions, would be waged wholly by "the people of South Vietnam" and conducted "by the Provisional Government of the People's Republic of South Vietnam" with its own zones of control and its own armed forces in South Vietnam. It will be a war between two opposing states in South Vietnam. We are being trapped in a "delicate" situation due to the new international environment and we can expect more and more difficulties in our continued struggle for survival against an armed force that only fairly recently did not have any significant control of either population or terrain but that now has been recognized as "a reality" to contend with.

It is a mistake to remain complacent in the belief that the U.S.S.R. and the People's Republic of China will observe their pledges to reduce military aid to North Vietnam in order to help end the war in Indochina. Such pledges will remain good as long as they go, because the Communist strategy of invasion will ever remain flexible depending on the situation. Although the Soviet Union and China have agreed with the United States to stop aiding North Vietnam militarily, we can still expect a sudden renewal of all-out war any time in the future. In sum, the various preparations by the Communists in the zones under their temporary control after Jan. 27, 1973, are not strictly aimed at simply consolidating their areas politically and economically to prepare to live in peace.

[JUNE 1973]

Eleven

Seeing the Plot behind an Attack*

IN THE PREVIOUS ARTICLE, written in the month of June 1973, we outlined the Communist effort—both Northern and Southern Vietnamese Communists—to rebuild a road connecting the hilly region around Khe Sanh (in Quang Tri province) and south-eastward to Ham Tan, Dai Loc (Quang Nam province). This road ultimately hooks up with the northern extremity of Route 14, and from there open and easy access is provided to Kon Tum or to the coastal lowlands of Quang Ngai and Binh Dinh provinces. This road is essential for the Communist plan to set up a second state in South Vietnam. In addition to the area delineated by Khe Sanh, A Shau, and Kon Tum, this "state," which is gradually taking shape, also comprises territories east of the Mekong Delta and southwest of the Central Highlands. That is why that road does not end at Vo Dinh but branches out in a detour through Attopeu and reconnects with other networks of roads in the South: the road from Thien Ngon to Katum (Tay Ninh province), another from Tong Le Chan (Tay Ninh, Binh Long) to Loc Ninh (Binh Long province), and a stretch from Bo Duc to Bu Gia Map (in Phuoc Long province), the latter running in a northeast direction parallel to the Cambodian border and turning back into Quang Duc province, linking the two strong points of Bu Prang and Duc Lap. The road linking Bo Duc–Bui Gia Map–Bu Prang is called Route 14A, which runs parallel with the main Route 14 connecting Chan Thanh–Dong Xoai–Kien Duc (in Quang Duc province). Routes 14 and 14A intersect at Bi Prang and lead up to Ban Me Thuot. We have written at some length about this Communist network of roads because we wish to provide the reader with a detailed picture of a system of transport communications of prime strategic importance. As we have outlined this north-south road after reaching Quang Nam province and linking

* Please consult Map A (page 128–29) and Map B (page 140–41) for localities.

with Route 14 and pushing further southward to Vo Dinh about 30 km north of Kon Tum runs up against an area under the control of the Saigon government. In order to circumvent this area, the Communists had to build a detour into Laos. This portion of the road, we call a bridge. Naturally the mountainous area west of Route 14, although under the control of the Saigon government, is crisscrossed with narrow jungle trails that the Communists can use to move their infantry and light equipment, albeit stealthily. But they need a good road, a real axis of communications. The Communists were also hampered by the Bu Prang and Duc Lap base camps manned by GVN forces straddling Route 14A in the south, so that if the Communists want to move north, they would still have to use routes 520, 524, and 523 in Cambodia (they call this network "liberation trails"). In short, the Communist North-South axis of communications was disconnected at Vo Dinh, Duc Co, and Phuoc Binh (in Quang Duc province). The high command of the Communist armed forces in the South issued an order on Oct. 15, 1973, purportedly to instruct its units to mount counterattacks against land-grabbing operations by the Saigon government, but in reality it was designed to carry out Resolution No. 12R of the Central Office of the South Vietnam Labor Party in the North. The Resolution ordered Communist troops in South Vietnam to grab land from the Saigon government, to gain more control of the population, to carry on the struggle quietly and step by step, etc. But Resolution No. 21 also put special emphasis on the need to complete the North-South axis of communications.

The road in the North (in Pleiku province) passes through Le Minh base camp and in the South runs close to Bu Prang, Bu Dong, and Dak Song base camps. These base camps have been targeted for attack. On Oct. 22, 1973, units of the enemy 320 Division applied strong pressures against Le Minh, forcing evacuation of the base camp. The Communists did not move on, because the order given out on Oct. 15 only specified the targets without a time limit within which the objectives were to be achieved. Fighting broke out further south on Nov. 4. Two Regiments, Number 205 and Number 271, supported by tanks and armored personnel carriers from Armored Regiment 203, launched a combined attack on Bu Prang base camp, which controls the intersection of routes 14 and 14A. Regiment 205 was new to the area of operation. It used to belong to the Hau Nghia military zone but now was part of the Regional Command. But Regiment 271 had been operating in the area for some time. It was a unit of C30B Division, the main force division of the Eastern Zone Command.

During the 1972 Offensive, while Regiments 5, 7, and 9 were used to lay siege to Loc Ninh and An Loc and to mount ambushes against reinforcements moving up Route 13, Division C30B was responsible for diversionary attacks in Phuoc Binh and Hau Nghia and its Regiment 271 was used to spearhead the attacks against Go Dau Ha and Trang Bang. The Regiment was out of luck: after the attacks at Thien Ngon, Hieu Thien, and Trang Bang in April 1972, due to heavy casualties that reduced its effective strength by more than one half, the Regiment had to pull back for reorganization and recuperation in the Parrot Beak area. In May 1972, it was returned to the battle in Hau Nghia, but after failing in its attempt to cut Highway 1 between Trang Bang and Cu Chi and suffering more casualties, it again had to leave battle. There was a report that, after a second reorganization and recuperation, the same Regiment was again ordered to move out in support of Regiment No. 9, laying siege around An Loc. After an attack into Hau Nghia province town on the night of June 6, and blocking Highway 1 in that area, Division C30B only managed to secure temporary control of a few hamlets north of Trang Bang, until they were forced out by the 25th GVN Infantry Division. For a time, Division C30B disappeared from the battle map of III Corps. It was speculated that was the time when Regiment 271 was removed to the command of the 9th Division. After the long battle of An Loc, Regiment 271 received orders from the Regional Command to carry out harassment actions and to lay siege to the Tong Le Chan base camp while it still remained under the direct command of the 9th Division.

In Nov. 1973, Regiment 271 suddenly emerged in the attack of Bu Prang. In any case, it became clear that the Communists were determined to capture Bu Prang, Bu Dong, Dak Song, and possibly Duc Lap as well, in order to complete their North-South axis of communications unhampered south of Route 14. With the availability of the battle-hardened Regiments 271 and 205, the Regional Command probably did not have any doubt that the targets would be easily secured, especially when the attacks also had the support of more than thirty tanks from armored Regiments 203 and M-26, not including the entire 9th Division as reserve forces. The attacks were launched without hesitation against Bu Prang, Ba Dong, and Dak Song. Bu Prang was only defended by a Regional Force unit from the Quang Duc sector. It was supported by artillery fire from fire base Bu Dong manned by a Battalion of Regional Forces, an armored detachment, and two artillery units. Bu Dong was a firebase set on a low hill about 1 km northeast of Bu Prang. It was established toward the middle of Oct. 1972, at a time when there were reports that a new order of counterattack had just been issued by the COSVN. The firebase was responsible for providing support to Bu Prang and Dak Song.

At 0440 hours on Nov. 4, two Communist Regiments launched a concentrated attack against both Bu Prang and Bu Dong and captured the two base camps the same day. Enemy units planned to take three days for rest and recuperation before moving on to attack Dak Song on Nov. 7, cleaning up the border area of the presence of GVN control in Quang Duc province. After seizing the three outposts, enemy troops moved on in two lines of attack, in the southwest direction to attack Kien Duc and Gia Nghia, and straight up from Dak Song to overrun Duc Lap district town. The capture of Duc Lap district would enable the enemy to secure control of Route 14 and at the same time to completely isolate Quang Duc province. Quang Duc province town, which is also the Gia Nghia district town, is connected to the outside world by two main roads, one leading up from Chon Thanh, Dong Xoai (Binh Long province) and another leading down from Ban Me Thuot. The road to Chon Thanh has remained cut for a long time. Duc Lap district lay on the northern portion of the road. If the Communists succeeded in taking Duc Lap, Quang Duc province would join the fate of Phuoc Long province (province capital in Song Be), which has been completely cut off except by air.

In short, after the first phase of attacks overrunning the border outposts, the Communists intended to secure complete control of the three districts. But probably due to an error in their tactical calculations, and wary of unfavorable publicity in case of long-drawn-out fighting, the Regional Command decided to make use of both Regiments reinforced by units of the 9th Division. Because they wanted to launch successive attacks against several targets, the enemy ran into difficulties in moving their troops and failed to achieve all the objectives. The sieges of Gia Nghia, Duc Lap, and Kien Duc were broken by a Rangers Brigade from II Corps. The Rangers also relieved the pressure at Duc Lap and retook Dak Song, forcing the enemy to leave battle and retreat to the other side of the Cambodian border. The battle of Quang Duc ended on Nov. 24, 1973. The Communists did not achieve all of their objectives, but they still managed to close the gap in their North-South axis of communications south of Route 14A.

We have just described a battle, a battle in peacetime, nominally engaged at the divisional level, but the actual fighting remained at the battalion level, a battle waged at medium intensity with a view on both sides not to disrupt the peace. The size of the battle was insignificant compared to the terrible battles during the 1972 Offensive, but the political ramifications were of particular interest. The central intention of the Paris Agreement was the restoration of peace in South Vietnam based on the spirit of national reconciliation and concord. The two South Vietnamese sides, working in that spirit, will establish a supreme organ called the National Council for National Reconciliation and Concord that will encourage both sides to jointly form reconciliation councils at all levels, to carry out the terms of the Cease-Fire Agreement and to discuss other domestic problems. The National Council will also be responsible for organizing general elections to enable the people to elect their representatives in the government (Art. 12 of the Paris Agreement). But in the present situation, since the Communists only control a few districts and villages in remote areas or in the Highlands, with no economic potential and less than 3 percent of the total population, they will certainly lose in the general elections.

On the other hand, the Saigon side will have enormous advantages: President Thieu's Democracy Party has been organized down to the village and hamlet level, and the majority of the population has had bitter, firsthand experience with the Communists. Under these circumstances, the holding of general elections will have the effect of nullifying all Communist efforts during the past ten years. It seems unavoidable, then, that the Communists will have to try to interpret the Agreement in such a way as to deflect this course of development. As we have seen, they have tried to consolidate and build up their strategic zones, to connect together all the disparate zones with the building of a North-South axis of communications parallel with Highway 1, to delineate a continuous area of control, to set up an administrative machinery within their zones, as well as some simulacrum of industrial and production plants to create some semblance of a separate state for the National Liberation Front. After having consolidated their areas of control, the Communists would move out into the lowland to gradually expand their zones, encroaching on territories held by the Saigon government. Once they felt themselves strong enough, they would eventually agree to general elections with the help of a fifth column lying in wait within the various social classes on the side of the Saigon government. That is the plan of the Communists. Whether or not they can carry it out successfully is a different matter. So far, the industrial plants that they set up in the Duc Co area have failed to operate, there is still no electricity, and natural resources are scarce in some areas under their control.

Despite strict discipline and constant calls for doubling and tripling efforts for construction, the Communists have failed to turn their zones into a working economy. The control of techniques and the effective use of resources seem resistant to any dose of Marxist doctrine. There is also a morale problem within their ranks. Two thousand young women forcibly moved from North Vietnam to populate the Tan Canh and Duc Co areas have reportedly asked to be allowed to return to North Vietnam to be reunited with their families, their parents, and their children. Many Communist troops, except for the young, immature, and fanatical elements, have also become disillusioned. Many have defected to the Saigon government, others became lackadaisical, and still others just left their units to try to survive by themselves in the jungle or among the Montagnards in the Laotian or Cambodian highlands. The Communists call them the "B quay" (B turn), in the sense that they went to the South, "go B," but changed direction. The Communists have also run into serious difficulties in their effort to improve and build up their strategic network of roads because in many instances the lines of communications had to pass through thick jungles, high mountains, steep valleys, and fast-flowing waterways especially in the tri-border area. These roads also require constant back-breaking maintenance work to keep them from being washed out after each heavy rainfall. That is the situation on the Communist side. On our side, in these last days of the war, what shall we do for our own survival, to remain free from the yoke of a doctrinaire dictatorial regime, to be worthy of the sacrifices of hundreds of thousands of our soldiers, and hundreds of thousands of civilians killed in this bloody war that is coming to be viewed as just a mistake? This is the decisive moment, the final hour in a long war where the life and death of a whole people are in the balance. We shall not, and cannot, afford to slacken our effort if only because of some cankerous actions within our midst.

[NOVEMBER 1973]

MAP A
Mengtzu
HA GIANG
Nanning
CAO BANG
LAOKAI
QL1
QL2
LAI CHAU
LANG SON
TUYEN QUANG
QL1
SON LA
HANOI
HOA BINH
HAI PHONG
GIA
LAM
QL6
Samneua
THAI BINH
LUANG
PRABANG
GULF OF
TONKIN
QL1
HAINAN
Xieng
Khouang
LAOS
QL7
VINH
HA TINH
VIENTIANE
MU GIA
QL12
Nong Khai
Nakhon
Phanom
DONG HOI
SOUTH
CHINA
SEA
Udon Thani
Thakhek
QL1
THACH HAN
QL9
Sepone
QL9
QUANG TRI
LAO
HUE
Savannakhet

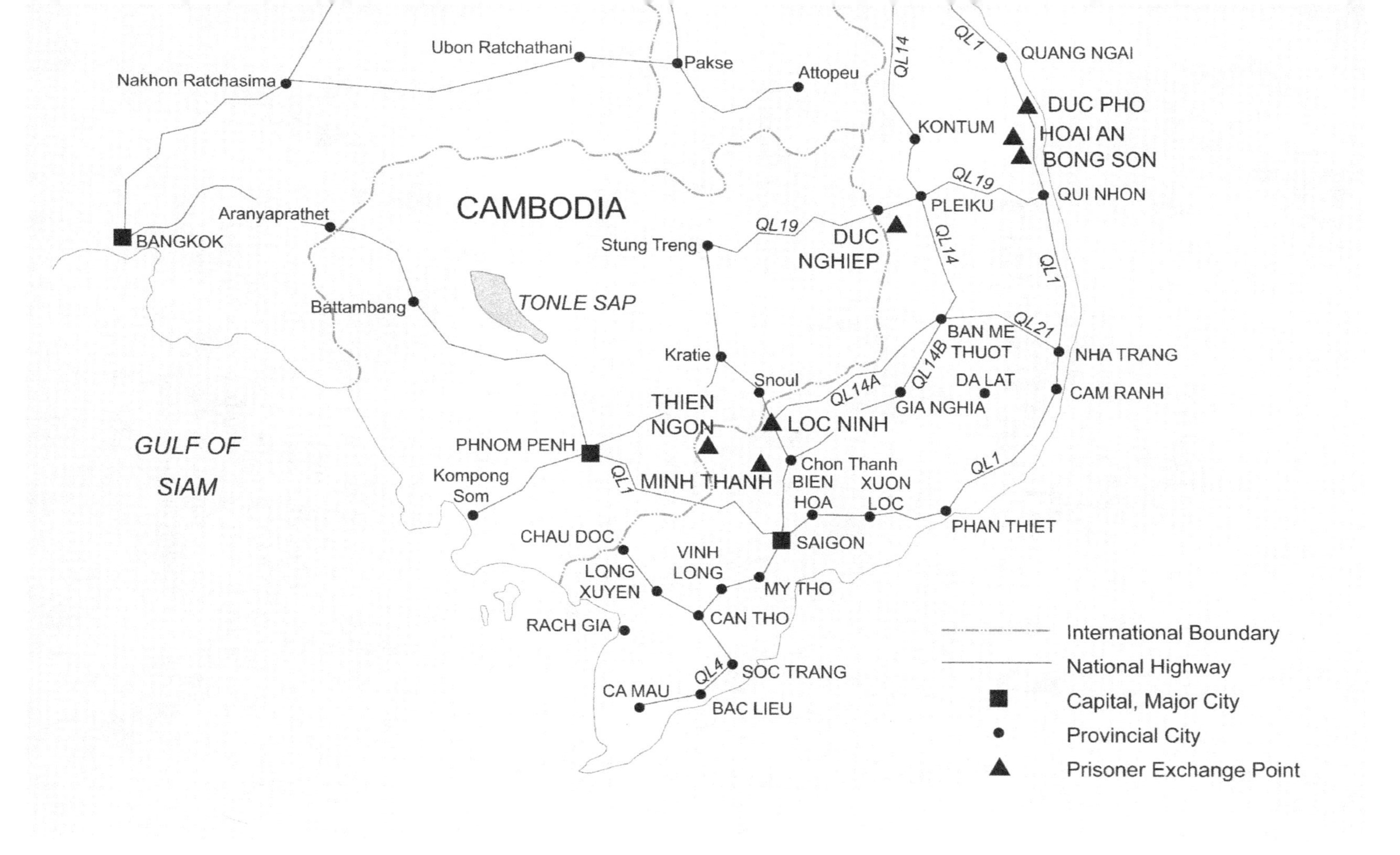

Nakhon Ratchasima
Ubon Ratchathani
Pakse
Attopeu
QL14
QL1
QUANG NGAI
DUC PHO
HOAI AN
BONG SON
KONTUM
QL19
QUI NHON
PLEIKU
CAMBODIA
Aranyaprathet
BANGKOK
QL19
Stung Treng
DUC
NGHIEP
QL14
QL1
Battambang
TONLE SAP
BAN ME
THUOT
QL21
NHA TRANG
Kratie
Snoul
QL14B
DA LAT
QL14A
CAM RANH
GIA NGHIA
THIEN
NGON
LOC NINH
GULF OF
SIAM
PHNOM PENH
Chon Thanh
QL1
Kompong
Som
QL1
MINH THANH
BIEN
HOA
XUON
LOC
PHAN THIET
CHAU DOC
SAIGON
VINH
LONG
LONG
XUYEN
MY THO
CAN THO
RACH GIA
QL4
SOC TRANG
CA MAU
BAC LIEU
International Boundary
National Highway
Capital, Major City
Provincial City
Prisoner Exchange Point

Twelve

Tong Le Chan—Or a Tear Drop for Peace*

WHEN MANY PEOPLE all over the world are ringing bells, uncorking wine bottles, and throwing confetti to welcome peace in Vietnam, fire flashes from the muzzles of guns like lightning on a day without rain in a remote corner of this country.

Tong Le Chan, a military outpost set up on a stunted hill not more than fifty meters high overlooking two rivulets between the two provinces of Tay Ninh and Binh Long, came under heavy enemy attacks. Taking advantage of the cease-fire, the Communists openly launched an attack against the base in plain daylight. This is ignored by the world as a small accident in a troubled country. Peace, a stale wine for the world to drink and to forget. Tong Le Chan, a battle in the late season of a long war, a battle that took place in complete indifference. Until today, this base has been under siege for 17 months of 510 days. We can't help feeling guilty if we can give ourselves a moment to think of it.

Stalingrad was encircled by the Germans for 76 days, American troops held on to Bataan for 66 days, and British and Commonwealth troops dug in at Tobruk for 241 days. In Vietnam, "paradise" of the gods of war, where violence knows no limits, we also have a history of long sieges, the best known of which must be Dien Bien Phu, which only succumbed after 57 days. More recently, during the 1972 Offensive, we had battles that should have been specially mentioned in any history of war. These were the battles in Kon Tum, An Loc, Quang Tri. The battles at Delta and Charlie firebases in Kon Tum province raged on for four days. The siege at An Loc lasted for 110 days. Quang Tri City, taken by the Communists on May 1, was largely freed from enemy troops by July 25, 1972. But Tong Le Chan, after 510 days under siege, should be recognized as the longest battle in the world history of war.

* Please consult Map A (page 128–29) and Map B (page 140–41) for localities.

Ever since May 10, 1972, the importance of this small military outpost has been largely eclipsed behind the great billowing fumes of war from An Loc, Quang Tri, and Kon Tum. Today, six months after the fateful peace has been decreed, there is an even greater tendency to forget about it in willful ignorance of the crimes of the Communists. This is a teardrop, a small prayer to the heroes of Tong Le Chan who have sustained combat for 510 days, a cry to the whole world—that crime has become synonymous with Communism, that Tong Le Chan has become the symbol of the unlimited capability for resistance of the South Vietnamese.

The base was set up on a low hill of about 50 m in elevation, looking down on the Takon and Neron rivulets, two of the many waterways flowing into the Saigon River and covering like a net over the two provinces of Tay Ninh and Binh Long. It is situated on the common border of the two provinces, about 15 km northeast of An Loc and about 30 km south of the Cambodian border, at the point of the Parrot's Beak, a needle on the side of the headquarters of the COSVN.

Tong Le Chan used to be a CIDG (Civilian Defense Groups) camp under the command of the Special Force set up in 1967. Except for the Ben Soi base camp, which is located deep within the territory of Tay Ninh province, all the other camps in III Corps, from Tay Ninh to Phuoc Long province, were set up right along the border with Cambodia to monitor enemy troops movements on the other side of the border and to interdict enemy infiltration and penetration across the border into South Vietnam. These were camps at Ben Soi, Thien Ngon, Katum, Tong Le Chan, Loc Ninh, Quan Loi, and Bu Gia Map. The camps also sent out patrols to search and destroy enemy units in their respective areas of operations.

Tong Le Chan's area of operations includes Combat Zone C, one of the most important sanctuaries of the enemy. Like the system of provincial roads that was built in 1960 and 1961 under President Diem's administration, the Special Forces camps were a pet project of President Kennedy, the most glamorous of the thirty-seven American Presidents. But the time has changed. This is 1973, and the Americans have returned to Clark Field, to Guam, leaving Indochina deep in the fog of war and the illusion of peace. The old Special Forces camps now manned by South Vietnamese troops are only lost objects in an indifferent world.

This is no longer war, and these are just the first seizures of a dangerous peace. And Tong Le Chan is left to suffer its long and senseless delirium. The foothills north of the base camps are traversed by Route 246 leading up from Tay Ninh and winding through the lush vegetation of Binh Long province. As a route connecting Combat Zones C and D, it is also an essential life line for the NLF. Tong Le Chan is also a choke point astride the portion of the Communist North-South axis connecting the headquarters of the COSVN with Dau Tieng, an infiltration route to Binh Duong and Gia Dinh provinces. Because of its tactical position, Tong Le Chan is not just any military target. This small base camp has a special importance because it can control both the east-west and north-south movements of Communist troops. As a matter of fact, it is situated right at the hub of the network of Communist communication lines, in the center of the enemy base area. Since the beginning, Tong Le Chan has never had a peaceful day.

It was called Tonle Tchombe by the local inhabitants. But the first commander of the camp, Major Dang Hung Long, changed its name into Tong Le Chan, and the troops would just call it Tong Le for short, which in Vietnamese means "Tear of Separation," a fateful name for an ill-fated camp. The CIDGs of the camp consist mostly of Montagnards of the Stieng tribe. In 1970, when the Special Forces camps began to be turned over to the South Vietnamese Armed Forces, most of them volunteered to stay on, and they were formed into the 92nd Border Ranger Battalion. In April 1972, with the opening of the front at An Loc and Loc Ninh, the Communists attempted to remove all the South Vietnamese border posts that hampered the free flow of their troops and equipment. Because of the emergency situation at the time, the Commander of the Ranger Forces in III Corps decided to close down all four bases at Thien Ngon, Katum, Tong Le Chan, and Bui Gia Map. But the commander of Tong Le Chan, citing the unanimous wish of the troops to stay back at the camp, requested permission to hold on to the camp and pledged that the defenders would be able to repulse any enemy attacks.

From that moment, the fate of the small base camp was sealed. The Rangers of the 92nd Battalion manning the camp were to become the unsung heroes in one of the last battles of the war, a battle which served to highlight the unlimited capability for endurance of the Vietnamese people in their struggle for peace. Peace in Vietnam. The poor dream of a whole people. The unknown heroes of the 92nd Battalion have at least made their contribution from a dark corner lost in the jungle of South Vietnam. Would this ever be recognized in the world kept in balance by a lame peace?

Because of its important position within the Communist network of communications, and because it served as a shield for the western defenses of An Loc, the commanders in COSVN came to the decision that Tong Le Chan had to be wiped off their battle map. In May 1972, all hell broke loose. After sappers had penetrated inside the defense perimeter, the enemy, with tank support, attempted to crush the camp by human wave tactics. But the camp withstood all attempts by the enemy to overrun it, and the commander of the camp, a twenty-five-year-old man named Le Van Ngon, had kept his promise. Ngon had graduated from the 21st Class of the National Military Academy in 1966, and in Sept. 1973, within record time, he was promoted to the rank of lieutenant colonel. But there was no envy. In fact, there can be no ground for such sentiment because it seems that all through the history of war there has never been any unit that was able to sustain up to 510 days of siege and still keep on fighting. Ngon and his 92nd Battalion were the exception. They represented the noble sense of responsibility of true soldiers of all times. Men everywhere have at times proved their capabilities for outstanding acts of heroism, whether on the island of Saipan, or in the cabins of the Zeroes, or in the bombing missions challenging deadly anti-aircraft fire over the skies of Europe.

In Vietnam, during the Tet Offensive, the 1971 Operation into Lower Laos, and during the 1972 Offensive, several units and individual soldiers of the South Vietnamese Armed Forces have proved their heroism. But Tong Le Chan shone with a special light. On June 8, 1972, An Loc was finally retaken after the 6th Airborne Battalion managed to hook up with the 8th at the south gate of An Loc. The enemy fled to the west, licking their wounds and vowing to return for a bigger offensive. Tong Le Chan was the only base camp left after all the other border outposts had been withdrawn by order of III Corps Command. The Vietcong 9th Division ordered its units to take turns putting the base camp under relentless fire for a whole year. On Jan. 25, 1973, two days before the Peace Agreement was signed in Paris, the Communists decided to get rid of the camp once and for all. The enemy wanted to "raze" the base camp to secure complete control of the border area from Tay Ninh to Loc Ninh. It was supposed to be D-Day for Tong Le Chan. But the attack failed and the base camp at this time, in Sept. 1973, is still there after having sustained 233 shellings, 20 ground attacks by human wave tactics, and 7 sapper attacks. The camp has been hit by a total of about 14,500 artillery shells during the first 220 days of peace in Vietnam.

The siege has been going on for 510 days and the casualties, in dead and wounded, have reached almost 100. It has been impossible to evacuate many of the more seriously wounded. The enemy has a dense net of anti-aircraft fire around the base camp, and the medical evacuation helicopters of the Vietnamese Armed Forces became drones for enemy anti-aircraft fire training. This is in blatant defiance of international law, of simple humanity, and certainly contrary to the spirit of national reconciliation and concord loudly and solemnly proclaimed by the Communists at the negotiating table and at the prisoner exchange location north of the Thach Han River. On Aug. 10, there was another failed attempt at evacuating the seriously wounded by helicopters. The UH-1 of Flight Group 233 was felled by enemy fire. The crew survived and remained at the camp until they were taken out by a most daring rescue attempt by VNAF Major Bao, a former classmate of Colonel Ngon, the camp commander, at the Dalat Military Academy. The flight took off at midnight from Bien Hoa airbase under the command of Major Bao. The flight also brought up some reward money from the people and soldiers of III Corps to the defenders of Tong Le Chan and a new rank of lieutenant colonel for the base commander. But there was another moving aspect to the evacuation: forty of the seventy-five wounded asked to be allowed to stay back. Besides injuries inflicted by enemy fire, the defenders of Tong Le Chan also suffered from malaria and trench rot because of the lack of medicine and of fresh food, and because of their long stay inside their bunkers and trenches during the long siege. Supplies had to be dropped in by parachutes. In July a supply mission almost failed because a special hook and cable for releasing the packages from the planes was out of stock and the crew had to resort to improvising, since missing parts had to be ordered from the United States and it would be a long time before they could be available. The improvisation worked, although not perfectly: 60 percent of the airdropped supplies landed outside the camp perimeter and fell into enemy hands. The reason was that the cable made of smaller strands had the effect of delaying the release time by a few seconds—enough for many parachutes to miss the small, enclosed space of the camp. Because of the difficulties in supplying the camp as well as the enemy's incessant shelling, the defenders often had to go hungry and sometimes had to survive even on cockroaches and other insects in the camp.

The long siege and the deprivations did not affect the endurance and morale of the defenders. During the siege of Dien Bien Phu, General Giles, commander of the paratroopers in the French Expeditionary Corps, called General Cogny and General Navarro on the phone and said, "Get me out of here! I have just spent six months in the rat hole of Nasan. I cannot endure any more of this claustrophobia!" Six months in the fortress of Nasan was enough to wear down a celebrated French paratrooper commander, although the fortress was known to be provided with all material comforts! What should we think of commander Le Van Ngon and his troops, sick, wounded, and starving, but still fighting after more than 510 days in the cold, dark trenches of Tong Le Chan when we compare them to some men of some other time, as brave and as tough as they were? What is even more painful is that Ngon and his men had to carry on the fighting when peace is supposed to have returned to South Vietnam—what a dishonest and tricky peace it is!

What can we do to be worthy of the heroism of these men? No longer necessary are the original functions of Tong Le Chan: to monitor enemy activities, to prevent enemy infiltration, and to send out patrols in search of the enemy. What it is is just a dramatic symbol, a dubious battle in an absurd battlefield where heroes are felled in the silence to lay bare a wicked and dastardly peace.

At the special session for top delegates held on March 17, 1973, upon the request of the Saigon side on the Joint Military Commission, Tong Le Chan was put at the top of the agenda. The chief of delegation of the Republic of Vietnam, General Du Quoc Dong, had three urgent proposals:

- That the Commission immediately dispatch a team to Tong Le Chan to investigate violations of the Peace and Cease-Fire Agreement.
- That the United States, as current chairman of the Commission, request the International Committee to start the investigation if the above proposal is rejected by the Communist side.
- That the National Liberation Front give immediate order to its units around Tong Le Chan to stay in place and not to fire on aircraft transporting the investigating party.

But, being deceitful as ever, and probably sensing that they would have to deal with an important proposal for which they had not received clear instructions, the National Liberation Front came to the meeting without being represented by its chief of delegation, General Tran Van Tra, who was supposed to have full authority to make decisions on the spot. Excusing the absence of General Tra, Colonel Dan Van Thu, the acting chief of the NLF delegation, chose to ignore completely the proposals presented by the Saigon side and instead launched himself into a long diatribe against so-called cease-fire violations by the Saigon side in Duc Pho and Sa Huynh (in Quang Ngai province), in Duc Co (Pleiku province), etc., and concluded without flinching that the Saigon government had violated the Cease-Fire Agreement. No mention of Tong Le Chan was made in his long speech. All the while, the head of the North Vietnamese delegation kept nodding his head in agreement, then delivered a similar speech with somewhat different wording.

Since the Communist delegations chose to ignore completely the three proposals, the Saigon side repeated the second proposal about a direct investigation by the International Committee. That proposal was also jointly rejected by the National Liberation Front and the North Vietnamese. They did not agree to the request for an investigation by the International Committee and, citing "the confused and insecure situation in the area," they declined to guarantee safety for the investigating team until such time as they found to be convenient. The session ended on that note. Such is the principle of unanimous decision! There can never be unanimity at meetings of the Joint Military Commission!

In order to further ensure that there will be no inspection, the NLF and the North Vietnamese also asked their comrades in the Polish and Hungarian delegations to reject the investigation request as forwarded by the U.S. delegation on grounds of safety. Perhaps to stress their goodwill stance, they set a conditional acceptance of the request: We would go if the delegation of the National Liberation Front could agree to send a liaison officer to accompany the investigators on the same plane they said. Naturally, that condition could not be satisfied because the NLF, having rejected the investigation, would never agree to send one of their men to go with the investigating team of the International Committee.

A whole week passed after the meeting of March 17. There was no movement to the urgent proposals of the Saigon side.

Every time the proposal was raised, the NLF delegation would say that "the situation in Tong Le Chan remains confused" and that they need instructions from higher echelons before they could give an answer to the proposals. And on the International Commission, the argument was that the Committee could not send out a team to investigate in the field without being accompanied by a representative of the National Liberation Front. It was the same shameless game of passing the buck among the four Communist delegations. And the issue was completely sidetracked.

On March 23, 1973, with only four more days to go for the 4-Party Joint Military Commission, the United States again made an urgent request with the Canadian delegate who was then Chairman of the International Commission to make direct arrangement with the National Liberation Front for an early investigation of

Tong Le Chan. The NLF, being pressed hard, had to agree to a meeting between Colonel Vo Dong Giang, their deputy head of delegation, and Colonel Lomis of the Canadian delegation to discuss the sending of a representative of the NLF to go with the International Committee investigating team to Tong Le Chan on March 24. Giang agreed to dispatch a liaison officer with the investigators, but only after the same officer had made contact with Vietcong units in the area. The plan was for the officer to depart from Tan Son Nhut airbase for Tong Le Chan, to make contact with Vietcong forces there, and to return to Bien Hoa airbase to wait for the team from the International Committee and accompany them back to Tong Le Chan. But the Vietcong liaison officer, after going to Tong Le Chan, returned to Tan Son Nhut instead of Bien Hoa as agreed, leaving the International Committee investigators to wait for a whole day in Bien Hoa for nothing. It was the same cheap deception again, and the investigation of Communist cease-fire violation at Tong Le Chan never took place.

Back at the Joint Military Commission, after a full week of needling and poking since the meeting of March 17, the Saigon side finally had the NLF delegation agree to jointly send liaison officers to Tong Le Chan to ensure safety for the evacuation of the wounded. But on March 23, the Vietcong liaison officer, instead of going to Tong Le Chan, asked to be taken to Con Tran village about 10 km west of Tong Le Chan because he said he needed to get in touch with the "local authorities" first. After searching in the jungle for a while, he returned to the helicopter and claimed that he had lost communications with the local authorities because of bombing by the Americans and the Saigon government. The helicopter returned to Saigon with no wounded soldiers on board. The Saigon delegation kept on with its requests and the NLF could no longer procrastinate. On March 24, the first and also the last twenty-two wounded soldiers were evacuated from Tong Le Chan. There is a price to pay in blood for the belief in the spirit of "national reconciliation and concord" of the National Liberation Front. The Tong Le Chan base camp will remain closed forever, and its tragedies will remain buried.

The Joint Military Commission continued to hold meetings both at the level of chief delegates and heads of subcommittees to try to give a sweeping solution to the Tong Le Chan issue. But, as people say, the Communists have a different perception of the truth. The Tong Le Chan affair became in their view a case of Saigon troops launching an operation in flagrant violation of the cease-fire agreement in an attempt at land grabbing in Tong Le Chan, an area in the "liberated" zone of the Provisional Revolutionary Government! In addition, the NLF claimed that the shelling of the base had been quite restrained and was only intended as a warning against any attempt by the base defenders to move out to attack the liberation forces. (How can a unit of more than two hundred men come to the attack of a whole division encircling them?) Asked to explain why the NLF forces had used loudspeakers to call on the defenders to surrender, the NLF delegation said it was only trying to explain the spirit of national reconciliation to the soldiers in Tong Le Chan, as stipulated in the Paris Agreement. Language has lost all meaning with the Communists!

The most absurd denunciations were inverted. The most unfounded accusations were aired over their radio station. Groundless protest notes were sent to the International Committee, which their Communist comrades in the Polish and Hungarian delegations would consider as the most serious matters. And who knows how many people in the world might have been misled by these protests from Tran Van Tra and Le Quang Hoa alleging cease-fire violations by the Saigon side? One of those protest notes was even carried by the official journal of the Vatican. When the Pope read those lines, would he know of the wretched defenders of Tong Le Chan praying for the first daylight in their cold, dark trenches? It is even more painful when many people in Saigon still don't know, or don't want to know, of Tong Le Chan and its desperate defenders, although the besieged camp is not more than 100 km north of the city.

And there are still others who insist on looking at the problem in an opposite way: the so-called peace lovers, men like Hong Son Dong, Ho Ngoc Nhuan, Ho Huu Tuong, Truong Gia Ky Sanh, Father Ngoc Lan, Father Chan Tin, etc., the people often quoted by the National Liberation Front in their denunciations of the Saigon Government. Has anyone ever wondered why are they acting as accomplices to the bloody crimes of the Communists? Twenty days after peace was declared, Tong Le Chan suffered four more killed in action and twenty-two more wounded. Who are they dying for? Aren't they dying for the defense of South Vietnam, where these people live, and in the name of "peace" they protested against the defense of it?

We are now in a strange situation of peace after twenty-six years of raging war. We have become used to the rumbling of artillery, the explosions of rockets, the sky-high flames of the Tet Offensive, the hellfire of An Loc and Quang Tri, so much so that at the first hint of peace, however painful that peace is, we want to get rid immediately of any traces of war, we want to forget all the terrible images of the past months and years, we have become too insensitive to concern ourselves with the image of a solitary combat for survival, for freedom, and for peace—a dream of the whole people. We have a part in that dream. What can we do for Tong Le Chan?

I wrote down this tragic call for Tong Le Chan in June 1973, at a time when Communist troops were getting ready to launch a final attack against the base camp during the rainy season of 1973. During the whole of 1973, the small base camp withstood numerous ground attacks and sustained tens of thousands of artillery shells, and Lieutenant Colonel Le Van Ngon had kept his pledge to defend the base to the death. His name seemed to have destined his fate with the base: Ngon, a man of loyalty, a man who keeps his words. Despite the constant threat of death, this hero, so young in age and yet so old in combat experience, has indeed become the purest symbol of the capacity for limitless endurance of the whole people. I feel ashamed in writing these lines when I think of his bravery. At the many sessions of the two-party Joint Military Commission in March and April 1973, the Saigon side has repeatedly denounced the Communist plan to launch a final attack against the base camp. According to the plan, the attack would be carried out by Regiment 271 with the close support of an artillery Regiment, an anti-aircraft Regiment, and an armored Brigade, not including reserve forces and forces used to ambush reinforcements. The Communists have had one year of probing, two months of study over sand tables and of rehearsal on similar terrain. The enemy used trench tactics combined with crushing firepower tactics to begin moving on the base on April 5. They finally came to terms with the defenders and captured the base at 0100 hours on April 11.

What else, what more could Lieutenant Colonel Ngon do with 259 men, including 50 already wounded in previous attacks and 20 in the last attack? The 92nd Battalion had fought longer than any combat unit in the history of warfare. Alamo, Saipan, Wake. Hundreds of thousands of fighting men in the world who have set examples of the sacred duty of the soldier. The greatest, brightest example was set by Ngon and his men. What is even more commendable is that Lieutenant Colonel Ngon and 259 Rangers defending Tong Le Chan were also soldiers for peace—peace for our beloved motherland. We are here, in this quiet town. What do we think when the news reached us that Tong Le Chan has fallen? Tears are welling up in our eyes.

[NOVEMBER 1974]

MAP B

VINH LINH
TRUNG LUONG
Ben Hai R.
GIO LINH
THACH HAN
DONG HA
Thakhek
Cam Lo
QUANG TRI
Huong Hoa
AN LO
Thach Han R.
Khe Sanh
My Chanh R.
HUE
Lang Vei
Co Bi
QL9
LAO BAO
Birmingham
Nam Hoa
HAI VAN
QL1
Sepone
A Luoi
Bastogne
Savannakhet
Ta Bat
A Sao
DA NANG
HOI AN
Dai Loc
Thuong Duc
Thu Bon R.
QL1
TAM KY
QL14
QUANG NGAI
Dak Sut
Gia Vue
QL1
DUC PHO
Ben Het
Tan Canh
Tam Quan
AN LAO
Charlie
HOAI AN
Dak To
Vo Dinh
BONG SON
Attopeu
Delta
KONTUM
QL14
Le Trung
QL19
Binh Khe
An Tuc
QUI NHON
PLEIKU
Duc Co
DUC

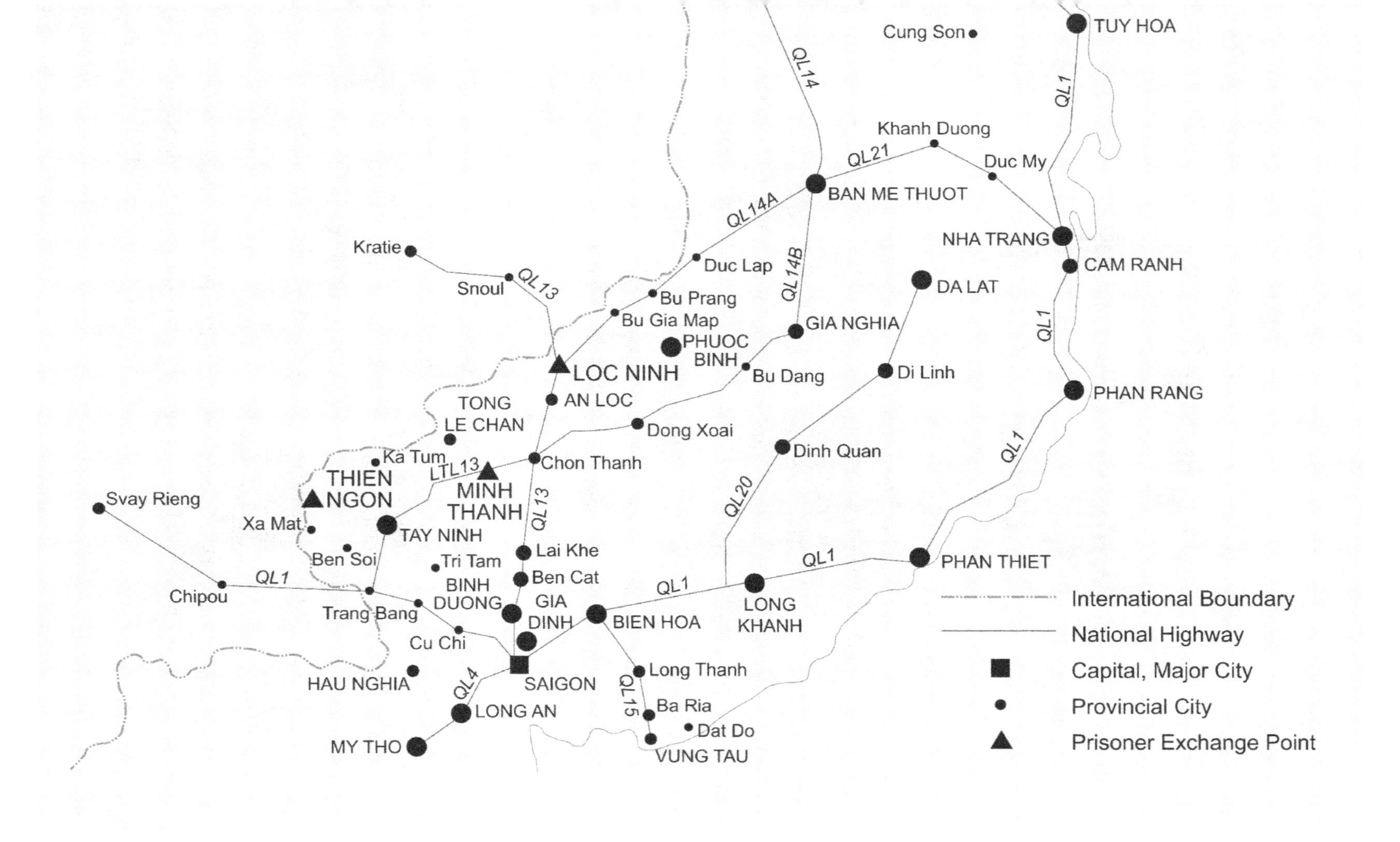
Cung Son
TUY HOA
QL14
QL1
Khanh Duong
QL21
Duc My
BAN ME THUOT
QL14A
NHA TRANG
CAM RANH
Kratie
Duc Lap
QL14B
DA LAT
Snoul
QL13
Bu Prang
Bu Gia Map
GIA NGHIA
QL1
PHUOC
BINH
Di Linh
LOC NINH
Bu Dang
PHAN RANG
TONG
AN LOC
LE CHAN
Dong Xoai
Dinh Quan
Ka Tum
LTL13
Chon Thanh
QL1
THIEN
NGON
MINH
THANH
Svay Rieng
QL20
Xa Mat
QL13
TAY NINH
Lai Khe
Ben Soi
Tri Tam
QL1
PHAN THIET
Ben Cat
QL1
BINH
DUONG
QL1
LONG
KHANH
Chipou
GIA
DINH
Trang Bang
BIEN HOA
Cu Chi
Long Thanh
HAU NGHIA
QL4
SAIGON
QL15
Ba Ria
LONG AN
Dat Do
MY THO
VUNG TAU
International Boundary
National Highway
Capital, Major City
Provincial City
Prisoner Exchange Point

Thirteen

A Prisoner Released, an Outpost Overrun

MRS. NGO BA THANH has finally been released from jail. She remains under house arrest pending trial. But this nevertheless represents a great improvement in her situation since it had been expected that she would be turned over to the National Liberation Front in late July 1973. This change is due to many causes—to various pressures applied for her release, and to the almost grotesque publicity stirred up by many groups and individuals around her person. Mrs. Thanh, who are you? She is probably supported by the religious left, or the Communists, or the Americans. It is painful to think about it. To think that one has spent several years of one's life to become, in the end, just a card for dark and devious plots. Her movement is called Movement for the Right to Live, but the people who should best claim the right to live, the poor, wretched soldiers and their families, are not represented and not given a voice in her Movement. Mrs. Thanh, the woman intellectual who has spent fifty-seven months in jail, has proudly declared: "I am the Third Force."

The Third Force, whether it does have force or not, is indeed the essential element to complete the Paris Agreement. Still, are the dreams and aspirations of our people well reflected in the ambiguous wording of the strange document? What has happened since then? The Le Minh base camp and the flight into the jungle of 293 soldiers and their families amid the rumbling of artillery. The breach made by the enemy K-2 sappers battalion and then the waves of assaults by troops of the North Vietnamese 320 main force division to clean up the base camp. Nobody talked of those 293 soldiers or would take a minute to try to conjure up the image of a soldier's wife, holding her infant child at her bosom, fleeing with her husband while ducking fire from the Vietnamese revolutionaries. It is supposed to be a Revolution made up of workers and peasants and supported by class-conscious people. The soldier, his wife, their baby certainly represent obstacles to the progress of the proletarian revolution. Do these people have the right to live? Why can't Mrs. Thanh include them in her Movement?

Perhaps it did not come to the realization of Mrs. Thanh's Movement for the Right to Live that these miserable people should also have a voice in the Movement? And there is a so-called opposition paper whose stated objective is to struggle for the real patriots. I wonder if the editors of that paper can ever picture in their mind the scene of a base camp on fire deep in the jungle, and the crazed yelling and shouting of the Hanoi troops? The release of Mrs. Thanh took place in this confused, nerve-wracking, phantasmagorical situation.

The personal achievement of this well-known lady is beyond doubt. Forty-one years old, PhD in international law, in and out of jail for a total of fifty-seven months in seven years—these are credentials that not anybody can pretend to equal. A woman with a PhD is still a rarity in our country, nay, even in all of Southeast Asia. Her doctorate in international law is proof of her competency in the field. Not everybody can keep up this spirit, retain the same determination to overcome any hostile environment, and remain unwavering in the pursuit of their ideals as Mrs. Thanh has proved that she can. Despite the fact that people have gone to jail and may have been tortured it's not ordinary that a woman rejected a quiet and peaceful life to take to the streets and get involved, willing to endure long months of confinement within the cold walls of a prison. She has got to have strong motivations, ambitious plans, and great aspirations of perhaps national scope. Mrs. Thanh is a woman who is willing to brave the storm and the fire, to accept sacrifices and to suffer pains. Such a woman is certainly worthy of our admiration.

But with all due respect for her personal qualities, we can't help feeling doubtful about the objective of her struggle. This could not be simply a lone struggle waged by a woman intellectual against a regime with several imperfections. It would be a naïve thought to have of such a very well-organized, multifaceted, and overall plan.

It may be useful to review the activities of the Movement in the past years. The Movement launched the struggle in support of the Disabled Veterans. It has called for the demilitarization of the schools. It was involved in a dispute over a piece of real estate between two Buddhist sects. Could it be that these short-term involvements in minor issues were only tactical moves of a Movement with such an ambitious objective—the Right to Live itself? And the Movement has ignored, or has not cared to reach out to, a whole class of people who should have the best claim to the Right to Live: the combat soldiers and their miserable families.

The Movement, by getting itself involved over the years in vain, pointless, stop-and-go activities, by championing even negative causes, has gradually laid bare its own true nature. This is not a Movement guided by declared strategy and objectives; it is just a pastiche known for its hyperactivities, and it has revealed itself to be nothing but an instrument, not so well designed, for stirring up the masses on some deliberate issues. What the Movement did in the years 1969 and 1970 called to mind actions of Communist vanguard elements in the streets of Saigon. I am most hesitant to express that feeling because I don't want to hurt the image of the leader of the Movement, a woman who has proved capable of such endurance, such flexibility, such forcefulness, a woman of intellect and with great self-control. But I tend to think that her doings in the streets of Saigon during the past years were just rehearsals for bigger tasks to come. It would be unjust to equate Mrs. Thanh with a middle-level cadre of the National Liberation Front in the city. It may be mere coincidence that the objectives of the Movement fit with the real intentions of the National Liberation Front.

If Mrs. Thanh does not work for the great national objectives, and if she is not just a middle-level cadre of the Communists, then how can we place her? Let us here permit ourselves a little digression: if Mrs. Thanh were indeed a top-level cadre of the Communists, then we can be sure that the NLF would never have wasted such talent in noisy and grotesque street demonstrations in years past. Through this subtractive analysis, we can only be a front for the real nature and intentions of the Americans. This is an unavoidable conclusion. This is a deplorable situation. Here is a brilliant individual, with firm intellectual knowledge, with fifty-seven long months in prison to her credit as a result of days of tedious street struggle, a person who has been given so much publicity and fanfare, and such a person in the end has turned out to be not more than a hidden hand in a game, paving the way toward the conclusion of the Agreement for the Restoration of Peace in Vietnam. This is a deceitful document that can easily lend itself to various interpretations, although it is supposed to meet the true aspirations of the Vietnamese people. As indeed Mrs. Thanh has declared: "[The Agreement] is a great victory. It proves that the right cause will always win in the end." Such a remark from Mrs. Thanh is typical of Communist phraseology. In fact, it simply duplicates a statement from the National Liberation Front commenting on Article 1 of the Paris Agreement: "The right cause shall win." A phrase that came from Ho Chi Minh and that has been widely publicized and often repeated among the Communist rank and file. But what is important is not the use of Communist phraseology. What is irritating is the way she gallantly announced, "I am the Third Force." The Third Force is certainly the talk of the town for the time being. Several names have been mentioned, and many of them have been living in exile for years: former Emperor Bao Dai, former Prime Minister Nguyen Van Tam, Ex-General Nguyen Chanh Thi, Senator Vu Van Mau, retired General Duong Van Minh. All of them antiquated figures, former opportunists who have been discarded in the dustbin of history and whose images are being re-polished in preparation for the new struggle in which the Vietnam problem has been removed, according to the new American strategy of Mr. Kissinger, the outstanding U.S Secretary of State. Among those who have been newly refurbished is Mrs. Thanh, with her pitiful arrogance when she offered herself as a representative of the Third Force—"I am the Third Force." But the Third Force does not have a place in our community. It is but a late creation, imposed on us from the outside, a necessary appendage for the masterpiece of Mr. Kissinger.

We have viewed the Agreement in its basic brutality. We have seen the sick and unformed state of the Third Force, the pointlessness of wasting away fifty-seven months in prison of Mrs. Thanh, the uselessness of her doctorate in international law, the grotesque publicity surrounding her in the local press, and we have felt anger. Too many people have tried to exploit the cause of patriotism, to pretend to serve the interests of the people for their own profit. Too many people have feasted upon the blood of this country, to which have contributed the 293 soldiers and their families from the Le Minh base camp. The Third Force, late guests to the banquet, don't let yourselves be carried away. There is no cause for enjoyment.

It is of grave concern to note that the Le Minh base camp is a test case for the kind of peace as envisioned in the Paris Agreement. That kind of peace is not the peace for Vietnam. Should we discard the case as just an accident without consequence and move on to gather a Third Force to carry out the last step of the Paris Agreement, or should we present the blood-and-guts issue for a vote of confidence before the people who have a good conscience, who love justice, who are straight and brave? We are now under siege, a siege of fire and deceit. All issues have been blocked. We are subjected to severe charges. We are being driven crazy by the barbarous cries from enemies on all four sides. The interview of Mrs. Thanh, and news of the base camp on fire, should give us food for thought. We have to make a choice between conscience and vain arguments, between righteous actions moved by the deepest sorrow or the role of passive accomplice and letting ourselves be driven away by the force of circumstances until the day when things will get out of control, beyond our grip.

[NOVEMBER 1973]

Fourteen

War of Words

THE MEETINGS of the 4-Party Joint Military Commission were held in an atmosphere of emergency. The Communist sides were well prepared. Their delegations included experts who had participated in the Paris conferences and had become well versed with negotiating procedures. They were also well coordinated and had learned to express themselves in long and fluent diatribes "in accordance with the spirit and the words of the Agreement." Nevertheless, they could not avoid getting themselves into snags sometimes because most of them did not have a firm grasp on the actual situation in South Vietnam. In theory, the Communist officers who came to Saigon to participate in discussions concerning the problems of South Vietnam were members of two separate delegations. But in actuality, most of them were either North Vietnamese or former cadres from Communist sectors in central Vietnam, such as the B-3 Front (the tri-border area), B-5 Front (Tri Thien area), or the Nam-Tin-Ngai sector (covering the area made up of the three provinces Quang Nam, Quang Tin, and Quang Ngai). These officers were not familiar with many geopolitical characteristics in the South despite the frequent study sessions they held among themselves.

Usually, after each meeting, they would return to their accommodations in Camp Davis where they would hold staff meetings—sort of evaluation sessions to review past activities, to analyze mistakes and achievements, and to prepare themselves for the next negotiating sessions. On the side of the delegation of the Republic of Vietnam, we have approached the first meetings in an atmosphere of confusion. The Saigon delegates, from the chief delegation (General Dzu, for the first month, in Feb. 1973) to his deputy (General Hiep), to the various heads of subcommittees were mostly commanding officers of combat units, or senior officers in other branches of the Army, and as such did not have any experience in dealing with the enemy across the negotiating table. These officers also came to the negotiations utterly unprepared. A case in point was the appointment of General Du Quoc Dong as head of the delegation. General Dong came straight to the negotiating table from being the commanding officer of the Airborne Division, and his only experiences were combat related. As a result, the first meetings in Feb. and March 1973 were conducted in a strangely uneasy atmosphere. The delegates would just deliver their prepared speeches and would simply ignore the questions or proposals presented by the other side. The following is a typical dialogue in a meeting of the subcommittee dealing with the issue of prisoners of war held on Feb. 12, 1973:

Colonel Dac (Republic of Vietnam):

-"We wish to inform you of the number of prisoners of war that we are planning to release tomorrow, Feb. 13. Tomorrow, we are going to transport twenty prisoners from Bien Hoa to the reception area north of the Thach Han River. The prisoners will be flown from Bien Hoa airport to Phu Bai airport and from there they will be transported by trucks to Quang Tri. Also tomorrow we will release six hundred military personnel to your reception area in Loc Ninh. They will be transported by air from Bien Hoa to Loc Ninh."

Colonel Russell (U.S.)

-"We wish to make a protest to the National Liberation Front because the release of American P.O.W.s has not taken place at Loc Ninh at 0800 hours today as agreed. The American delegation will send a protest note to the chief delegate of the National Liberation Front and Chairman of the International Committee. We wish to have the reaction of the National Committee. We also wish to have the reaction of the National Liberation Front on this issue."

Colonel Le Truc (NLF)

-"The lists of prisoners of war to be released will only be given to you prior to the actual release of the prisoners. On the question of the locations for the release of P.O.W.s, we have said that P.O.W.s of the Republic of Vietnam would be released at two locations only, and they are at Pleiku and Loc Ninh. On the question of civilian prisoners, we only have a list of 140 people, not thousands of people as insisted by the delegation of the Republic of Vietnam. As a matter of goodwill, we believe that, in the exchange of P.O.W. lists, prisoners should be released as soon as they are ready and should not be held back until full listings are made. [Note: The issue here is the lists of prisoners to be released. The Republic of Vietnam has a list of 5,081 Communist civilian prisoners that will be released to the Communist side. In return, while the Republic of Vietnam has claimed that the number of civilians held prisoner by the Communists should be in the thousands, the Communist side says that they only have a list of 140 civilians ready to be released. The release of civilian prisoners was held up on that hitch.]"

Colonel Tran Tan (North Vietnam):

-"We wish to comment on the problem of the civilian prisoners in Bien Hoa. One hundred civilian personnel of the Provisional Government refused to board the plan to Phu Bai from Bien Hoa this morning (Feb. 12). This is because of political reasons. These civilian prisoners are strictly personnel of the Provisional Government and should not be returned to us, as stipulated in the Paris Agreement on the problem of military and civilian prisoners of war on all sides in the South. [Note: The North Vietnamese delegate had in mind Art. 2 of the Annex concerning the P.O.W. problem. Basically, in South Vietnam, there are only prisoners of the two sides of South Vietnam.] We regret that the Republic of Vietnam did not send a representative to go to Hanoi this morning to witness the first release of American P.O.W.s in Gia Lam airport."

The four problems presented by the four delegations at the meeting were completely unrelated, but the delegates remained straight-faced and held on to their positions. The delegations also differed greatly from one another. The American delegation was pragmatic, and they had a simple military task. Their responsibilities as specified in the Paris Agreement were also extremely clear: they would receive the P.O.W.s, they would neutralize the mines in Hai Phong, and they would withdraw their troops. Members of the American delegation were professional military men. They viewed the problems in a simple and logical way, and they presented the issues in a clear-cut manner. The delegation of the National Liberation Front, as mentioned, was made up mostly of cadres from North Vietnam or Central Vietnam who did not have a firm grasp of the situation in South Vietnam and, moreover, did not have the authority to make any decisions, even on procedural matters; as a result, they would only read prepared speeches at the negotiating sessions or limit themselves to well-rehearsed statements of positions or principles. Whenever confronted with problems presented by the Republic of Vietnam side or the American side, problems that they felt they could not avoid or reject out of hand, they would declare that they would take note of the ideas or the proposals, that they would give them due consideration, and then they would never respond to them. In this tight negotiating strategy, the North Vietnamese delegates likewise did not have authority to discuss any problems and besides, like the Americans, their responsibilities at the negotiating table were also simple and well defined. Usually, they would just repeat the same ideas that had been expressed by the NLF delegates, albeit in a different order and with somewhat different wording, in support of their protégés.

The delegation of the Republic of Vietnam, to the contrary, found themselves in a position of having to repulse attacks from both sides. They were also saddled with a friend whose pragmatism sometimes bordered on cold insensitivity. The South Vietnamese delegates were also involved in too many responsibilities, confronted with too many problems to be solved, and presented with too many demands to be satisfied while they had to face an uncompromising attitude of the enemy, and subjected to prodding and sometimes even pressures from their allies to work against the restrictive time frame as defined in the Agreement. Since they were also unprepared, they were soon plunged into confusion because of the heavy workload, and the negotiations sometimes would take strange turns as exemplified in the above.

To go back on the NLF's proposition that ARVN (Armed Forces of the Republic of Vietnam) prisoners would only be released at Loc Ninh and Pleiku—the reason the NLF's delegates presented that proposal was because they were completely ignorant about the disposition of the Communist P.O.W. camps. In the tri-border area, ARVN prisoners were kept at three locations. A number of them were held in place and would later be released at Vo Dinh (Kon Tum) and Duc Nghiep (Pleiku). Other ARVN prisoners captured in the same area were moved to North Vietnam. Some of them were to be released from a location on the north bank of Thach Han River while the rest would be moved back to the area of the Communist B-7 Front (comprising the four provinces of Quang Nam, Quang Ngai, Quang Binh, and Phu Yen and under the command of General Chu Huy Man) and would be released from locations in Quang Ngai and Binh Dinh provinces. The reason the NLF's delegate, Colonel Le Truc, insisted that ARVN prisoners would only be released from two points in Duc Nghiep and Loc Ninh was probably because in the beginning the Communists gathered all ARVN prisoners into these two locations. North Vietnam had planned to help build Duc Nghiep (Duc Co, in Pleiku province) into a kind of industrial center, a showpiece for the National Liberation Front, and Loc Ninh evidently had been considered as a capital for the NLF. Afterward, however, the Communists dispersed ARVN prisoners to eleven areas spreading from Quang Tri to Ca Mau in an attempt to use the exchange of prisoners as an indirect way to claim recognition by the International Committee (to supervise the cease-fire) that the NLF did control vast continuous areas all through South Vietnam. Le Truc's insistence was probably due to the fact that he had just come back from the Paris Conference and was still unaware of the latest developments and the plan of the NLF to lay claim to territorial control through the modalities of the exchange of prisoners. Because of their unfamiliarity with the situation, the NLF's delegates would sometimes present strange proposals such as the time when they proposed to receive their P.O.W.s at Hon Quan airbase in An Loc, which is GVN (Government of the Republic of Vietnam) territory. Or, probably they wanted, by creating a precedent, to force upon the Saigon side de facto recognition of safe corridors of communications between areas under their control and those under the control of the Saigon government. That was a tough question that would remain unresolved after more than one year of discussions at the military subcommittees. The negotiations at the Joint Military Commission thus were bound to create numerous headaches. Absurd proposals were presented, such as "the use of Ai Tu airport as a location for prisoners exchange." That proposal was seriously and thoroughly discussed at the Commission until all four sides reached the agreement that an inspection was in order to see if the airbase could accommodate C-130 transport planes. All four sides in the negotiations were completely unaware (or pretended to be ignorant of the fact) that the Ai Tu airbase had been severely damaged and the perforated steel platings on the airstrip torn up by heavy bombs and artillery shells after the withdrawal of the 3rd ARVN Infantry to Quang Tri city in April 1972. The inspection took place anyway in all seriousness and enthusiasm on Feb. 11, 1972.

But despite all the zigzagging and confusion the Commission did achieve real progress after two months of seemingly unending sessions: all P.O.W.s whose lists had been exchanged in Paris were released. And so, despite all the confusion and mistakes over procedural matters and the way in which the negotiating sessions were conducted, and in spite of the inexperience of the military officers in the Commission, a part of the Paris Agreement had been duly carried out.

After March 27, 1973, the 4-Party Joint Military Commission became the 2-Party Commission. On the Saigon side, General Du Quoc Dong was replaced by General Pham Quoc Thuan as head of the delegation. General Thuan was former Commander of the 5th Infantry Division, the elite division in III Corps, the most used division in all of South Vietnam. The 5th Infantry Division had been engaged in fighting in Combat Zone C, Combat Zone D, Secret Zone Ho Bo, and Secret Zone Bo Loi. It also took part in numerous operations into the Iron Triangle and the headquarters of COSVN. The 5th Infantry Division was responsible for an area of operation of the most strategic importance, and General Thuan, as Commander of the Division, had led it into the first conventional battles of the war when Communist guerillas were turning to the offensive in the early 1960s. Although a professional soldier, General Thuan, with his brilliant mind and his sharp political sense, was admittedly a good choice to lead the GVN delegation at the negotiating table.

The appointment of General Thuan came at a time when great changes were expected at the negotiations. But the conference did not move in the direction of peace as outlined in the Peace Agreement. General Tran Van Tra went to Hanoi with the North Vietnamese delegation and did not come back. It was learned later that he made a trip to France to coordinate with the NLF's cadres in Paris and returned to the NLF's secret zones in South Vietnam. There was no explanation for his departure from the Joint Military Commission. There was some speculation that he actually had been relieved because he was deemed soft and not quite in line with the tendency in Hanoi to complete the invasion of South Vietnam by force of arms. But this and others were just hypotheses. People had to wait until the negotiations at the Military Commission reached such impasses, and the discussions became colored with such hostility, to finally see what had really led to the precipitous departure of General Tra.

General Tra was born in 1918 in Quang Nam province and participated in the first days of the Viet Minh movement. Like the provinces of Hghe An, Ha Tinh, and Quang Ngai, Quang Nam is a land of unending turmoil and conflict, where bloody clashes between the various political factions had taken place. The province has spawned the most fanatical Communist cadres, but it was also the training ground for the most fervent nationalist patriots. General Tra, one of the first Communists in the province, had stirred up the local movement of protest against increased tax collection, against recruitment by the colonialists of cheap labor for the plantations. General Tra also led the terrible massacres in Thang Binh and Dai Loc around 1945. After 1945, he was assigned to the South, where he reached the highest position of commander of the Quyet Thang Regiment in the Dong Nai area before being moved to the North after the 1954 Geneva Agreement. In the North, he was promoted to brigadier general and given the command of Division 330, one of the two main force divisions formed from troops evacuated to the North as a result of the Geneva Agreement. The other division, Division 338, went under the command of Dong Van Cong, a Communist senior cadre from Ben Tre in the Mekong Delta.

In 1960, Tran Van Tra returned to South Vietnam under the secret name of Tran Nam Trung and, as Commander of the Eastern sector and concurrently

Political Commissar in the South, he set up his headquarters of COSVN in War Zone D. In June 1969, after the National Liberation Front formed a Provisional Government to take advantage of new political opportunities, General Tra was appointed Minister of Defense. The Communist leadership probably decided that General Tra, with such political and military credentials, could be put to much better use outside the negotiating table, where the communists were planning to create impasses anyway. As a member of the Communist delegation to the Joint Military Commission, even as chief delegate, General Tra, like any other Communist negotiator, would not be able to make any independent decisions or express personal opinions, and his role would be limited to carrying out instructions. However, because of his political and military standing, General Tra, while he was still on the Commission, sometimes would not be so reluctant to have wide-ranging ideas, possibly going beyond the instructions given to his delegation. In response to a question about ARVN prisoners still held in North Vietnam, General Tra said that

-He would try his best to clarify that issue and would keep the Saigon delegation informed of any progress made. . . .

Not much, but that was the most encouraging, the most positive response from the Communist side of Joint Military Commission. Afterward, when the question was raised again, Hoang Anh Tuan (replacement for Tra) or Vo Dong Giang (deputy chief of the NLF's delegation) would only give evasive answers. Basically, their answers were:

-"Those captured in Laos or Cambodia, that is outside of South Vietnam, were under the responsibility of the Pathet Laos or the Khmer Rouge; the National Liberation Front was not aware of ARVN prisoners, if any, being held by the Democratic Republic of Vietnam in North Vietnam."

Between the two answers, the answer from General Tra evidently was the more open and reasonable. That attitude completely disappeared after March 27, 1973. Hence, General Tra, being so conscious of his powers, was probably found to be unfit for the role of a puppet and, therefore, had to be replaced by General Hoang Anh Tuan.

In order to further understand the change in the nature of the conference, it may be necessary to look deeper into the personalities of Tuan and Giang (Giang has remained in his position as deputy chief of the NLF's delegation).

Tuan's real name was Ho Xuan Binh, a native of Hue. In the period after 1945, Tuan was battalion commander in the Tri-Thien area (Quang Tri and Thua Thien provinces). He was captured by the French, released to the Viet Minh and moved to the North after the 1954 Geneva Agreement. In 1960, he was returned to combat in the South with the rank of Colonel. He was appointed to head the NLF's delegation at the Joint Military Commission under the secret name of Hoang Anh Tuan and with the bogus rank of Brigadier General. Tuan had the original, heavy accent and intonation of people from Hue. At the meetings, he had a way of stressing words with guttural sounds as if he was suffocating with repressed anger, but after some time, he appeared to be an uninhibited, even simple-minded man, a man seemingly unable to harbor dark plots and evil intentions. Tuan indeed was far from being an imaginative man: he would tirelessly repeat the same words, the same ideas, the same expressions over and over again, and his pronouncements were an exercise in banality. He also had to rely on written texts repaired in advance, even for very short requests or announcements. Thus, during the meeting on May 10, he read the following from a piece of paper: "The Republic of Vietnam has restricted the privileges and rights granted to the delegation of the National Liberation Front as has been agreed upon. The NLF's delegation requests that these rights and privileges be restored in order to enable the Joint Military Commission to work normally and effectively. Without these rights and privileges, the NLF's delegation would be unable to perform its duties and to cooperate with the delegation of the Republic of Vietnam to carry out the work of the Joint Military Commission." General Tuan was not affected with a speech disability. He just did not have the courage, or the willingness, to express himself freely outside of the written texts. In fact, he did play truthfully his role at a time or during a standstill in the negotiations.

Giang, Tuan's deputy, was actually his opposite. Giang, with the rank of colonel, was also political officer of the delegation and as such assumed the position of spokesman for the delegation ever since the first day of the negotiations. A native of Quang Ngai, Giang was on the staff of General Tra and put in charge of students and youth affairs and relations with the press. Thanks to his varied experiences, Giang came well equipped to the negotiating table and soon proved to be a brilliant tactician on the NLF's delegation. Contrary to Tuan, Giang would often go beyond the main points of the issues, weaving his arguments, mixing the subjects, slowly spilling out his ideas with fluidity and in complete self-confidence. The most admirable thing about him was that he knew how not to cause antagonism and instead had a way of getting the listener involved in what he had to say, in whatever subject he chose to expound on, including his sharp criticisms or even verbal attacks. An exchange during one of the meetings of the Joint Commission could serve as an illustration.

One day, the delegation of the Republic of Vietnam criticized the lack of reaction of the National Liberation Front after China had seized the Spratley Islands off the coast of Vietnam. In response to the charge, Tuan, in an angry voice and toeing the line as usual, said, "The Revolutionary Army, born from the people, engages in fighting for the people and the motherland. It is inadmissible to pose as an issue that the Revolutionary Army could act as an accomplice to an army of invasion as in the case of the Army of the Republic of Vietnam vis-à-vis the French Expeditionary Army before and America now. . . ."

Giang, on the contrary, used a well-calculated evasive action and, ever so sweetly, quipped, with a smile on his lips, "Speaking of the problem of the Spratley Islands, let me tell you a story I happened to glean from a press conference yesterday. So, yesterday, during the press conference, a foreign correspondent asked a question: What do you think when the Republic of Vietnam tries to exaggerate the importance of the affair of the Spratley Islands and to make a big issue of it. . . . Now those expressions, to make a big issue and so forth, came from the correspondent, not from me, and since the problem is again mentioned today I just want to relate word for word that question from the foreign correspondent for you to think about. . . ."

Giang was a specialist in flank attacks that seemed much more effective than the frontal, straightforward way of Tuan.

So Tra left behind those two characters (there was another colonel, Colonel Si, who was second deputy chief of the NLF delegation and since he only had a secondary role, he was not included here). Despite their differences, they still made a good combination and were quite successful in their attempt to deflect the discussion to their advantage and to cause the negotiations to drag on.

From the first meetings of the 2-Party Joint Military Commission (March 23, 1973) until the day he left his post as chief of the Republic of Vietnam delegation, General Thuan only attended the more important meetings, such as the one following the issuance of the Joint Communique of June 13 between Kissinger and Le Duc Tho, and the session held to try to solve the impasse in the exchanges of prisoners held on July 23. For the other meetings, General Hiep or Colonel Doa attended as acting chief of delegation. The reason was because General Thuan far outranked the chief delegate of the other side and because he knew that nothing significant could be achieved at the conference table, the sole purpose of the Communists being to try to prolong the negotiations as much as they could, and as part of this plan they appointed representatives with no authority to solve any problems. The negotiations indeed reached an impasse because of unresolved conflicting views, and during that period the Commission did not achieve any results or reach any agreement even on simple matters of principle or procedure.

The problems that remained unresolved were cease-fire, formation of joint commissions at the regional level, and the setting up of teams at the lower, local level. There were supposed to be seven principal regions: Quang Tri, Danang, Pleiku, Nha Trang, Phan Thiet, Bien Hoa, and Can Tho; within each region there would be several teams—for example, in Bien Hoa, there would be a team operating in An Loc, another team for Vung Tau, etc., totaling thirty teams in all of South Vietnam. The two delegations also did not reach any agreement concerning the problem of the ports of entry, replacement of weapons, and rights and privileges for the Communist delegation. An example was the cease-fire issue. Concerning that problem, the Saigon delegation put forward a seven-point proposal:

- The four sides of the Agreement issue jointly an urgent call for cease-fire;
- 48 hours after the appeal is made public, all units will cease-fire in place;
- Areas of control from the level of platoon will be clearly delineated and neither side is allowed to cross a white line into the other side;
- All units will return to their respective positions prior to January 28, 1973;
- Formation of joint commissions and teams at all levels to supervise the cease-fire on the whole territory in accordance with the Peace Agreement and the Annexes to the Agreement;
- Applications of procedures for investigating cease-fire violations with the cooperation of the International Committee;
- Meetings between commanders in the field.

The National Liberation Front had a four-point counterproposal:

- The two sides in South Vietnam issue a joint cease-fire appeal; the appeal will be announced by the most effective means available to all armed units, paramilitary units, main force units, and regional units of both sides;
- Immediately after the appeal has been communicated to all units, the cease-fire will take effect immediately and all units will remain in place;
- All obstacles, mines will be removed from the roads and rivers and the people on both sides will enjoy freedom of movement, freedom to choose a place of residence, freedom to engage in trades, etc. Field commanders on both sides will meet in the spirit of national reconciliation

and concord to ensure effective maintenance of the cease-fire and to determine their respective areas of control;

- Formation of Joint Commissions at the regional level and Teams, etc. . . .

At first glance, the two proposals seem quite similar, although one contained seven points and the other only four. In reality, while the two proposals had the same objective, which was the cease-fire, they reflected two completely contradictory points of views. The position of the Republic of Vietnam was that the cease-fire appeal should be made by all four sides in the Paris Agreement to be effective and to reflect the reality of North Vietnamese participation in the war in South Vietnam. The appeal, in the view of the Saigon side, was only the first step toward an actual cease-fire, which could only be effected after all the Commissions and Teams had been set up to supervise the cease-fire. The NLF had a different view: According to them, there was only need for two sides in South Vietnam to issue the appeal and the cease-fire could be effected immediately after the order for the cease-fire had reached all units.

On the problem of meetings between field commanders, the Saigon side specified that field commanders would have to be divisional commanders because only divisional commanders could have enough authority and means at hand to order subordinate units to cease-fire. Divisional commanders could also work with province chiefs on the problem of territorial delineation for troops stationing. The NLF however proposed that meetings could be held between field commanders at all levels down to foot soldiers. The following dialogue between General Hiep (Republic of Vietnam) and General Tuan (NLF) would serve to illustrate the conflicting points of view.

General Hiep:

-"It is our view that divisional commanders would have enough authority to effect maneuvers in the field as well as to ensure coordination with other branches of the armed forces such as the Artillery, the Air Force, Logistics, etc. . . . Therefore, only field commanders at that level can be authorized to meet with field commanders at an equivalent level of your side to effect the cease-fire. According to your opinion, meetings of both sides in the field could be between division commanders as well as between commanders at the unit level. We wish you could explain to us what you mean by 'unit level'?"

General Tuan (NLF):

-"By 'unit level,' we mean the divisional level, the regimental level, the battalion level, the company level, the platoon level."

General Hiep:

-"Does that mean that there is no more unit level under the level of platoon? We want to make sure that the 'unit level' in your understanding stops at the level of platoon and that term does not apply to the level of the squad or the detachment or team. In other words, the platoon level will be the lowest level where the cease-fire order can be issued to the subordinates. . . . Do you agree with that understanding?"

General Tuan:

-"The term 'unit level' could be more broadly defined. In our statement we stopped at the platoon level but actually there is also squad level and team level."

General Hiep:

-"I suppose the team level is the lowest level?"

General Tuan:

-"No. By 'unit level' we mean down to the individual foot soldier, because the soldier is also a unit that can take orders and carry out orders."

General Hiep:

-"Are there other meanings to the term?"

General Tuan:

-"In our exposé, we have mentioned only the military levels. However, on the political side, there is also the provincial level, the district level, the village level, the hamlet level. . . ."

The above excerpt was enough to illustrate how two proposals toward the same objective and containing almost the same wording could be so conflicting. The order of the steps to be taken in the two proposals could also lead to serious disagreements. On the Saigon side, a meeting between two sides at the divisional level could take place in three steps:

1. The Joint Military Commission will pick a test location. The Commission will also pick the time for both sides to jointly order a cease-fire in place in their respective areas of responsibility;
2. The Joint Military Commission will immediately dispatch a Team to the test site. Team members will be officers at the rank of colonel, and they will serve both as intermediary and witness at the meeting between the divisional commanders;
3. The two divisional commanders from both sides will hold subsequent meetings to discuss the modalities and other details of the cease-fire as well as the maintenance of the cease-fire in their respective areas of responsibility. . . .

This plan would be applicable only after all the Teams and Regional Commissions had been in place. At the same time, the International Committee for Supervising the Cease-Fire should have deployed four members representing four nations at the various locations that had been determined in accordance with the Appendix to the Agreement. And meetings between field commanders of both sides should be limited to the divisional level because only divisional commanders could have enough authority and means to order a cease-fire to all units under their command with proper coordination and effective maintenance.

The National Liberation Front, on the other hand, viewed the meetings in a different way and according to a different process: After the cease-fire order has been made public, both sides in South Vietnam will refrain from all hostile actions, will remain in place, will dismantle all defensive systems, clear all the mines and booby traps, and elements from both sides will meet first at the lowest level, gradually going up to the higher level to ensure a total and long-lasting cease-fire. . . . The wording was the same and the phrases were the same, but the two proposals were totally contradictory. The Saigon side requested several clarifications from the NLF:

- Suppose there is a meeting between a private first class in the Republic of Vietnam Army and a local guerilla of the NLF—What is the purpose of their meeting? What can they resolve among themselves and how can they carry out the cease-fire?
- Who is going to play the role of the arbiter to all the confusing meetings taking place everywhere in the country, without proper preparation, without a schedule and program, and especially without supervision by representatives of the Joint Commission and the International Committee? That is the reason why the Saigon side has proposed urgent formation of the various Teams and Commissions at the regional level (Item 7 of the proposal).

Response from the National Liberation Front:

- As a unit level, each soldier, each individual cadre has a particular set of tasks and responsibilities. They are the opposing sides on the battlefields and therefore they have to meet first to further mutual understanding and to discuss the spirit of the Agreement so that they could really cease fire. Similar meetings will be held upward to the higher level.

- The NLF delegation also requests that the Saigon side respect all rights and privileges according to the delegation of the NLF (freedom of movement, freedom of assembly, freedom to hold press conferences, freedom to raise their flags, etc.) so that its members could perform their duties. The NLF also affirms that the formation of teams should proceed on a ratio of 2 to 5, that is, two teams in Republic of Vietnam areas versus five teams in disputed areas. . . .

In fact, when they presented their respective proposals, the two sides never entertained any hope that their own proposal would be accepted by the other side knowing how far apart their positions were. How could the NLF accept meetings at the divisional level when all of the North Vietnamese divisions were stationed on the border areas and three main force divisions of the NLF, the 5th, the 7th, and the 9th, were only capable of holding on to some scant territory in the three provinces of Tay Ninh, Phuoc Long, and Binh Long, also along the border? To meet at the divisional level only would mean the abandonment of all their guerilla forces, their underground network, and the areas that the NLF had managed to infiltrate into during the 1972 Offensive. Likewise they could not accept the idea of supervision of the meetings by members of the Joint Commissions because in that case they would not be able to claim the existence of a border zone between the GVN areas and the Communist-controlled areas—and that was an important point that went into all the Communist calculations.

On the other hand, the Saigon side couldn't accept the idea of multilevel meetings before the formation of all the Teams and the Regional Commissions. Such meetings would create a most confusing and dangerous situation where Communist guerillas, political cadres, and soldiers would emerge everywhere, mingling with the people, stirring up disturbances, and possibly moving on to take over the local administrations, all based on the spirit of national reconciliation and concord.

The Saigon side naturally had to stick fast to their position concerning the prior formation of the Regional Commissions and the Teams since these could act as a kind of security force—their missions being to control and to supervise—against all violations of the cease-fire.

The NLF insisted that the rights and privileges be granted to them so that "their delegations can plant their flags on their cars to move from their areas to the Saigon government areas and to be able to work in the zones in between." Even this would help give supporting evidence—before the International Commission, before the people, and before the world—that there were in actuality two separate zones under the control of two separate armies and two separate governments. That was a strategic point that the NLF had been struggling to achieve, by hook or by crook. That was on the mind of every one of them from the General at the negotiating table to the Communist soldier standing guard at Loc Ninh—every word they uttered, every reasoning they resorted to, every effort they spent had been aimed at that one objective: to win recognition that there were two zones of control, two armies, and two governments in South Vietnam. The visit of Fidel Castro to Nguyen Huu Tho, chairman of the Provisional Government of the Republic of South Vietnam, and the presentation of credentials by the Algerian and the Eastern European Ambassadors were staged with the sole purpose of proving the existence of the Government of the National Liberation Front.

Naturally, the Saigon side had to reject that reality. The argument presented by the Saigon side, whether at the chief delegates meetings or at the sub-committee meetings, was that a government should have certain attributes such as a well-defined territory, population, international recognition, a system of currency, etc. The Saigon delegates pointed out that NLF's government only controlled about 3 percent of the total population in South Vietnam, in remote areas along the border, that the people in their zones also used the Saigon piaster as a means of exchange, that they were only recognized by a few counties, including some non-aligned countries, and therefore there was no separate government of state in South Vietnam beside the Republic of Vietnam. Moreover, all through the Paris Agreement, the National Liberation Front was only designated as an opposing side, and there was no specific mention of such a government in the text of the Agreement. In short, by argument based on reality, by referring to the text of the Paris Agreement, the only legal document in international law where the role of the NLF was mentioned, the South Vietnamese delegates had repeatedly pointed out the "reality" of this so-called Government.

The conflicting points of view led inevitably to an impasse. From March 28, 1973, the first day of the second phase when the 4-Party Joint Military Commission was reduced to the 2-Party Joint Military Commission, to June 13, 1973, when the Kissinger-Tho joint communique was issued in a last-ditch attempt to get the negotiations out of the impasse, the Commission did not come to any significant agreement. On Oct. 15, the leadership of the NLF issued an order to all their armed units to counterattack and the directive was "to attack to achieve substantive results without creating any noises." The order of Oct. 15 was issued in execution of the COSVN Resolution No. 12R, which was actually North Vietnam's Central Committee Resolution No. 21 re-codenamed for camouflage purposed.

After the counterattack order of the COSVN was issued on Oct. 15, the military situation became extremely serious. On Oct. 20, a Regiment of the Communist 320 Division launched a concentrated attack forcing the Rangers to abandon the Le Minh base camp southwest of Pleiku. On Nov. 4, the battle at Quang Duc broke out and the fighting, at divisional level, went on for half a month. These were the most significant battles since Jan. 28, 1973, and they were carried out in accordance with the policy of "attacking to get results, not to create publicity." Resolution 12R, which was the same as Resolution 21, directed all units in the South to go on the counter-attack, combining the three points (armed attacks, political attacks, and propaganda attacks with GVN troops), maintaining the initiative on all three fronts [military front, political front, and diplomatic front], and making advances in all three areas [areas under the control of the NLF, areas under the control of the Saigon government, and disputed areas]. The instructions were widely distributed down to each soldier and each village and hamlet cadre to study, to clarify, and to execute.

While the military situation warmed up and ceasefire violations increased both in frequency and in scale, at the negotiating table, the NLF applied a new tactic, dubbed the tactic of "chewing rubber band and spitting phlegm" by Colonel Doa, deputy chief delegate of the delegation of the Republic of Vietnam. Hoang Anh Tuan and Vo Dong Giang launched into a series of attacks against the Saigon government on the two issues of cease-fire violations and exchanges of prisoners. The main document used by the NLF delegation to denounce the Saigon government was the transcripts of the Liberation Radio news broadcasts. These broadcasts naturally contained only exaggerations and slanderous charges against the ARVN from I Corps to IV Corps. A typical denunciation at the negotiating table would run as follows:

- The Saigon government has been engaging in land-grabbing and land sweeping operations for the purpose of gathering the people into concentration camps, and plundering the rice and the money of the people. Units of the 3rd Infantry Division have indiscriminately carried out these operations in hamlets west and southwest of Dai Loc, in Duy Xuyen, and in Que Son in Quang Nam and Quang Tin provinces. The 2nd Infantry Division has mounted attacks and shelling attacks against the liberated areas in Son Tinh, Mo Duc, and Duc Pho in Quang Ngai province. The 1st Battalion of the 4th Regiment of the same division, reinforced by Battalion 102 of the Regional Forces, and supported by an armored unit,

> launched an operation with an attempt to completely destroy the two hamlets Pho Phong and Pho Duc of the district of Duc Pho.

The NLF chief delegate paid particular attention to this area, often giving elaborate details in his charges, because he knew that General Hiep was former commander of the 2nd Division, and the former armored commander stationed in the Quang Ngai and Quang Tin areas for a long time. General Hiep had also been commander of the Quang-Da Special Sector (Quang Nam and Da Nang) and hence was quite familiar with the terrain and with each unit in that area. At one of those sessions, Gen. Tuan, while launching into a long denunciation of cease-fire violations by the Saigon government, mentioned a hamlet in Hoa Vang district close to Da Nang (Quang Nam province) and he alleged that the Saigon government had used a significant number of troops in a ground and shelling attack into the hamlet with the purpose of destroying it and forcing the local population into concentration camps. The reaction of General Hiep was immediate:

-"The whole of the district of Hoa Vang, in Quang Nam province, lies close to the city of Da Nang, as close as the districts of Go Vap and Tan Binh are to Saigon. No hamlet in that district has ever fallen into the control of the NLF. The sole activities of the NLF in that area have been limited to some occasional terrorist attacks, to the distribution of anti-government leaflets and planting of NLF flags. There have never been any armed unit of NLF operating in the area that would require the GVN to launch a battalion-size operation in that area. Moreover, most of the population in Hoa Vang district are members or followers of the Dai Viet Party which has been in bloody coNLFict with the Communist side for the last several years. I would advise you to pick another area to engage in your slanderous charges."

The NLF delegation subsequently chose to stay away from that area (provinces of Quang Nam, Quang Ngai, and Quang Tin).

The NLF delegation shifted their attention to the Highlands. Any time there was an attack by Communist troops and a reaction by the government forces the NLF delegation would call it a cease-fire violation by the Saigon government. When government troops moved up to try to recapture Le Minh and Plei M'rong base camps, the NLF delegate would point to that as a serious cease-fire violation by the Saigon government. They charged that the Saigon government had mobilized up to three or four Ranger Brigades and up to two or three infantry Regiments supported by aircraft, artillery, and armored units to attack and destroy areas that have long been under the control of the National Liberation Front. They had similar denunciations in the case of the Duc Lap and Dak Song base camps in Quang Duc province. Concerning the III Corps the NLF delegate said, "The revolutionary armed forces are determined to counter-attack to defend liberated areas north-east of Trang Bang (Hau Nghia province) and to consolidate areas under Front control by removing the roadblocks that the Saigon government has illegally set up north of Route 13." This charge was used to cover up the land-grabbing operations of the NLF northeast of Trang Bang and north of An Loc, where the roadblocks have been set up by the Communists themselves. Similar charges were made in Long An, Dinh Tuong, and other areas in the Mekong Delta down to the Seven-Mountain area in Chau Doc province.

Along with charges of cease-fire violations, the NLF chief delegate also made slanderous denunciations of corruption, rapes, and plundering by the Saigon government. The Communists always tried to make their trumped-up charges sound more convincing by including seemingly concrete details, accompanied by further elaboration, and by repeating the charges again and again. For example, in making a charge of cease-fire violation by the Saigon government at a certain specifically named area, the NLF delegate would add some vivid and elaborate details. They would say, for example, that the second company of such-and-such battalion had stolen fifty chickens from a Mr. Le Van Sau at hamlet No. 1, village of Pho Phong, etc. After a while, in order to make the story new and enticing, the NLF delegate would add more gory details to their charges, such as murder, rape, etc. These were perhaps attempts by the Communists to up the ante in the face of the denunciations from the Saigon side.

The Republic of Vietnam delegation often based their charges of Communist violations on the daily reports of Communist terrorist activities released by the National Police Command every morning at 0700. These reports, compiled from local police reports from all over the country, gave full details of every incident, complete with time, locations, the nature of the incidents, the number, and even the names of the victims.

The more systematic and important terrorist acts of the Communists often were targeted at a certain region or group of people and would sometimes point to a certain trend or intention of the Communists. For example, on March 9, 1974, nearly a hundred children were killed and wounded by an 82mm mortar shell in Cai Lay district. That was an inconceivable crime, causing great consternation in the nation and in the whole world, but perhaps, to the specialists, it was something that should have been expected. In any case, it was a "great achievement" of the National Liberation Front. Following is a list of Communist terrorist activities committed since the release of the Joint Communique of June 13, 1973, between the two Nobel Peace Prize winners.

On June 20, 1973, to celebrate the anniversary of the signing of the Geneva Agreement, the Communists fired twenty 82mm mortars into a populated area southeast of the Cai Lay market, killing and injuring five people.

On July 27, 1973, the Communists fired one 107mm artillery shell into Bung hamlet, south of Cai Lay district, killing one child and injuring four adults.

On Sept. 17, 1973, a bridge 3 km north of the district town was damaged to 70 percent by the explosion of a mine.

On Sept. 18, 1973, Communist terrorists fired two B-40 rockets into a truck, killing two lumbermen on the spot.

On Oct. 8, 1973, two rockets exploded just outside the perimeter of the district headquarters, killing one civilian and injuring three others.

On Nov. 18, 1973, Communist guerillas fired three 60mm mortars into Nhi Quy city, killing six civilians.

On Feb. 5, 1974, five 61mm mortar shells landed on the village of My Thanh.

On Feb. 6, 1974, a tri-lambretta light truck moving on provincial road No. 29 between Cai Lay and Kien Tuong received sniper fire; three passengers were killed.

On Feb. 9, 1974, a B-40 rocket was fired into a private house in the village of My Thank Trung, injuring three children.

On Feb. 27, 1974, a plastic charge was hurled into a private house, wounding two people.

On March 4, 1974, an M-79 grenade was fired into a crowd about 7 km southeast of Cai Lay district, injuring two people.

On March 9, 1974, a 60mm mortar was fired into a populated area about 3 km north of Cai Lay, injuring five people. . . . On the same day an 82mm mortar shell hit a public school in Cai Lay. Another one was fired into the Bung hamlet, but this one only achieved a "moderate" result with one civilian injured.

The violations were noted and compiled into a white paper on the crimes of the Communists. The Saigon side built the charges on this concrete evidence. Since the NLF could not reject out of hand all of these accusations, they adopted a new tactic by upping the ante. In response to a charge that the Communists had abducted a hamlet chief, for example, the Communist side would invent a story of premeditated murder, rape, or even wholesale massacre committed by the Republic of Vietnam Army. Probably because they did not have communications with their local units and did not receive accurate reports on illegal acts (if any) committed by soldiers of the South Vietnamese Army, the Communist delegates would often assign these crimes to ARVN units engaged in operations that they knew were ongoing. In this connection it must be noted that the Communist delegation did receive reports on military operations from their cadres in the field, and was kept well-informed of these operations, down to the company level. But sometimes the stories invented by the NLF delegation proved awkward and unconvincing because they lacked credibility, due to their need to have newer and ever more horrible stories. General Tuan and Colonel Giang of the NLF would not hesitate to deal low blows whenever they could. They would say:

-"As true revolutionaries, we are always ready to accept sacrifices and miseries in our struggle for independence and freedom for the country and people. Conversely, going against the aspirations of the people, and killing the people, is the true nature of your army. We are here not to bring judgment on that true nature, but since you brought up the subject, we had to point out these criminal acts—the plundering, the rape, and the immolation of innocent people committed as a joke among yourselves. Your officers and men are continuing to commit on the Vietnamese people the acts that the French invaders have committed here thirty years ago. This is after all not surprising because you are simply the products of the French Expeditionary Corps and the mercenaries of the American neo-colonialism!"

The chief delegate of the NLF made frequent use of this malicious diatribe because General Hiep looked very "Frenchie," with his luxurious beard, his straight nose, his deep-set eyes—at first look, he really appeared to be a Frenchman speaking Vietnamese! But that was not true, because General Hiep was 100 percent Vietnamese. As a matter of fact, his "French" appearance did cause a lot of trouble for his military career. Under the Diem government, the Diem brothers felt they could not trust his "French" appearance and so let him be locked at the rank of captain for almost ten years. The NLF delegates would poke fun at his "French" appearance once in a while, probably because they were mistaken about him as well. General Hiep would not pay attention to these malicious attacks, but Colonel Doa, a fast-talking Vietnamese of Northern origin, would not take any quibbling without lashing back in kind. He would challenge:

-"If you want to criticize, we will have a lot of criticism reserved for you. If you want to waste time in lengthy diatribes, rest assured that we have a lot more to say. As a matter of fact, we can talk for days if necessary, and you can bring out a couch here and lie down and listen to us. We are surprised that you keep bringing up stories of rapes at this negotiating table. Our troops after each operation can return to their families right away in their quarters in the base camps. This arrangement in our army is not conducive to any wayward acts by the troops. On the other hand, we know that rapes are committed on your side, but they are camouflaged under such phrases as 'support for the troops,' or 'participation to the revolution,' or 'gratefulness to the troops,' etc. . . .

"We know that women in Tam Quan and Hoai An districts (Binh Dinh province) have been forced to have sexual relations with your troops when these areas temporarily fell under your control during your offensive in the summer of 1972. But of course you camouflaged these acts under the designation 'acts to prove gratefulness toward the troops!' General Vo Nguyen Giap took as his wife Mr. Dang Thai Mai's daughter, who used to call him uncle. We know that back in 1945 a celebrated beauty in the Mekong Delta, Miss Thoa, was forced into a marriage with Le Duan, under pressure from the Party. We know that Nguyen Khanh Toan, the comrade and close confidant of Ho Chi Minh, had the help of the Party in his third marriage to a seventeen-year-old girl when he was already seventy years old. Those are some of the facts reflecting the true policy of the Party in accordance with the new morality in which gang rape is called the 'cultivation of a new generation!'"

Seeing that their denunciations of crimes and violations by the Saigon government had provoked devastating counter-attacks, the NLF delegation probably concluded that they had all been counterproductive but pending other instructions from their headquarters in Loc Ninh, they would not give up stories of rape and murder. However, they turned to the tactic of using clippings from the Saigon press as supporting evidence for their allegations. Naturally the Saigon press (with the exception of the blatantly pro-Communist newspaper *Dien Tin*) never could suspect that the NLF would make use of reports published in their own papers in their attacks against the Republic of Vietnam government. The NLF delegation would declare:

-"The Saigon press, although constantly threatened and gagged by the authorities could not remain silent before the crimes that your troops have been ordered to commit against the people!"

Next in the order of priority, the NLF exploited to the full press reports of cases of corruption and abuses of power by government officials. In making these denunciations, the point that they wanted to make was that all those alleged crimes were just the natural products of a corrupt society, an inhuman policy maintained by the Saigon government, an instrument of American neo-colonialism. These alleged crimes were committed, the NLF said, because the Saigon government always wanted to expand their areas of control, to deny the reality of two governments, two armies, two areas of control . . . in other words, the Saigon government had not acted in accordance with the spirit and the words of the Paris Agreement and the spirit of national reconciliation and concord! So, a drunken militia man, a committing a bad action in the night, had acted in collusion with a corrupt hamlet chief to sabotage the Peace Agreement, ruining the peace that the National Liberation Front has painstakingly brought about after defeating half a million Americans, and the Korean and Thai mercenaries, etc. The Communist delegates have managed to weave all the disparate bits and pieces into a real fairy tale!

The NLF's campaign of "reading the Saigon Press" was counterattacked by Colonal Doa:

-"You people come here to negotiate or to pass the time reading newspapers? If you want to negotiate, you have to discuss the issues raised in the Paris Agreement to find ways to carry out the cease-fire and to really restore peace and not to pull out a pile of newspapers. Actually, you have not read all the papers, you have misread and misquoted them. Did you read the story about the Chinese invasion of the Spratley Islands? Did you read the story about your guerilla throwing grenades into Ba Xuyen? Did you see the BBC broadcast reproduced in the Saigon papers about the massacre of children in a school in Cai Lay? Those were really crimes against the people."

The riposte of General Hiep came from a different direction:

-"All the bad deeds published in the Saigon press were committed by a few individuals, and if they are found to be guilty, they will be punished by the law. These bad deeds came to light because our press is a free press, they can publish both the good and the bad things in society, unlike the press in Communist paradise where only the good things are allowed to be reported. Can your press write anything on their own, or rather is everything that is published in your press done according to the order and instructions from the Party?"

The military solution became more and more tense by the day. After Le Minh, Duc Lap, and Chi Linh, came the turn of Duc Hue, Tong Le Chan, Kon Tum, Hau Nghia, and Dinh Tuong. As the Communists pressed on with their land-grabbing operations and the crackling of the rifle fire went to a crescendo in the field, back at the negotiating table, Communist delegates also spent more and more time reading the papers and the discussions intended to work out the case-fire were consumed in mutual recriminations and lengthy denunciations of murder, plunder, rape, corruption, abuse of power, etc. The NLF had a logical explanation for the alleged misdeeds of the Saigon government:

- These bad deeds reflect the slavish policy of the Republic of Vietnam, a policy that will surely lead it to an impasse. That is what the Americans want. They want the Saigon government to be dependent on the United States, they want them to be just an instrument for their neo-colonialism policy.

With the "neo-colonialism" argument as a point of reference, the NLF delegates aimed all denunciations, all slanderous charges toward the one conclusion: that the Saigon government has to recognize the reality of two zones of control, two armies, two governments, and the reality of the Provisional Government of the Republic of South Vietnam.

The year 1973 had come to an end. The Lunar New Year was coming. Then it would be the first anniversary of the signing of the Paris Agreement. The Republic of Vietnam had created favorable conditions to get the negotiations out of the impasse through the exchanges of prisoners of war. Both sides had achieved some progress in that direction. . . . There was hope that the changes would soon be completed so that civilian prisoners from both sides could reunite with their families during Tet. Although both sides agreed on the principle of this humanitarian issue, the two positions remained poles apart when it came to discussing the details of the problem. The Republic of Vietnam side wanted to solve the problem of prisoners exchange in a general way, by solving the question of the release of ARVN prisoners captured in Cambodia and Laos, as well as those captured in the years prior to 1972 (95 percent of the ARVN prisoners that had been released were prisoners captured by the Communists during the 1972 Offensive.) On the side of the National Liberation Front, the problem was conceived differently: The prisoner issue was only the remainder of the P.O.W. exchange plan that had been agreed upon on July 23, 1973. In other words, the Saigon government would have to release the rest of the 5,081 Communist civilian prisoners and 410 P.O.W.s at Duc Nghiep.

The plan of July 1973 gave the Communists several advantages because if the rest of the 5,081 civilian prisoners were returned to them the National Liberation Front would have the needed manpower to build up their infrastructure that had been overwhelmed by the North Vietnamese influence. If the exchanges could get underway, prisoner exchange locations would gain de facto recognition as zones under their control. In addition to locations north of the Thach Han River, in Loc Ninh, and in Quang Ngai that had been used before, others had been added in Dai Loc (Quang Nam province), Ky Que (Quang Tin), Vo Dinh (Kontum), Due Nghiep (Pleiku), and location in the foothills in Khanh Hoa province, one location north of Xuyen Moc (Phuoc Tuy), U Minh (Kien Giang), and Nam Can (An Xuyen).

Of the 637 civilian prisoners held by the NLF, 195 had been released to the Saigon government north of Thach Han River in May 1973. For the remaining 442, the NLF wanted to release them from 11 different locations all over South Vietnam to prove that their presence and their zones of control are widespread all over the country. That intention was clearly recognizable when the Communist designated the two locations at Vo Dinh (Kon Tum) and Duc Nghiep (Pleiku) that are so close that there could be no other justification, especially when it was learned that only eight civilian prisoners would be released from Vo Dinh. At the end, however, both sides still could not reach agreement on the exchanges of prisoners. By that time Tet for the year of the Tiger had passed.

After Tet, in the beginning of Feb. 1974, the prisoners exchange issue was brought up again. There was renewed hope, inside the country as well as in the world at large, that both sides would reach agreement on the exchange of prisoners, and that would lead to other results such as the formation of the Council for National Reconciliation, an effective cease-fire, the delineation of zones of control, and finally general elections. The country was rife with speculation and rumors about the effective execution of the terms of the Paris Agreement and other urgent tasks for peace. But all these turned out to be just wishful thinking. The exchange of prisoners had ended miserably. . . .

Of the 410 ARVN P.O.W.s to be released from Duc Nghiep, 31 were missing. The NLF explained that 15 had died of sickness contracted before their capture and that 16 had taken advantage of the "leniency" of the guards to flee. The same situation happened at other locations. In Quang Ngai, 70 prisoners were released instead of 71, in Khanh Hoa 5 instead of 6, in Vo Dinh, 2 were missing in a list of 8. The total number of prisoners unaccounted for amounted to about 12 percent of the number that had been listed for release. Most seriously, Communist troops at roadblocks on Route 13 from Chon Thanh to Loc Ninh (the recognized air corridor for the transport of prisoners between Saigon and Loc Ninh) were ordered to fire on VNAF helicopters on the returns that took place on Feb. 26 and March 7, the same day the Republic of Vietnam unilaterally released 76 military personnel to the Communists. The second firing caused the death of a crew member of the Chinook CH-47. Although the Saigon side kept to the schedule, a VNAF aircraft was fired upon for the second time on the same day, at about 1550 hours. In justification of this inhuman and absurd act, General Tuan laid the countercharge that VNAF aircraft had strayed out of the accepted corridor and had violated procedures that had been agreed upon for the release of prisoners. The NLF delegate also denied any firing despite the bullet hole in the aircraft and the body of the air force sergeant. Tuan said:

-"In reference to your protest note of July 8, you have invented the story of a Chinook helicopter being fired on during a prisoner exchange mission in an attempt to cover up the numerous cease-fire violations that you have committed in the past. We have many times condemned your abuse of the corridors, your abuse of the name of the Joint Commission to fly your aircraft in reconnaissance missions, in bombing and strafing missions against areas under the control of the Revolutionary government. In the recent prisoners release, in complete disregard of our repeated recommendations, you have flown a number of aircraft close to the aircraft of the International Committee to effect a bombing mission west of Route 13 on Feb. 14. On Feb. 19, taking advantage of a mission to Loc Ninh, your aircraft has also engaged in reconnaissance, and has committed provocative acts over our roadblocks. Our liaison officer on the plane witnessed the fact and has lodged a warning. On Feb. 22, during a prisoners release mission from Vo Dinh, you have also used your planes to attack an area west of Route 14. On Feb. 28, you have flown fighter planes alongside the aircraft transporting members of the International Committee on a mission to supervise the release of prisoners at Loc Ninh and these planes engaged in provocative acts against our ground forces. This has been witnessed by the Ambassador of Iran."

Tuan concluded:

-"Even if one of your planes has been shot down—not just warning shots—that firing would still be an appropriate reaction against your covert violations. You certainly have no ground for protest."

Tuan had used a classic Communist tactic, never admitting their crimes. During 1973, thousands of helicopter mission had been carried out along Route 13. Every time they passed over the Communist roadblocks on Route 13 they would see Communist troops on the ground wave their hands in greetings and the helicopter crews had become thoroughly familiar with that image. That was also observed by members of the Joint Military Commission and of the International Committee. On the prisoners transport mission of Feb. 8 and other subsequent missions, the crews also used the same corridor and the same altitude of about 50 m alongside Route 13. Why the new order to Communist troops to fire on the aircraft on Feb. 26 and March 7?

The charge by General Tuan that an L-19 had violated the airspace of Duc Nghiep (Pleiku) was even more absurd. The same charge was repeated to me by an NLF Major at the prisoners release at Duc Nghiep on March 5.

On March 10, at the Joint Military Commission, Colonel Doa had a stronger protest:

-"We are sure that the men who hold the rifles on the ground would not commit that brutal act for no reason, even if there were provocations. We are also sure that they did not fire on our helicopter because they just felt like doing it. They've got to have received prior instructions. They've got to have been instructed in advance not to fire on the aircraft on the outgoing trip from Bien Hoa, but to fire only on its return trip. All the violations until now have been committed on helicopters returned from Loc Ninh. We want to stress that point."

-"Who are the enemies during these days and these months, here in the South, in the cabin of the aircraft on a mission to release prisoners?"

That the exchanges of prisoners had ended in blood and death had destroyed all hopes that the two sides could move on to solve other problems toward building a foundation for peace. That painful ending was still very much on the mind of the people, distressed to see that the road to peace had reached an impasse, when on March 9, 1974, Communist cadres fired an 82mm mortar round into the Cai Lay Public School, killing forty-three children and wounding seventy others in their terror and pressure campaign in Cai Lay district in preparation for Communist infiltration into Dinh Tuong province and subsequent attacks in May 1974. The crime exploded like thunder in a day without rain. Its effect was like a giant wave from the bottom of the ocean washing out the whole city within the wink of an eye. The sight of forty-three small bodies and of the seventy other children writhing in pools of blood shocked the whole world. That was a crime that went beyond the limit of imagination. It took place on March 9, but not until March 15 did the NLF delegation say that they could not conceive of such horrible "achievement" by their armed cadres. But because of the low level of artillery training of the guerillas, and because the launching tubes for their 107mm and 122mm rockets were improvised from bamboo trunks, most of their rockets, as well as their 60mm and 82mm mortar rounds fell outside the populated areas. And that explained the shock of the NLF delegates when they received the news that the shelling of March 9 had caused the horrendous result of forty-three children dead and seventy injured. The NLF delegates remained silent until March 15, when they made a solemn denunciation:

-"The Saigon government has been engaging in a campaign of slander. They warned that the 'the Communists are planning a dry season offensive.' They have made up stories about our troops blowing up mines against civilian buses and firing into crowds. But since their campaign has failed to shock the public opinion, they have invented the story of 'Communist shelling into a public school in Cai Lay.' This is to cover up a large military operation being mounted by the Saigon government in which 17 battalions of the 10th and the 11th Regiment have been used in an attempt to encroach upon the areas under our control north east of Route 4, north of Cai Lay district. Their field operation headquarters has been maneuvering field forces in attacking and destroying villages and hamlets, and in mounting indiscriminate shelling in populated areas."

The argument was totally illogical. The 10th and 11th Regiments of the 7th Infantry Division had always had the area under secure government control for more than ten years. The 82mm mortar shell that landed on the Cai Lay school was Chinese made. ARVN troops only had 60mm and 81mm mortars in the arsenal while Communist troops used mortars larger by 1mm (Chinese made 61mm and 82mm mortars) so that they could also accommodate 60mm and 81mm rounds in their tubes. This argument of the NLF would sound completely absurd to those who had some knowledge on the disposition of troops in the area and the use of firepower of both sides. But General Tuan continued:

-"The shelling of the school in Cai Lay was only an attempt to cover up the many violations that the Saigon side has committed. We will conduct a thorough investigation to find out the true cause of the incident. The Revolutionary Army was not born yesterday or today. It has been in existence for thirty years. It was born from the people to fight for the people. Your attempt to invent this and that crime in order to denounce and to slander us will prove to be in vain."

With this argument, therefore, Tuan has acknowledged that the massacre at Cai Lay did indeed take place, but he accused the Saigon government as being the perpetrator of the massacre. Tuan intoned:

-"Do not believe for a moment that your shedding of crocodile tears over killing and wounding of children in Cai Lay could help you prove your humanity, your love for children, for the people, for the country. Do not believe for a moment that you could instantly transform yourself from a crow into a peacock through sheer imagination. If this incident did really grieve you, then why didn't you hold an emergency meeting right after it happened, why did you wait until today to bring it out for official discussions at this table. Do not deceive yourself into believing that you could use the blood and bones of the children to turn truth into falsehood. It is clear from the true natures of the two armies who was the perpetrator of the crime. The revolutionary armed forces, born out from slavery, from oppression, have taken up arms to fight against one imperialist aggressor after another. We are the vanguards of the general struggle for independence, for freedom, and for the happiness of the people. You said that we committed the shelling into the Cai Lay Public School. Then how do you explain the fact that a foreign correspondent was prevented from coming into the area to film the scene of the crime even though he had received authorization from the General head of your Political Warfare Department? Was it because you are afraid that the correspondent would discover the evidence that would incriminate you? The order to prevent that correspondent from coming in to gather evidence was issued by General Nghi, the tyrant of the IV Corps Command."

That was supremely unconscionable. That National Liberation Front had waved aside, without the least embarrassment and without flinching, such a toweringly horrendous crime! They did not only deny the story, they even turned over the responsibility to the Saigon government with cold and blatantly inhuman expertise!

After all, this strange behavior could be traceable to the capacity for flexibility of the Communist man who can coldly accommodate himself into any situation without letting shock and anger overtake them—such as we often would. We were not sure whether the order to close off the area came from General Nghi or from the Dinh Tuong province chief, but evidently that order had opened an excellent route of escape for the criminal—it had provided a bridge for the murderer to flee. That absurd order had laid a shroud over the mangled bodies of innocent young victims. The observers, the public opinion in the country as well as in the world at large, after the first shock, had been overwhelmed by a scene of depression and had let the criminal get away so easily under cover of the smokescreen that we ourselves had created. Was it possible that the Dinh Tuong province chief had wanted to cover up the crimes of the enemy so as to prove that he had the area under his responsibility completely secure, that his province was safe, that, under him, population and territorial control was achieved up to 100 percent—all in the hope that he could get his first stars when his turn came up on April 1, and that he could again be among the favorites of Thieu after having botched the mission of moving smuggled goods from Dinh Tuong to Long An entrusted to him some time ago? In any case, the order to seal off the area from the press on March 9 and 10 had provided a most needed route of escape to a cornered enemy.

Afterward, the province chief of Dinh Tuong did have another act: he organized a demonstration of protest against the International Committee when Committee members came down to investigate the incident. During the demonstration, probably because things got out of control, some young demonstrators had inexplicably hurled rocks against members of the investigating team. Taking advantage of that incident, the liaison officer of the National Liberation Front, citing the insecurity of the area, advised their Polish and Hungarian comrades on the investigating team to put an end to the investigation. What was most deplorable was that one of the victims of the rock throwing was the Indonesian delegate, the most fervently anti-Communist component on the International Committee. Even the Saigon delegation on the Joint Military Commission was shocked. It had been no small achievement to get all four members of the International Committee to agree on the need for an investigation. The investigation, which promised to bring about results most profitable to the Saigon side, had to be cut short because of the rock throwing incident. . . . What was on the mind of that province chief? People shook their heads in disbelief. Could it be possible that the Dinh Tuong province chief was in reality an underground Communist agent who was given the duty of finding a route of escape for the enemy? Was he out of his mind, or was he just a stupid person? That was not too much to say because after the rock throwing incident the NLF delegation was overjoyed and confidently went on to more denunciations:

-"Do you know who committed the crime at the Public School in Cai Lay? If it were we who did, then why did the local authorities organize demonstrations to throw rocks and prevent the International Committee from conducting the investigation. Was it because they were afraid that the International Committee would discover the trace of the criminal?"

During the session, I was sitting in the observer's room, taking notes, but I was overwhelmed with angry emotions, my hand trembled, and I felt as if the walls of the room were closing in on me, crushing me and suffocating me. I felt suffocated as if a flame of fury contained within myself was about to explode in a hellfire. That was probably the reason why we were still locked in precarious struggle with the Communists despite the fact that we were intrinsically stronger, our troops were brave and our cause was right? Why have we not won the war? We had not won the war because there were still elements like the Dinh Tuong province chief and his accomplices in our midst.

However, even with the help of quislings within our own ranks, and despite the trickiness and deceitfulness, the denial of the NLF chief delegate did not have any single effect at the negotiating table because of the monstrosity and the utter brutality of the crime through which had been laid bare the true violent and savage nature of a policy built on the blood and the bodies of the people. The death of the children had spotlighted all the dark corners of the Communist Hell. The tragedy was like a shock that cornered the NLF delegates, Tuan, Giang, into a situation where they found their hands bound. Even the Politiburo probably did not know how to deal with the situation. In response to the denial by General Tuan, General Hiep read a thirty-minute-long document reviewing all the crimes committed by the Communists during the past week, from the firing at aircraft on prisoner exchange missions, to the random killing of innocent people at the Tam Soc Pagoda in Bat Xuyen province, to the shelling of children in Cai Lay. The session took place in an atmosphere of tragedy, and the NLF delegates, despite their usual coolness and unruffled attitude, had to sit there and grimly listen to the speech. General Hiep said:

-"You have again talked about the shooting down of our Chinook helicopter on the way back from prisoners release missions resulting in the death of one of our crew members. From your presentation, we see two points. First, I assume that by proposing discussions on possible measures to be adopted in order to avoid the recurrence of similar regrettable incidents in the future, you have admitted that a violation of the cease-fire has been committed by your side. Second, you have raised the problem again to discharge all responsibilities over to us and to deny and wrongdoing on your part.

"You have used modern weaponry for the mass killing of children, as reported by the mass media during the past few days. The British Broadcasting Corporation in London, it its news broadcast at 2215 hours on March 9, had this report: 'In South Vietnamese, 23 children from five to 11 years old have been killed and about 40 others injured when a Communist mortar round hit a school in Cai Lay about 65 km southwest of Saigon. According to the latest reports, the number of fatalities may have reached 40, and among the injured there was a teacher and another adult. The explosion occurred when the children were filing into the classrooms. Army experts confirmed that the shrapnel indicated the mortar was Chinese made and had been in use in the North Vietnamese arsenal.' The excerpt that we just read to you was from a news report by an independent foreign news service. Unlike past shellings, in violation of the cease-fire which used to occur under cover of the darkness, this time the terrorists have chosen to carry out their act in plain daylight at the time when all the pupils of the Cai Lay Public School were still in the schoolyard.

"Because we have a different conception of things, we, the South Vietnamese people, as well as people in the whole world, have expressed our shock and have condemned this massacre of innocent children. What would you feel when you received the news that your own children had been killed on the way to school?"

The shelling of the Cai Lay Public School was like the straw that broke the camel's back. The situation became suffocating and tense and the negotiations reached serious impasses. All the subsequent meetings on March 8 and 12 were cut short. During the meeting of March 15, the Saigon chief delegate, after reading the speech, refused to take up the cease-fire problems in the agenda. On March 22, the NLF delegation at La Celle-Saint-Cloud put forward a six-point proposal as follows:

1. Both sides stop firing in execution of the cease-fire. The armed forces Command of both sides in South Vietnam jointly issue an identical appeal, calling on all levels of the administration, all units, all armed police forces under their command to strictly observe the cease-fire.
2. Both sides complete the exchanges of military and civilian personnel. The numbers include 200,000 civilian personnel belonging to the National Liberation Front and the Third Force, and 15,000 military personnel of the NLF captured prior to Jan. 28, 1973.
3. The rights of freedom and democracy of the people will be guaranteed.
4. Both sides speed up the formation of the National Council for Reconciliation and Concord, recognize the reality of two separate governments, two armies, two zones of control, three political forces, within three months of issuance of the joint appeal.
5. Organization of general elections in freedom and democracy within one year after the formation of the Council for National Reconciliation and Concord; a National Assembly will be elected to draft a Constitution and to work toward formation of a government for South Vietnam.
6. Both sides will reduce the size of the armies, return the soldiers to the land, and work toward the formation of one unified army,

Like the other proposals in the past, this six-point proposal was merely a trap. The proposal, through the choice of words and the order of execution, put all the blame and responsibilities to the other side. In point 1 of the proposal, for example, the Saigon government would have to dismantle its police force while on the Communist side, since it was not mentioned, the formidable party apparatus would still remain in place. The other points of the proposal also followed in the same vein, especially points 4 and 5 concerning the formation of the Council of Reconciliation and organization of general elections. The National Liberation Front laid all the blame on the Saigon side for the current impasses: it was implied that the Saigon side had not accepted the reality of two separate governments, two armies, two zones of control, and three political forces, and the setting up of the essential prerequisites (National Council, general elections) in order to delay the execution of the Paris Agreement as the NLF had proposed. At the Joint Military Commission, in the true spirit of a military commission, and as is the conduct of military men, Colonel Doa mounted a decisive counterattack against this proposal without mincing words:

-"Before pointing out the deceitfulness in your six-point proposal, we wish to say that this is just fake merchandise that you want to pitch on us; and of course you would accuse us of badwill when the proposal is rejected. This is like a saleswoman going around trying to unload some counterfeit goods on innocent customers. She would travel to all corners shouting her sales pitch: 'Ladies and gentlemen, come and buy my wares, this is new, this is good, this is what you need.' Then, when she sees she cannot get the attention of anybody (presumably they know that she is the dealer of fraudulent merchandises), she would cry her innocence and blame the customers for suspecting her and her goods. I expect you would have a similar reaction after we pointed out the fraudulent nature of your proposal."

The six-point proposal, after creating some mild commotion for a few days, was soon forgotten amid the rumbling of cannons northeast of Kon Tum, at Duc Hue (Hau Nghia province), at Chia Linh base camp (on Route 14, northeast of Chon Thanh, Binh Long province), etc. At first, people who earnestly aspired for peace and who were exhausted of the war wishfully thought that these battles were only the last battles of the war, the last eruptions before peace would be finally restored. And likewise, the whole world had become so tired of the war in Vietnam and did not wish to hear any more about death and destruction, even death and destruction in the darkest bottom of despair. Such was the tragedy of those wretched people who had aspired for peace, a peace that would come in blood, in death, and in tears. In those tragic days of unseasonal war, the Vietnamese people, more than ever, wanted to cling to their dreams of peace, the dreams crystallized from their boundless sufferings, and they saw in these battles the first signs of the elusive peace, the last surgical interventions to cut away the cancerous organs and return the body to health.

But all that was just a dream. As soon as the guns fell silent in Kon Tum, Duc Huc, and Chi Linh, the fumes of war rose on Tong Le Chan. Tong Le Chan, the biggest eruption of the "post-peace" war in Vietnam. The base had been under siege since summer of 1972 had set An Loc on fire. Exactly two years had gone by. Two years under siege! There was no such precedent in world military history, especially not in this century, the era of blitzkriegs, of modern wars, of space wars. The tiny base, not more than 300 feet in length, had withstood enemy pressures for more than 700 days in a strange phase of the war, the phase of war in peace. Excluding the period from April 1972 to Jan. 28, 1973, when the Agreement was signed, during the whole 1973, Tong Le Chan stood there, suffering, like a balloon used to gauge the disturbances of peace, a thermometer to measure the temperature of the war in a situation of "reconciliation and concord." Tong Le Chan, the exhaust valve, the respiratory tube, the main blood vein of the Peace Agreement. On April 14, 1974, the beleaguered outpost finally fell. The peace balloon was punctured, the dream for peace faded away like a mirage.

The negotiations at the Joint Commission was no longer the place to discuss the terms of the Peace Agreement, to talk about peace and reconciliation and concord. The air was filled with hatred, the exchanges were tense with mutual recriminations. In the past, the two sides would use the negotiating table to denounce each other, but the denunciations were made concerning the subjects on the agenda (mainly the cease-fire problems and the exchanges of prisoners). From the beginning of April 1974 onward, at chief delegates meetings, such a simulacrum was finally put aside, and both sides no longer made use of the agenda as a basis from which to exchange accusations—it was a free for all. There was no agreement even on the agenda. The conference became an arena where anything was permitted. There was even no time limit and meetings frequently would go on to accommodate the lengthy verbal attacks of the two chief delegates. A typical duel:

Colonel Giang (National Liberation Front):

-"All your attempts at turning black into white could not hide your nature, your plot to escalate the war, destroy the peace, and sabotage the Agreement. More blatantly, the United States has introduced more F-5E aircraft into South Vietnam and you have tried to justify this serious act by empty jokes. Meanwhile, a number of American politicians at the White House and at the Pentagon have engaged in insolent statements, threatening all-out intervention if we should dare to commit aggressive acts. Every time the Americans escalated their war of aggression, and every time the Pentagon issued threats of war, you would join in echoing their threats and denunciations. Recently, the Americans and you issued the warning that North Vietnam would increase the attacks before or after Tet, and denounced that North Vietnam was repairing airbases in South Vietnam. Afterward, you committed a savage bombing campaign into the zones under our control, including the populated areas. When there was no attack from us, you would say: the Communists did not dare to attack! And then you invented stories of our attack in Kon Tum, you made up stories in Cai Lay, you dreamed up the affair at Cay Dua or something like that. Not surprisingly, everything was part of a systematic plot to start the war in accordance with the instructions from the Americans."

Colonel Doa (Republic of Vietnam) counterattacked:

-"I wish to commend Colonel Giang for his good voice and the way he expresses his ideas nodding his head in a very artistic manner. Colonel Giang has rolled his eyes when he comes to the attack, thrusting out his head, pushing in his chin, leaning to the left, veering to the right, like a good actor performing. As a matter of fact, I also wish to give high praise to the North Vietnamese Communists for having produced a good actor. . . . Unfortunately, his clownish performance would be of some use only at a training class for abducted people, (?) or for teenagers. (?) But here, I advise you not to take any provocative stance, because that would lead nowhere."

Colonel Doa continued:

-"Now, we wish to respond to each of the points that he has just raised. Since you denounced us for having received F-5E aircraft, you will have to answer to this question. Since the signing of the Paris Agreement, how many SAM rockets, how many artillery pieces, how many rockets, how many 130mm artillery pieces, and 85mm cannons have you and North Vietnam brought into South Vietnam? Concerning your attempt to evade responsibilities by denouncing that the United States is still involved in the war and is still encouraging the war. This is something very special, because you have waited a month and a half before denouncing 'American aggression.' During the past month and a half, you have remained very quiet, not a single word about 'American imperialist aggressors' has been used in your speeches. You must know more than anybody else the situation you are in, the Spratley affair is still there, it is stuck in your throat, and you can't talk. You must still remember that the Republic of Vietnam delegation has suggested that both sides issue a joint communique denouncing all imperialist aggressors who encroach on Vietnamese territory, but you have avoided it because you are afraid that the Spratley affair would be like a string strangling you if you signed that communique. You have remained silent even though the

Communist newspaper *Pravda* has repeatedly denounced the People's Republic of China for taking over the islands. You know that Americans have to have entry visas to come to Vietnam but the Communist Chinese travel freely in and out of Quang Tri without having to apply for a visa. Perhaps they came to the Spratleys in the same way, without the invitation of the National Liberation Front? On the basis of that good spirit of friendly relations between you and the PRC, we understand the thanks that Chairman Mao extended to Nguen Huu Tho 'for the long struggle of the National Liberation Front' to mean that the NLF has provided an opportunity for China to invade Vietnam.

"Since you are in such a bind, we would advise you from now on not to mention the word 'imperialism' anymore, or if you wish, you can talk about 'Chinese Imperialists,' because China is the imperialist country which has caused so much bereavement to the Vietnamese people through many centuries. You can reread history and see for yourself that in any century of its thousands of years of history Vietnam was subjected to attacks from China. You criticized the Republic of Vietnam for asking for economic aid from the United States, but it is your side, your leaders in North Vietnam that have been yearning for American dollars! You're sad your economy has gone bankrupt, but the economy in North Vietnam is just a tragedy, it is the poorest country in Southeast Asia! Why? Because North Vietnam has had to feel all manpower and resources into the war in South Vietnam, because they have to feed your armed forces and their invading army so that they can continue to sow destruction in the South. North Vietnam's economy has become so desperate that Hanoi had come to trade corpses for dollars. On returning the remains of twenty-three American soldiers Hanoi has not forgotten to remind, to beg the Americans to remember to give them money in return for the bodies!"

Colonel Giang, of the National Liberation Front, took careful notes of Colonel Doa's speech, scribbling notes in his notebook, paying close attention to each word, each phrase, his head nodding. After Colonel Doa finished his speech, Giang delivered his countercharge:

-"The Spratley incident has been used by your side as a diversion from a most serious threat: the intervention of the United States into the situation in South Vietnam threatening the Paris Agreement that all four parties have signed on. You created a lot of noises, but just look at the Saigon press and you will see how isolated you are! Many newspapermen have asked me the question: 'Do you know why they are creating so much noise about the Spratley incident?' I gave them the answer and they said: 'We thought you didn't know!' Now let me explain. Why did Chairman Mao extend thanks to Chairman Tho? I think you know very well but you just wanted to find ways to slander us despite your knowledge. That is why I will have to point it out to you. The whole world is grateful to the Vietnamese people under our leadership because if we did not accept sacrifices in our struggle to defeat the Americans, Ngo Dinh Diem would have turned South Vietnam into an ideal base from which to attack the North. Ngo Dinh Diem has called for filling out the Ben Hai River and marching up to the North, sabotaging the 1954 Geneva Agreement and putting all of Vietnam under the yoke of American neo-colonialist policy. Had that been realized, then what would have become of the peace in Southeast Asia?

"That is why not only China, but the U.S.S.R. as well, are grateful to us. Let me further explain. Why is America falling behind the U.S.S.R. in the race for strategic arms, so much so that ever since Johnson the United States has had to try its utmost to catch up? Because if we did not cause the United States to have to spend tens of billions of dollars in this war, the United States would not have to shift their military budget from being spent on strategic arms to conventional arms for the conduct of the war in Vietnam. If America had maintained superiority in strategic arms, then what would happen to the world? It is common knowledge that the United States, through many Presidents, always has the basic policy of preparing for the Third World War. If they gained superiority in strategic arms, what would happen to the U.S.S.R.? What would happen to the world? We are not only talking of the socialist world, we are talking of the whole world, because the capitalist world and the Third World are also grateful to us.

"Why is the Third World grateful to us? Because even as they were conducting a Special War in South Vietnam, they have openly declared that they were using South Vietnam as a test site for their Special War strategy and they believed that kind of semi-war would not lead to the Third World War and would provide them with experiences to snuff out all armed liberation movements and to suppress all national liberation movements in the world. I don't think Colonel Doa is not aware of all that, but I have to lay it our because he has insisted on putting out slanderous obfuscation in the face of the truth. Because of the time limit, we cannot quote all the expressions of thanks that we have received from true representatives of countries the world over. When the United States rushed great numbers of troops into South Vietnam, many had thought that nothing could stop the march of the Americans. I have had the opportunity to personally observe that feeling during my visit to many foreign countries. But, when the war in Vietnam has reached its highest point, when the United States has used up most of its reserve forces and is still defeated, when the Nixon Administration has had to shift the strategy to Vietnamizing the war, the forces friendly to the National Liberation Front have seen, to their satisfaction, that the United States is not invincible. This is only a small country, with only limited territory and population, but that does not mean that anybody can freely impose their will here if people are determined to carry on their struggle. This is not my conclusion. The whole world has come to that conclusion. I can freely and amply quote on this subject. Even in America, where the people used to be quite arrogant, there are those who have had to admit that they have a debt of gratefulness toward the Vietnamese people, and they are grateful to us because through us they have seen that their government has been obviously covering things up from them! Therefore, it is not hard to understand why Chairman Mao had to express thanks to Chairman Tho!"

The meetings of the Joint Commission became as tense as if both sides were ready to pull the trigger on each other. The air was highly charged, as if ready to explode. Meanwhile, the military situation had grown much worse. Communist troops openly went on attacking all of the four Corps regions. Outposts in the foothills of Quang Nam and Quan Ngai provinces came under fire and were captured by the enemy. The Dakpek sector, the extreme north fortress of Pleiku province, a thorn in the side of the Communist B-3 command in the tri-border area for the last ten years, the place where the yellow flag has been snapping the wind as a symbol of the unchangeability of the Republic of Vietnam in defiance of numerous attempts by the Communists to capture it, finally fell to the enemy. The Pleiku airbase was shelled for the second time. There were proddings along Route 13. . . . After removing the Chi Linh outpost north-east of Chon Thanh, the Communists prepared to move in a two-pronged attack against Chon Thanh, Lai Khe, and Ben Cat.

The war broke out as something that has been expected, proving the complete impasse of the way to restore peace as indicated in the Paris Agreement, a worthless document designed as a compromise between alien forces rather than as a real formula for peace in South Vietnam. . . . The Republic of Vietnam army counterattacked in accordance with the phrase from President Thieu: "We have to strike first, we have to keep them on the move." Back at the negotiating table, the Saigon delegates also changed their strategy: they would no longer engage in discussions of general issues and instead would concentrate on specific problems, such as the restoration of the functions of the International Committee to Control and Supervise the Cease-Fire. The South Vietnamese delegation proposed that both sides jointly request the International Committee to conduct investigations of cease-fire violations at such or such specific location.

The National Liberation Front delegation also returned to the specifics and they posed a pre-condition that they would only move on to discuss other problems until after the Republic of Vietnam had agreed to grant them the Specific Rights and Privileges. The Rights and Privileges were contained in an eleven-point document that had been agreed upon by the 4-Party Joint Military Commission and they were designed to facilitate the activities of the NLF delegation during the period from Jan. 28 to March 29, 1973. After March 28, 1973, the 4-Party Commission was reduced to the 2-Party Commission and the Saigon side suspended the special rights and privileges to the NLF delegation, arguing that the new situation mandated it. The NLF delegation insisted that the agreement should be maintained. At the same time, they also demanded that these rights and privileges should be broadened to give the NLF delegation a status equivalent to diplomatic delegation. During all that time, the Saigon government temporarily accepted a number of privileges for the NLF delegation, such as the right to hold press conferences, the right to communicate with Loc Ninh, etc. These rights were further severely restricted after March 7, 1974, following the shooting of the Chinook helicopter, the shelling of the Cai Lay school, and other Communist violations such as the attacks at Duc Hue, Chi Linh, and Kon Tum.

The unreconcilability of the issues and the utter hostility at the negotiating table led the conference to total collapse. The two sides could not even agree on a common agenda, least of all reach agreement on any issue. The meetings were no longer held to negotiate, they became the place where both sides would come to hurl insults at each other. A typical meeting on April 30, 1974, proceeded as follows:

Republic of Vietnam:

-"Let us go directly to the issue at hand. If there can be no agreement on the question of inviting the International Committee to investigate the cease-fire violations as we have proposed in the agenda, then perhaps we can take up some issue that we think should receive special attention."

National Liberation Front:

-"You have interrupted us for the first time."

Republic of Vietnam:

-"We also take note that for the first time you have evaded discussions on the cease-fire problem—a most urgent problem at this time."

National Liberation Front:

-"For the second time, you have interrupted us."

GVN: (Government of Vietnam, or Republic of Vietnam)

-"For the second time, you have refused to hold discussions on the agenda."

NLF:

-"For the third time, you have interrupted us."

GVN:

-"For the third time, you have turned away from discussions on the cease-fire problem."

NLF:

-"You are requested not to take advantage of our composure to say anything you want."

GVN:

-"Not at all! You are far from being composed. Proof is that Colonel Giang has rolled up his sleeves, indication that he is ready to make verbal attacks against us."

NLF:

-"How many times have we been interrupted?"

GVN:

-"The fourth time, or if necessary the tenth time, the hundredth time, the thousandth time. We will be most patient in calling on you to return to the agenda and take up discussions on the concrete issue of the cease-fire."

NLF:

-"You have interrupted us for the sixth time. Let me make it clear that you should not take advantage of our respect for negotiating procedures to engage in talking on any issue you choose. You are not allowed to interrupt us when comes our turn to speak."

GVN:

-"Let me tell you that we are not interrupting you, we are just warning you."

NLF:

-"Once again you are requested to stop sabotaging the meeting by interrupting the speech of our delegates."

GVN:

-"We request that the most concrete problem should be taken up for discussions, and that we should refrain from mutual criticisms at a time when soldiers from both sides are spilling blood on the battlefields because the level of cease-fire violations has dangerously increased. We believe that to refuse discussions of concrete issues is to run away from duties."

NLF:

-"You have interrupted us for the tenth time."

GVN:

-"You are wrong! That was just the eighth time!"

NLF:

-"If you wish, that means ten less two."

GVN:

-"That means that we have warned you for the eighth time!"

NLF:

-"So, are you done with the warnings?"

GVN:

-"You don't have to ask. You understand it so well."

NLF:

-"We have to make sure."

GVN:

-"You don't have to ask. You can see it for yourself!"

NLF:

-"This is the thirteenth time that you have interrupted us. We have to declare that the meeting today cannot proceed any longer."

GVN:

-"It is your right."

Meeting would break up that way until finally the NLF delegation declared unilaterally that all meetings, at the level of the chief delegates as well as at the level of the subcommittees, would be suspended starting May 10, 1974. Two days later, the NLF delegation at La Celle-Saint-Cloud went much further by declaring an indefinite suspension of the high-level negotiations and their readiness to return to Vietnam.

On May 20, 1974, the front from Binh Duong to Ben Cat erupted ferociously. From their secret zones of Ho Bo and Boi Loi, Communist troops poured out into An Dien with the intention of crossing the Thi Tinh River to capture Ben Cat, isolate Lai Khe and, pushing down Route 13, attack Binh Duong. In the east, the front at Phu Giao (on the border between Binh Duong and Binh Long) also boiled up: the Communists advanced in two wings, from the northwest and the northeast, toward Binh Duong and Bien Hoa. From there they could thrust into Gia Dinh and Saigon was just a small step beyond. All through the more than ten years of the Second Indochina War, that was the first time that Communist tanks went closest to Saigon, only 30 km on a straight line. Thirty kilometers that was the last phase of their march to liberate South Vietnam. Communist guns were in place, ready to tear up the sky of peace over Saigon with their shell fire. Peace—Oh, what a dream it seems!

Latest reports said on May 4, 1974, a public school in Vinh Long, named Song Phu, was hit by Communist artillery fire, killing seventeen children and wounding seventy. Nobody had the courage to go through all the details of that massacre. This will serve to conclude this article. I do not have enough strength to add one more word to it.

[MAY 1974]

Fifteen

Memories of War in a Time of Peace

JAN. 27, 1973, was the date an Agreement was signed to restore the peace in Vietnam. Under a deep blue sky in the dazzling golden light of a brilliant sun, or on the white background of a snowbound landscape, well-dressed, civilized people in mansions or out on the streets of the big, modern cities in the world were throwing confetti and flowers and raising their glasses to toast the welcomed arrival of Peace in Vietnam, the distant country at the other end of the world, on the other side of the Pacific, beyond the continents. Here was unending darkness, with the stars twinkling in the sky, and on earth, trampling the dark soil, the enemy was closing in, marching in deadly silence and pointing the cold muzzles of their guns forward, and the wind seemed to bring the first echoes of exploding shells. . . . Far away, in the civilized world, in Paris, in Rome, in Washington, in New York, people were drinking, shaking hands, hugging, laughing, warmly welcoming the peace and progress for mankind. Peace, the victory of light over darkness, of reconciliation over hatred, of the will to build over the will to destroy. But in Vietnam, on the night of Jan. 28, 1973, there was only the whimpering and groaning and horrible screaming of those on the point of death, butchered in the prime of their lives. . . .

Early on the morning of Jan. 28, 1973, like every morning that dawned on this miserable land, the Vietnamese people clasped their hands together in an effort to contain their emotions and asked themselves if this was really the first morning of peace. In Saigon, the militia went around knocking on doors calling on the people to put the flag out in front of their houses, marches were played on the radio in between communiques and announcements reminiscent of the days of coups and countercoups of 1965–66. Nobody knew for sure whether there was really something like peace in that morning of the 28th. I walked in the streets of Saigon, and my heart was filled with misgiving, as if someone was pointing a gun at me.

The battle at Cua Viet (Dong Ha) exploded; the Communists set up roadblocks on Highway 1 north of Trang Bang district and north of Xuan Loc in Long Khanh province; Route 15 connecting Saigon-Phuoc Tuy-Vung Tau was cut at two points north and south of Long Thanh; company-size and battalion-size battles took place between Communist troops pouring out of the secret zones onto Highway 1 and Saigon troops guarding the highway running close to the coastline between the Binh De, Deo Nhong, and Deo Ca passes. In the foothills of Quang Tri, Thua Thien, in the area of the Ong Do cave and the hills of Tan Teo and Truong Phuoc, North Vietnamese troops raised their heads above their trenches and waved to soldiers of the 1st Infantry Division and the Airborne Division, after 300 days of fighting since April 29, 1973. At two o'clock a man clad in a khaki uniform of Nam Dinh, wearing a pith helmet adorned with a red star, his feet shod in canvas boots (Communist uniform), left his trench and strode across sixty meters of rough terrain to shake hands with First Lieutenant Thang of 94th Company, 9th Airborne Battalion. Cups of warm tea were brought out and Dien Bien cigarettes were exchanged for GVN Army-issued Ruby cigarettes. So, we are reconciled, they said, so we will live in concord, they said, in accordance with the spirit and the words of the Agreement. "You are not afraid coming over to us all by yourself?" the paratrooper asked with laughter, and reassured the man: "No, I am not going to fight you, we are now friends!" Half an hour later twelve paratroopers in camouflaged uniforms walked over to the other side to return the visit. One hour passed and still they did not return. No shots were heard: they probably used their bayonets. That was the eighth hour of Peace in Vietnam. Not one among us could affirm that Peace had returned. Peace had only rested on the document, on the negotiating table in Paris. The dregs at the bottom of the glasses of wine raised in toast.

The poor people in South Vietnam for a moment felt they were like Cinderella, bestowed the gift of peace by a fairy; they thought they saw in their hand the shining diamond of peace, crystallizing the long-cherished dream of a miserable people. Nobody could believe in this miracle. As the day wore on in the harsh light of the hot sun, the dream would still remain a dream. The Vietnamese shook themselves out of the dream and told themselves: "This is just an illusion, a mirage, a simple dream." But was that peace that they just felt at the tip of their hands? Nobody could live in a dream, but if there were no dreams of better days, and if you would not believe in dreams, then what is there left for them to live on? We only had dreams and we were only given hopes.

I felt great tremors within myself walking the peaceful streets of Saigon on that first morning of Peace.

The first meetings of the 4-Party Joint Military Commission took place in conference rooms to the humming of the air conditioners. The exchanges were civil and conciliatory, and also empty. In the beginning, I participated in the negotiations with the enemy with all my enthusiasm and sincerity, but even with the generosity and tolerance of my young age, I finally had to conclude that behind the seemingly frank laughter, the firm handshakes, the phrases of reconciliation and concord so profusely quoted, the Communists did not have anything more to give to Peace. Regardless of who was sitting across from you at the conference table, whether it be Lieutenant Colonel Tuan Anh (North Vietnam), with his obvious sincerity in both his words and acts, or Major Ngoc Dung (a woman delegate of the NLF), with her sweet and honest smile, they were just puppets of a tough policy. That is why, while I had shown all sincerity, all attentiveness toward them, I always had to tell myself when crossing the Thach Han River or when going to Loc Ninh on prisoner exchange missions: "Watch out! Be on your guard! Be prepared to attack! Be careful in the defense!" I had to put myself in the position of readiness to pull the trigger even while receiving from them a cup of hot tea in the slightly intoxicating air of the rubber plantations in Loc Ninh. The Communists had taught me to be suspicious and deceitful. Peace had taught me that this was only another face of war—the hideous face of Peace.

I quickly became familiarized with the work and acclimated to the new environment that required frequent face-to-face contacts with the other side. On one hand, I felt sincere respect for the people on the other side because they were my elders and because they looked ascetic and obviously had suffered many miseries. On the other hand, I was always ready to attack them mercilessly, to pull no punches because I realized that they were also extremely deceitful and dangerous adversaries. On the plane to Pleiku, I gave a light to Major Si and, with sincere solicitousness, reminded him to keep himself warm because of the cold weather in Pleiku and because he was old and weak. That was deeply felt advice that I gave him as I looked at the strands of white hair covering his furrowed forehead. But once at Duc Nghiep, I put away my conciliatory behavior and, pointing at their flag, I yelled: "I didn't see this flag at Thach Han. Neither did I find it in the offices of members of the Joint Commission in Loc Ninh, or Minh Thanh, Quang Ngai. Then why is this here? Is it because you are outside that so-called-government of yours and belong to an invading army, an alien army? If you use your flag here then we will exhibit the flag of the Republic of Vietnam in the offices and conference rooms of the Joint Commission in Saigon. You accused us of violating the airspace of Duc Nghiep. Are you joking? Who says that Duc Nghiep belongs to you? Who can delineate the airspace of a 'liberated' hamlet from the airspace of a hamlet under government control? What you are saying is absurd, things that nobody with the least military and legal knowledge could accept. You said that we violated the airspace of this prisoner release point. But the release point is an imaginary point defined by longitudes and latitudes, and the theoretical airspace of this point is a perpendicular line going straight up from this imaginary point into space. And what evidence do you have when you said that our aircraft crossed into 'your point of space?' Or was it that you heard the noise of the plane flying overhead? No such thing as a 'noise violation' was stipulated in the Paris Agreement."

I did give a hard time to the Communist officers; all of them must be about fifty years old or more, their hair white and their faces green as leaves because of malaria. I could be without pity and I could be quite solicitous, and I could quickly and readily shift from one attitude to the other. Those cold and cruel tricks were all I learned in the work for peace with the Communists.

I was at meetings of the 4-Party Joint Military Commission, I was at meetings of the 2-Party Joint Commission. I had gone on dozens of prisoner exchange missions, I had been to all eleven prisoner exchange locations from the Thach Han River to the point of Ca Mau, and I had met all of them. There was the "heavy-faced combatant" standing guard at the gate at Loc Ninh. There was the lieutenant colonel, commander of the Gio Linh region. He wore glasses and his hair was all white and he could tell you lies just like that—"I am native of Gio Linh and I went to the hills to join the fight against the Americans for national salvation, now I am back here to take over control of Quang Tri."—He spoke with a clear North Vietnamese accent from either Nam Dinh or Thai Binh province. It was clear he was a Major in the North Vietnamese Army. The Party, the Politburo had turned all of them into thorough, shameless liars, from the baby-faced sixteen-year-old soldiers to the aging colonels just on the other side of death. He claimed he was from Quang Tri. This base lie must have been directed from the brilliant minds of Vo Nguyen Giap, Le Duan, and Pham Van Dong. Oh God! How could they still win? Thus I was supposed to be reconciling myself with those people. I remembered what Hoang Anh Tuan said in an apparently sorrowful tone: "On the tragic massacre of our nieces and nephews in Cai Lay, we will conduct thorough investigation to find the criminals!" And then one month late there was the Song Phu incident in Bien Hoa. And then there was the university professor Nguyen Van Trung, who with a straight face posed the issue: "The problem could be viewed fundamentally like this: There are Vietnamese who are not Communists. In other words, basically, they only differ on the choice of a socio-political regime and on the way to conduct the struggle for freedom and independence, not on patriotic ideas." And there was the writer Son Nam who affirmed in an interview: "I think the two regions, North and South, could find reconciliation and concord through culture." And the politician Ho Ngoc Nhuan: "Reconciliation is the last resort of the people."

I agreed, I agreed with all of you, men with diplomas and with credits in the fields of politics and culture. But I looked around me for a whole year, and I listened to Hoang Anh Tuan and Vo Dong Giang at the conference table, I talked to Lieutenant Colonel Phung in Gio Linh, Major Giang at Thach Han, Lieutenant Colonel Nam Tich in Loc Ninh, and Major Dung in Rach Gia, and I could guarantee one thing: there was just no way to enter reconciliation with these cadres. Neither could I reconcile myself with the Communist soldier standing guard on the pier north of the Thach Han River, and I found that out just after a brief talk with him. I asked him: "Where did you go to school? Was it Hanoi?" He immediately launched himself into an angry retort, spitting saliva: "I am not from Hanoi! Don't you slander the Agreement and sabotage the spirt of reconciliation and concord. I am from Quang Tri!"

Damn it! He was 100 percent North Vietnamese all right, and not a bit from Quang Tri! Then with whom were you supposed to be reconciled? To be reconciled with somebody would mean to live in harmony with him. The same with a group of people. I remembered a sermon by a Catholic Father at a church in Tan Dinh. He was preaching on Modernization and Concord: "Let's bow our heads with the enemy and send him our love. Have the courage to love our enemy as you love yourselves." Amen! God hath said so because God hoped that the love of God would neutralize the hatred within the enemy. But if you knew that the enemy was secretly holding a knife and that he was waiting for the first opportunity to butcher you, then you would have to adopt a different attitude. I was not a radical anti-Communist, and I was not fighting against the Communists for pay and for pension. I just happened to know more about them as a soldier, and I was soon to leave this position to become a completely free man under no pressures from any direction. So the question to be posed was this: Reconciliation was all to the good, but how and with whom? How could we reconcile with an adversary who in reality remained opposed to us and who was ever ready to destroy us? There was a Buddhist monk who said, during a seminar at the Catholic church in Tan Dinh: "You can only reconcile the same elements together, like water to water, not water to oil." I would say even further: "How can you mix blood with acid!?"

Meeting at the chief delegate level on March 15, 1974. General Hiep was delivering a denunciation of the shelling of the school in Cai Lay by the Communists. General Tuan of the NLF responded with a weak argument. I was listening to them and I had some remarks with people sitting near by: "This guy is hesitant in his response because he hasn't found a way to evade the responsibility and besides he is probably a little nervous because this is too big. The guerilla who did this thing in Cai Lay is sure to be severely punished." I realize we had unwittingly cleared the Communists of their crime. The thought in our mind at the time was that mass killing was probably an accident, that the mortar round was probably intended for the Cai Lay sector where the operational headquarters for the region was located. We thought that because of inexperience the Communist gunner had accidentally fired the mortar round into the school. That thought was in some way justification for the absurd and barbarous crime of the Communists. How could they fire on the children, what liberation task was built on the corpses of innocent children, those who still had not the least idea about the doctrines, whose mind was not yet tainted by any hatred? We could not bring ourselves to believe that this crime of extreme absurdity could be premeditated, directed by a deliberate policy, and carried out by creatures called men. But frankly we had been wrong, we had been totally wrong, because the Communists would soon have similar combat achievements, at Song Phu on April 10 and at Bien Hoa on June 3.

There could no longer be any doubt. The Communists really did have a deliberate policy of murder. That I could definitely affirm. They killed children because the children were the children of traitors, and they killed civilians because these civilians were reactionary. They killed because they wanted to build their glory upon fear, and their achievements upon the blood and bones of the people. The Revolution needs the stimulant of the hatred. The Vietnamese proletarian revolution had many stimulants: the French colonialists, the Japanese fascists, the landowners, the wicked and corrupt village officials, the feudalists, the Americans, and Diem, and Thieu, and Ky, and American neo-colonialism. In this year 1974, all those stimuli had ceased to exist and the Communists needed new stimuli, new corpses. They needed to create more objectives for their killing: puppet army, puppet government, reactionary clique, who did not seriously carry out the Paris Agreement. And these targets for murder were us, and the children in Cai Lay, and the civilians in Tam Hiep, Bien Hoa.

Progressive elements, left-leaning and opposition politicians, you were unwittingly playing the role of cheer leaders for a band of murderers, in a game of murder and you had encouraged the committing of the crimes with your good phrases for peace. Peace was just an abused word. Communist rhetoric was saturated with it: Dance of Peace, an Army of Peace, the Geneva Agreement dividing the country was a Peace Agreement, and now in these days of 1973 and 1974, that much-abused word was utilized again on a much grander scale. "Reconciliation and concord in accordance with the spirit and words of the Paris Agreement." Strange that those simple words could still be used to cover up crime after crime. On the evening of May 31, 1935, before rushing 300,000 troops into the Rhine, Hitler, in a speech designed to reassure Britain, France, and the League of Nations had this conclusion: "Germany needs peace and hopes for peace." After every blitzkrieg and after every victory, Hitler would again revert to the theme of Peace and would say amid the tolling of bells: "Peace be with us! Amen!" Or he would say, "God, give us freedom to build peace in Germany and in Europe. . . ."

The use of the word Peace would be the first intimation of a great offensive in the offering and it would be the aftermath of a massacre. It was strange that there was no more connection between words and deeds. Despite the fact that those two words had become so mutually destructive, a great many people, particularly people in civilized societies, still believed in their true meanings. After Hitler had pushed through Poland and shaken hands with the U.S.S.R. (another force for peace!) at Brest Litovsk, he declared, "I offer peace and I will not launch a war against France and Britain!" And all Europe believed him! As with Hitler, and as with Stalin, the whole world today again unwittingly acted as accomplices to the murderer by giving the Nobel Peace Prize to Le Duc Tho. And even more painful and ironic was that on the same day when a hundred rockets fell into Bien Hoa on June 3, 1974, "liberating" children and innocent people by the most horrible and barbarous means imaginable, the government of the U.S.S.R. bestowed upon Nguyen Thi Binh the Lenin Peace Prize. Peace again! Could it be that the language of man had changed, had lost all meaning? Could it be that this age of ours had become the age of deceit and tyranny where man used the noblest words only to cover up the most dastardly, miserable crimes? Peace, that word is now being used by the Communists as the sign of death.

Two years. It seemed to me that I had gone a long way to Hell. I asked myself: "Why is it that we are not left to live in peace for just one day, one day without the sound of gunfire, one day without cheating, one day outside the time frame of a policy, a strategy. Oh just one day of peace for our beloved country, for our great people who have suffered a great deal and who should well deserve it. . . ." I also asked myself, "Why is this that in the seemingly endless war, where hundreds of thousands of soldiers, fighting for the noble cause of freedom, have paid their price in blood, there is still no plan to honor them as heroes, as martyrs, as people who have sacrificed their lives for the country?" On the contrary, the soldiers and their families in these days of so-called peace are the first to be cashiered, stripped to the bones, and left to be drained away to the last drop of blood. Let's consider the case of Lieutenant Colonel K., an Airborne Brigade commander ten years ago, who now is seen biking to work, his badge of rank and his beret hidden away, clutching a small ball of rice for his day's sustenance. Or Lieutenant Colonel H., my former boss, now a decrepit old man, happy to bum a cigarette. And there were others, many others, all of them, as piles of white bones of the dead soldiers, the hundreds of thousands of them whose blood had seeped through to the entrails of this land. There was a war widow and her four children who committed suicide at the tomb of their husband and father, the soldier who just died for peace and was buried in the military cemetery. And that other war widow who killed her two children with poison before committing suicide herself because the death benefits of her late husband were far from enough to feed the children. And others, such as the wives and children of soldiers searching for cactus roots to feed themselves on the sunbaked land of Quang Ngai.

Whom did these soldiers die for? Did they die to nourish a miserable few like the Dinh Tuong province chief and the Long An province chief, and others who had smuggled hundreds of millions of piasters of goods worth of fertilizer, or received bribes up to the hundreds of millions of piasters for a signature authorizing lumber quotas? Why? That was a heart-rending question. A question with such explosive force that it threatened to cause the body to disintegrate and each cell to break up. Why? Why? God is silent, the Buddha remains indifferent, and Christ is resigned.

In the end, the war was still as it had always been, as the miserable and suffering life. It was like a never ending nightmare in a thousand-year-long night. War as a permanence, a fact of life, an ugly reality that was ever sticking to us. Our country and the war were one, there could be no one without the other. I would continue to accompany my friends to the cemetery. I walked behind the flag-covered coffin of Colonel Nguyen The Nha, my former battalion commander, the soldier who, after twenty years of the most horrible combat, finally was felled by a mortar round at La Son base in Hue. His soul might still be wondering about the murderous trap that the ill-conceived peace laid out for him, he who during his long military career had fought and survived at the DMZ, in Hue during the Tet Offensive, in Tay Ninh, in Lower Laos. . . . He died with rage in his heart, forever unrelieved. I had no doubt about it. In the end, peace, that shadow of a dream, was only a cruel irony, a symbol of miserable deceit, a call in a coded radio message for murderers to spring up for the killing.

Fighting broke out again in An Dien, on the other side of the Thi Tinh River. Again the same scene, refugees streaming out on Route 13, with their meager belongings in baskets balancing at both ends of bamboo poles across their shoulders, again the same sight of children, their bodies crippled and pierced with shrapnel, of shriveled old women whose eyes, opened to the horrors in the last dying light of their days, no longer gave any more sign of life. I did not have the courage to read through the war news, or watch the newsreel on the refugees, I fell prey to a terrifying sorrow, I was plunged into the most abysmal distress. An Dien at the Thi Tinh River. I was there ten years ago as a young Second Lieutenant. It was in December 1964. I could see myself, in airborne camouflage uniform, a red ascot around my neck, striding heroically at point after the crossing of an old cement bridge, leading the whole battalion in a thrust deep into the lush green jungle. Yes. Ten years ago it was. That night bivouacking at the plantation of a Mr. Thinh, the flash of the exploding grenade, the fleeing shadow of the Vietcong in the firelight, and the pulsating red light of the medevac helicopter, and the thumping of the mortar rounds. . . . Ten years, and the same scenes are still repeating themselves, basically years ago, my airborne battalion, combined with the 4th Marine Battalion, was enough to sweep from the Thi Tinh bridge to An Dien, then up to the Alimot and Bussy plantations, and around to the plantation of Mr. Thinh and back out to Route 13. The weapons at the time consisted of M2s and 81mm mortars. Today, we would need a divisional size force, and each direction of the attack would require a full Regiment supported by an armored detachment and a battery of artillery. Years ago, the band of guerillas that lurked in the rubber plantations used mortars to shell and grenades to harass the outposts. Now, those furtive shadows are no longer. In their places, denser than the trees in the forest, are Regiments upon Regiments of North Vietnamese regulars ceremoniously escorted by T-54 tanks. . . . For ten years, that small world in Ben Cat district, like thousands of other villages all over the country, had only the mournful honor of being the battlefield, see-sawing between two sides.

Strange that in the Vietnamese language we can form so many words with the prefix "war"—"war and conflict" meaning a conflict involving war, "war-terrain" meaning almost the same thing, "war-achievement" being another way to say victory, "war-instrument" used for both weapons and equipment. But the word "Peace" in Vietnamese can only stand alone, indeed a loner, and a very passive and frail loner, amid the forest of swords and lances of the war words. It is all the more miserable that word, Peace, has been abused, pushed around, and drained of all its meaning. Peace—is it true that it is no longer for man to enjoy, is it no longer for us? We are nearing the anniversary of the signing of the Joint Communique of June 13, 1974, and next would come the Day of National Shame, July 20, 1954, anniversary of the signing of the 1954 Geneva Agreement.

[JUNE 1974]

The End

The Naval Institute Press is the book-publishing arm of the U.S. Naval Institute, a private, nonprofit, membership society for sea service professionals and others who share an interest in naval and maritime affairs. Established in 1873 at the U.S. Naval Academy in Annapolis, Maryland, where its offices remain today, the Naval Institute has members worldwide.

Members of the Naval Institute support the education programs of the society and receive the influential monthly magazine *Proceedings* or the colorful bimonthly magazine *Naval History* and discounts on fine nautical prints and on ship and aircraft photos. They also have access to the transcripts of the Institute's Oral History Program and get discounted admission to any of the Institute-sponsored seminars offered around the country.

The Naval Institute's book-publishing program, begun in 1898 with basic guides to naval practices, has broadened its scope to include books of more general interest. Now the Naval Institute Press publishes about seventy titles each year, ranging from how-to books on boating and navigation to battle histories, biographies, ship and aircraft guides, and novels. Institute members receive significant discounts on the Press' more than eight hundred books in print.

Full-time students are eligible for special half-price membership rates. Life memberships are also available.

For a free catalog describing Naval Institute Press books currently available, and for further information about joining the U.S. Naval Institute, please write to:

Member Services
U.S. Naval Institute
291 Wood Road
Annapolis, MD 21402-5034
Telephone: (800) 233-8764
Fax: (410) 571-1703
Web address: www.usni.org

CPSIA information can be obtained
at www.ICGtesting.com
Printed in the USA
LVHW010830140920
665910LV00005B/7